Developing Quality PSHE in Secondary Schools and Colleges

Developing Quality PSHE in Secondary Schools and Colleges

Edited by Sophie-Lauren McPhee and Victoria-Marie Pugh

BLOOMSBURY ACADEMIC
LONDON • NEW YORK • OXFORD • NEW DELHI • SYDNEY

BLOOMSBURY ACADEMIC
Bloomsbury Publishing Plc
50 Bedford Square, London, WC1B 3DP, UK
1385 Broadway, New York, NY 10018, USA
29 Earlsfort Terrace, Dublin 2, Ireland

BLOOMSBURY, BLOOMSBURY ACADEMIC and the Diana logo are
trademarks of Bloomsbury Publishing Plc

First published in Great Britain 2024

A catalogue record for this book is available from the British Library.

A catalog record for this book is available from the Library of Congress.

ISBN: HB: 978-1-3503-3696-4
         PB: 978-1-3503-3695-7
         ePDF: 978-1-3503-3697-1
         eBook: 978-1-3503-3698-8

Typeset by Integra Software Services Pvt. Ltd.
Printed and bound in Great Britain

To find out more about our authors and books visit www.bloomsbury.com
and sign up for our newsletters.

Contents

Figures

Tables

List of Contributors

Victoria-Marie Pugh is Assistant Director of Accreditation for the Council of International Schools (COBIS), formerly responsible for PSHE and SENDI provision across the Initial Teacher Education programmes at the University of Worcester, UK. She was a primary teacher and PSHE teacher working across key stages from nursery to secondary education. Victoria is the lead author and series editor of the *My Life* Collins PSHE schemes of work and co-editor of the book *Teaching PSHE and RSE in the Primary School: Enhancing the Whole Curriculum* published by Bloomsbury Academic. Victoria has an X account: @MrsVPSHE.

Sophie-Lauren McPhee is the Trust Lead Professional for PSHE & SMSC at The Mercian Trust, based in the West Midlands, UK. She has led PSHE at Queen Mary's Grammar School in Walsall since 2016, in which year she also set up the personal development programme for sixteen- and seventeen-year-olds called Change Your Mind. She now travels across the UK and delivers webinars in order to help other schools and colleges set up this programme. Sophie is currently training to become qualified as a Transactional Analysis psychotherapist and runs her own private practice, Stoney Meadow Counselling. X: @TheOther16Hours.

Nickael Briggs is Vice Principal for Personal Development and Safeguarding at Ark Acton Academy, UK, where she oversees PSHE. She has worked as Curriculum Leader for Citizenship, Sociology, RE and PSHE in three different secondary schools and is an experienced teacher educator. She has led sessions at UCL on how to successfully implement GCSE Citizenship into secondary schools. As a teacher educator, she coaches staff at varying levels and uses evidence-informed strategies to promote high-quality teaching. Most recently, Nickael was listed in the Guardian's top 100 inspirational teachers list for her co-curriculum work and commitment to character development.

Stephen Lane has been teaching for over twenty years and is Chaplaincy Lead at Lichfield Cathedral School, UK. A common face on the ResearchED circuit, Stephen has been seeking to build an informed approach to pastoral leadership – the topic of his book *Beyond Wiping Noses*. Stephen has now moved into school chaplaincy. Stephen completed his doctorate in 2021; his thesis sought to construct a (post)critical ontology of a teacher who tweets. Stephen died in 2014 but thanks to the kiss of a stranger he woke up and is now an occasional fundraiser for the British Heart Foundation. Stephen can be found on X @sputniksteve.

Chris Farman is Wellbeing Lead at Denstone College, a co-educational boarding school for children aged four to eighteen in Staffordshire, UK. He has previously held the role of Deputy Head Pastoral in a central London secondary school, and other roles such as Head of Year and Head of PSHE. He is also part of the safeguarding team at his current school.

Kimberley Hibbert-Mayne is Senior Lecturer in Education at University of Worcester, UK. Her MA in Education and other research projects have predominantly focused on areas of social psychology and initial teacher training in secondary and physical education. Her most recent publication is *Differentiated Instruction in Secondary Education across Countries: Measurement Invariance and Comparison* (2022).

Charlotte Ross is a lecturer for the Secondary Physical Education PGCE and the Enhancement Activity Lead for PSHE and Citizenship at the University of Worcester, UK. Her research interests include examination PE and exploring paper to practice in secondary teaching and teacher education. A recent publication was *Played in England, Made around the World: The Origins of Badminton through the Commonwealth* (2022).

Dave Woodward is Senior Lecturer and Course Leader of the Secondary Physical Education PGCE at the University of Worcester, UK. His research interests include behaviour management, meaningful experiences in physical education and fundamental movement skills. His most recent article was *Learning about Meaningful Physical Education: How to Get Started* (2022).

Annie O'Neill is Company Director and School Nurse at OM Health & Wellbeing Consultancy Ltd and a committee member of the Schools and Public Health Nursing Association (SAPHNA), UK. Her interests focus on quality RSE and a whole-school approach to wellbeing and mental health.

Fiona Spargo-Mabbs is the Director and Founder of drug education charity Daniel Spargo-Mabbs Foundation, which works with young people, parents and professionals across the UK. Fiona is considered to be one of the leading experts in drug and alcohol education, speaking across a range of platforms, informing and influencing policy and practice at a national level. She is author of *I Wish I'd Known: Young People, Drugs and Decisions – a Guide for Parents and Carers* (2021) and *Talking the Tough Stuff with Teens* (2022) and has been awarded an OBE for her work. www.dsmfoundation.org.uk

Zahara Chowdhury is Head of Diversity, Equality, Inclusion, Wellbeing and PSHE Lead at Beaconsfield High School, UK. She is Head of Partnerships for Global Equality Collective, the first DEI app for schools. Zahara is founder of the blog and podcast 'School Should Be', a platform for students, parents and teachers to explore diverse topics in education. She is also a trustee for the charity Solutions Not Sides, which works with students and teachers on education about Israel and Palestine. Zahara was previously a Head of English and Associate Senior Leader at a secondary school.

Elizabeth Swan is an education and neurodiversity consultant. Drawing upon her twenty years' experience as a qualified teacher, SENDCo and head teacher working in both mainstream secondary schools and special schools, her postgraduate study of psychology, and lived experience as an adult with ADHD, Elizabeth works as a teacher, coach and education consultant, finding or creating learning and working environments that empower neurodiverse people to thrive. In addition, she helps parents and caregivers navigate the complexities of the special educational needs systems so that families flourish and their children's needs are met. Working in partnership with professionals and policymakers, she provides high-quality, evidence-informed training to remove stigma and improve outcomes for neurodiverse people.

Hannah Wilson is a leadership development consultant, coach and trainer. She co-founded #WomenEd during her Deputy Headship at a large London-based MAT and she co-founded #DiverseEd during her Executive Headship at a start-up school in Oxfordshire. She speaks, trains and writes about Diversity, Equity and Inclusion, Coaching and Mentoring, Mental Health and Wellbeing, Resilience and Leadership. The book she edited with Bennie Kara, *Diverse Educators: A Manifesto*, was published in 2022.

Holly Parker-Guest is Strategic Lead for PSHE at Kingsthorpe College in Northampton, UK. Holly oversees the strategic vision and planning for PSHE in the curriculum and whole school agenda. She is also passionate about equality and diversity and the importance this plays both within PSHE and school life.

Kit Marie Rackley (they/she) is an ex high-school teacher who provides teacher continuous professional development (CPD) and training. They are a consultant with the UK's Geographical Association and the National Association of School-Based Teacher Trainers (NASBTT). They are a published educational author, including works with National Geographic Kids and Diverse Educators. Kit Marie is a strong and passionate advocate of youth voice and empowerment, decolonizing the curriculum, and inclusive and intersectional education. Much of their work revolves around the climate crisis, focusing around framing it as a school safeguarding issue. Kit Marie runs an educational resource blog at Geogramblings.com.

Sophie King-Hill is Senior Fellow in the Health Services Management Centre at the University of Birmingham, UK. She specializes in sexual behaviours and first-point assessment in children and young people, sexual health, controversial issues, policy implementation, transfer and success frameworks. Sophie currently holds an ESRC NI grant as principal investigator; this project is seeking to understand what currently constitutes sexual behaviours – both online and offline – in children and young people aged thirteen to eighteen in the UK.

Mel Gadd is Co-founder and Manager of Cwmni Addysg Rhyw – Sex Education Company. She has been a sex educator and trainer since 2002. She specializes in working with young people who are autistic and/or have learning disabilities, or who have other challenges in their lives. She is author of *Masturbation, Autism and Learning Disabilities; A Guide for Parents and Professionals* (2021).

Emily Setty is Senior Lecturer in Criminology at the University of Surrey, UK. Her research focuses on young people's experiences of sex and relationships, including in their online cultures. She has published studies about young people's perspectives on harmful sexual behaviours, including online, and how best to address the challenges they face in their contemporary youth sexual cultures. Emily has published a book: *Risk and Harm in Youth Sexting Culture: Young People's Perspectives* (2020).

Nicola Butler is a mathematics and finance teacher at Ysgol Eirias Secondary School in North Wales. Nicola has a first-class honours degree in Banking and Finance from Bangor University. Following a long career in banking, Nicola now uses her previous experiences to give students a real insight into the importance of sustaining their finances over the long term. Her teaching and learning methods earned her The Personal Finance Teacher of the Year Award in 2021. Nicola's current focus is on embedding financial education across the whole school curriculum.

Elena Lengthorn is Senior Lecturer of Teacher Education at the University of Worcester, UK. Her research interests focus on education for sustainable development, our climate and ecological emergency and geography education. Her most recent article is 'Worcester Educator Climate Assembly: Promoting Sustainability Leadership through Participation. A Community Approach to Education in Climate Emergency' (2021). Her most recent chapter publication is 'Weather and Climate' in *Sustainability Education: A Classroom Guide* (2022).

Sarah Dukes is Sustainability Coordinator and English Teacher at The Chase School in Malvern, UK. She passionately feels we must adapt our school curriculum to include explicit teaching on the climate crisis, sustainability and nature connectedness. She has spoken on Green and Climate Education, has published on *Climate Change and*

Sustainability in Practice for The Teaching Times (2022), and has contributed to the World Wildlife Fund's *Sustainability Schools Guide* (2022).

Georgina Beard is Sustainability Coordinator and Mathematics Teacher at Nunnery Wood High School in Worcester, UK, who has an Environment and Business Management (BSc) degree from Cranfield. She has a real passion for climate education, conservation and connecting students back to nature, working directly with a variety of students to create nature spaces at school. She is a strong advocate that Environment should be a subject of its own throughout education at all levels. A keen enthusiast, she supports the World Wildlife Fund with new sustainability training and works with local environmental communities.

How to Use This Book

This book offers support to curriculum leaders, teachers, teaching assistants, support staff, student teachers and others involved in PSHE education. It aims to support the planning, delivery and assessment of a secondary school or college's PSHE curriculum, covering both statutory and non-statutory elements. Each chapter focuses on a key area within the PSHE curriculum and is informed by current research and best practice. There are opportunities throughout the chapters to engage with examples from practice, reflection questions and considerations for settings. The areas covered within the book are by no means an exhaustive list but are used as interesting and thought-provoking examples which can enhance classroom practice and whole-school implementation.

Within Each Chapter

Examples from Practice

Each chapter contains examples from practice which are designed to promote discussion and reflection within your own setting. They are an opportunity to explore PSHE areas of study and research in a practical and engaging way whilst giving snapshots of lesson activities and pedagogical strategies which have been successfully implemented by our authors.

At the End of Each Chapter

Reflection Questions for You and Your Setting

After each chapter, there are a set of reflection questions which have been designed to support you to unpick theory, research and examples given within the chapter and consider how this knowledge will develop your own practice or practice within your setting. This feature encourages you to explore the conversation within your wider school community. These questions or ideas can be used as discussion starters in staff meetings, development meetings or governors' meetings. They offer ways to encourage whole-school approaches to the planning, delivery and assessment of PSHE and R(S)HE and to explore the issues and opportunities available to particular settings. The questions are an opportunity to enable consideration of your next steps.

Recommended Resources

Listed here are suggestions of useful material, reading matter and websites which provide further understanding and resources on specific topics within PSHE.

Introduction

Victoria-Marie Pugh and

Sophie-Lauren McPhee

This book explores key aspects of the Personal, Social, Health and Economic (PSHE) education curriculum. It is intended to be an overview of the subject for trainee or pre-service teachers as well as those teachers and tutors who are experienced PSHE education providers. Within each chapter we explore some of the opportunities and challenges which come with key aspects of PSHE education and provide discussions on ways to explore the topics within each key stage, provide recommended resources and reflective questions within your own practice or that of your setting.

What Is PSHE?

PSHE has had many names, acronyms and foci over the past twenty years. In 1999, the Government's ten-year Teenage Pregnancy Strategy for England was published (Wellings et al., 2016). This national strategy aimed to reduce the rate of teenage pregnancy and ran from 1999 to 2010, with a goal of halving the under-18 conception rate, which was achieved, as evidenced in the under 18's conception rate 2014 data.

In July 2000, the government published the 'Sex and Relationship Education Guidance: Teacher, Headteacher and Governing Bodies' documents which laid out guidance for teaching Sex and Relationships Education (SRE). In February 2015, a report entitled 'Life Lessons: PSHE and SRE in Schools' was published as the direct result of an Educational Select Committee inquiry. This report made recommendations for statutory SRE and highlighted the importance of quality SRE in schools.

Finally in 2017, sections 34 and 35 of the Children and Social Work Act saw the introduction of newly named Relationships and Health education as a statutory element of education in primary schools and Relationships, Sex and Health Education (RSHE) in secondary schools. Table 0.1 shows the statutory requirements of RSHE as per the DfE guidance document (2019):

Table 0.1 Statutory requirements of RSHE as per the DfE guidance document (2019)

Relationships education	Relationships and sex Education	Health education
All schools providing primary education, including all-through schools and middle schools (includes schools as set out in the Summary section).	All schools providing secondary education, including all-through schools and middle schools (includes schools as set out in the Summary section).	All maintained schools including schools with a sixth form, academies, free schools, non-maintained special schools and alternative provision, including pupil referral units.
		The statutory requirement to provide Health Education does not apply to independent schools – PSHE is already compulsory as independent schools must meet the Independent School Standards as set out in the Education (Independent School Standards) Regulations 2014.
The statutory requirements do not apply to sixth form colleges, sixteen to nineteen academies or Further Education (FE) colleges,* although we would encourage them to support students by offering these subjects. These settings may find the principles helpful, especially in supporting pupils in the transition to FE.		

*Sixth form colleges and other 16-19 institutions that provide education for 14-16-year olds under an agreement with the Department for Education or its agencies are required by that agreement to follow guidance which covers a number of areas including the curriculum. The current guidance sets out the need to include the teaching of sex and relationship education in accordance with sections 403 and 405 of the Education Act. From September 2020, these institutions will need to teach the new subjects of Relationships and Sex Education and Health Education and to follow this guidance.

Although the statutory status of RSHE was welcomed by PSHE providers and educators across England, it did highlight the exclusion of a range of important topics such as climate justice, economic education and bereavement, to name a few. Given the omission of wider aspect of PSHE it is imperative that PSHE education goes beyond that of RSHE requirements so that it fulfils the needs of pupils both now and in their futures.

The chapters in this book therefore go beyond the statutory guidance requirements because we strongly believe that all areas of PSHE must be taught in order to provide the skills and knowledge that pupils need to lead healthy, informed lives. We acknowledge, however, that we have not covered citizenship in this book, even though some schools choose to include it as part of their PSHE education curriculum and name the subject 'PSHCEE', for example. This intentional omission is due to the fact that Citizenship is a subject in its own right and can be studied at GCSE level; however, it is not offered at every secondary establishment. Therefore, there may be many practitioners who, when developing their PSHE education curriculum, go beyond the scope of this book and also include such themes as the structure of UK local and national government; democratic rights and processes such as petitions and voting; radicalization, extremism and terrorism; and types of crime.

Despite this, it is safe to say that even each of the topics we have covered could easily be individual books of their own, so this book serves as a starting point and a springboard for further discussion, especially as PSHE education is the one school subject which is constantly changing. At the end of each chapter, we have referenced sources of information and research which have been cited and that can provide even more detail for individual topics covered.

Where to Begin?

For those who are new to PSHE education or leadership of PSHE, there are some steps which may make the introduction to PSHE easier:

- A personal audit: Considering any topics or areas of PSHE with which you might not feel as comfortable or confident teaching will enable you to identify areas to focus your CPD efforts upon. This can be personal reading of the resources recommended in this book or a more formal course or training such as those provided by the University of Worcester Diploma in PSHE or training courses run by organization such as the PSHE Association. Becoming a member of the PSHE Association as an individual or as a school is a vital step to accessing up-to-date research, resources and subject updates.
- A curriculum audit: Consider to what extent your curriculum meets both the statutory RSHE requirements and wider elements of PSHE such as the 'Living in the wider world' strand from the PSHE Association Programme of Study. Speaking to pupils, teachers and parent/carers about when topics are delivered can be a powerful way to co-create the curriculum so that it is relevant and informative for each key stage. The PSHE Association has a curriculum audit which is available for members to use.
- Staff training: Although we make the argument for specialist PSHE teachers with this book, it does need to be acknowledged that this is not possible in every setting. Nevertheless, all staff teaching PSHE must have an understanding of the statutory requirements and how these fit in with wider school or setting priorities such as safeguarding, SMSC, British Values and Personal Development. Quality CPD is important to ensure that PSHE is developed as a whole-school approach and feeds into personal development for pupils.
- Leadership: If you are a PSHE leader, ensure that you have regular communication with your safeguarding lead, pastoral team, Senior Leadership Team (SLT) as well as pupils, parents/carers and teachers. This level of communication

can support your understanding of pupil needs as well as any areas of the curriculum, delivery or assessment which may need to be adapted. If you are a PSHE teacher do not be afraid to speak to your PSHE lead if you have ideas, questions or need support for a particular aspect of PSHE.

- Curriculum development: You may use a commercial scheme of work or have created your own; either work as long as you have made the curriculum bespoke to your setting and can evidence this. Using local data and statistics such as crime rates, health data and national data can be supportive in working out what the key priorities are for your setting. For example, if your local community has high rates of knife crime or domestic violence, these elements need to be a priority within the PSHE curriculum. It is also important that your curriculum content is research-informed on a wider level too, and revised on an annual basis, as the PSHE landscape is ever-changing. Additionally, it is important that your curriculum is not reactive when a significant event occurs in the local, national or global community, but that each topic is woven into a sequenced, spiral curriculum.

- Lesson plans and resources: There are many excellent pre-prepared, research-informed PSHE lesson plans and resources. However, as we would teach our pupils in lessons on media, be critical consumers of these materials; for example, be curious as to who has funded them. This is not to say that pre-prepared materials should be rejected outright, but it is always advisable to adapt them to your circumstances, including considering the amount of time available and who will be delivering them.

- External speakers: It is important to be careful when considering external resources or speakers and ensure that there is no agenda behind the resources or presentation prior to using them. Be sure to obtain endorsements from other schools and colleges beforehand and best practice would be to check through any presentation slides in advance and have a discussion about what exactly will be delivered, and how pupils will be safeguarded. A member of the school or college staff should always be present during talks and workshops, so that any concerns can be raised – or indeed, so that the speaker can be verified as one to go on a list of recommended providers.

As an absolute starting point, however, all secondary educators, whether working in PSHE or another subject, should have a basic understanding of adolescent brain development. In PSHE education, such knowledge can link directly to topics such as mental health and relationships, but on a wider level, it can help us better understand the young people in front of us and why they think, feel and behave the way that they do, helping us in turn be more compassionate and understanding educators. From there you can start to think about how you can make your classroom a calm and caring environment, not only by creating ground rules, which we have covered throughout the book, but maybe also by using grounding exercises at the start and end of lessons, such as breathing exercises – especially useful when covering difficult topics such as bereavement. As a PSHE educator, you will need to be hyper-aware of the language, phrasing and tone that you use so that it is inclusive, and aligns with the physical space you want to create and the values you wish to help cultivate.

Why PSHE Education Is Vital Work

Whilst those of us working as PSHE education specialists wish to help pupils to make informed decisions for a happy and healthy existence as a positive contributor to society, it is inevitable that schools and colleges will want to focus heavily on raising academic attainment. The link between pupils' health and wellbeing and attainment was documented by Public Health England (2014, p.4), where it was stated that 'promoting the health and wellbeing of pupils and students within schools and colleges has the potential to improve their educational outcomes and their health and wellbeing outcomes'.

Aside from this, however, we are living in difficult times. The post-Brexit, post-Covid era of rising living costs, war in Europe and the climate emergency, to name some examples, could give us all reason to despair. However, good PSHE education is fuelled by hope, by faith in the capacity of people to make decisions – and the right decisions at that – and in turn fuels optimism that there is a future we can all look forward to. Thank you for being a part of it.

References

Public Health England (2014), *The Link between Pupil Health and Wellbeing and Attainment*. Available online: https://www.gov.uk/government/publications/the-link-between-pupil-health-and-wellbeing-and-attainment (accessed 3 July 2022).

Wellings, K., Palmer, M.J., Geary, R.S., Gibson, L.J., Copas, A., Datta, J., Glasier, A., Scott, R.H., Mercer, C.H., Erens, B., Macdowall, W., French, R.S., Jones, K., Johnson, A.M., Tanton, C. & Wilkinson, P. (2016), Changes in conceptions in women younger than 18 years and the circumstances of young mothers in England in 2000–12: an observational study, *The Lancet (British edition)*, 388(10044): 586–95.

1

How to Implement a PSHE Curriculum in a Secondary School or College

Nickael Briggs

Aims of This Chapter

- How to plan your curriculum in PSHE, advantages and disadvantages of different methods of delivery and how to create a lesson plan.
- How to work as part of the wider pastoral team.
- How to make the PSHE curriculum inclusive and the need for specialist teachers.

Curriculum Planning in PSHE

Implementing an impactful PSHE curriculum in a secondary school can be daunting due to the multifaceted nature of the subject. An effective PSHE curriculum is one that is designed to ensure that all pupils can acquire specific knowledge which is based on the most coherent and tested ways of conceptualizing the world that we have. The recent new guidance for Relationship, Sex and Health Education (RSHE) (DfE, 2019) is a welcome one due to societal changes which have seen the expansion of technology and an increase in societal pressures that young people face today. According to the PSHE Association (2018b, p.12) for RSE to be effective it ' … should always be taught within a broader PSHE education programme'. A high-quality and carefully sequenced PSHE curriculum (which includes RSE) will strongly enhance safeguarding and strengthen any whole school approach to additional school priorities such as Personal Development, SMSC and British Values. Reference to the PSHE Association is included to show how secondary school and college PSHE leads and teachers can use their 'programme builder' as a starting point for creating their own bespoke PSHE curriculum. Lastly, a compelling case will be put forward to promote the need for inclusivity in PSHE and for specialist teachers to deliver the subject.

Ofsted and the ISI (Independent Schools' Inspectorate) highlight the importance of PSHE education when judging personal development in schools. PSHE greatly contributes to fulfilling this judgement due to the emphasis on the curriculum and character development which schools must provide for students. Under the Ofsted judgement for personal development, schools must ensure students are given opportunities to develop their resilience, confidence and independence, and help them know how to keep physically and mentally healthy (EIF, 2021). Schools that evidence this well will have in place a high-quality PSHE curriculum which gives students opportunities to learn how to keep themselves safe. Similarly, the ISI state that 'the curriculum provided, including personal, social, health and economic education' will be a key measure to check whether students know how to stay safe and understand how to be physically and mentally healthy, particularly in terms of diet, exercise and a balanced lifestyle (ISI, 2019, p.13). Schools must therefore think deeply about their PSHE curriculum in order to ensure it delivers on these aims.

Curriculum planning is no easy job. There is a wealth of information out there to help assist with curriculum planning. Bruner (1960) cited in McLeod (2019) could be one way teachers could plan through what he referred to as the spiral curriculum. This involves information being structured so that complex ideas can be taught at a simplified level first, and then re-visited at more complex levels later on. The spiral analogy derives from the idea that subjects could be taught at levels which gradually increase in difficulty over time. In PSHE, teaching in this way could lead to students being able to solve problems themselves which strengthens the aims and rationale for PSHE learning.

Furthermore, a useful metaphor by H. Stanley Judd cited in Myatt (2010) highlights the importance of thinking of planning as a *roadmap*. Myatt states, 'A roadmap shows the destination but provides a number of routes to get there.' The roadmap metaphor can be a useful way of thinking about curriculum planning in PSHE. Context dependent, there are many routes a teacher can take to ensure students get the most out of their PSHE learning.

Planning backwards from the destination, teachers should ask themselves questions along the way that will lead students down the correct route for them. Starting with an overarching question in a Diversity topic for example: 'In what ways does knowledge of diversity, prejudice and bullying help us to make positive relationship decisions?' This can open ideas for the content which could be taught in the medium-term plan. Example diversity topics a teacher may explore could be:

- about identity, rights and responsibilities
- about living in a diverse society
- how to challenge prejudice, stereotypes and discrimination
- the signs and effects of all types of bullying, including online
- how to respond to bullying of any kind, including online
- how to support others

PSHE Curriculum Rationale

When creating a curriculum for PSHE, it is good practice to have a clear vision for your school which outlines the importance of the subject. Below is an example of secondary school PSHE curriculum rationale with guided questions for writing a curriculum vision.

Questions to Consider When Writing Your Curriculum Vision for PSHE

1 Why is your subject worth teaching?
2 What are pupils learning and why is it valuable?
3 What are the aims of your subject within the curriculum, including the knowledge and understanding to be gained at each stage?

An Example PSHE Vision Statement from Ark Acton Academy

Today's children and young people are growing up in an increasingly complex world and living their lives seamlessly on- and offline. This presents many positive and exciting opportunities, but also challenges and risks. In this environment, children and young people need to know how to be safe and healthy, and how to manage their academic, personal and social lives in a positive way. Personal, Social, Health and Economic (PSHE) education allows pupils to develop the knowledge, skills and attributes they need to manage their lives, now and in the future. These skills and attributes help pupils to stay healthy, safe and prepare them for life and work in modern Britain. PSHE education helps pupils to achieve their academic potential, and leave school equipped with skills they will need throughout later life. From making responsible decisions

about alcohol to succeeding in their first job, PSHE education helps pupils to manage many of the most critical opportunities, challenges and responsibilities they will face growing up. Pupils will learn to identify and articulate feelings and emotions, learn to manage new or difficult situations positively and form and maintain effective relationships with a wide range of people.

Our PSHE curriculum (Key Stages 1–5) aims to develop skills and attributes such as resilience, self-esteem, risk-management, teamworking and critical thinking in the context of three core themes: health and wellbeing, relationships and living in the wider world (including economic wellbeing and aspects of careers education). We want to prepare pupils for the future by encouraging the development of characteristics for life such as a love of learning, resilience, integrity, team work, critical thinking and independence.

Inclusivity in PSHE

Organizations such as Diversity Role Models and the Equality Human Rights Commission provide information and resources to support schools with the delivery of sensitive content. In schools where incidents of discrimination take place, teachers should be supported with resources to ensure content taught is in an inclusive and respectful way for all. Referencing and referring to the law and British Values (Department for Education, 2014) when teaching about protected characteristics can be an effective way of helping reduce or eradicate further incidents of discrimination taking place. In addition, regular coverage of protected characteristics and discrimination should permeate the whole school PSHE provision. Discrimination will not be solved through a one-off PSHE tutor session or drop-down day alone; therefore, schools are encouraged to explore their importance frequently. As directed by the DfE:

> Schools should ensure that all of their teaching is sensitive and age appropriate in approach and content. At the point at which schools consider it appropriate to teach their pupils about LGBT, they should ensure that this content is fully integrated into their programmes of study for this area of the curriculum rather than delivered as a standalone unit or lesson. (DfE, 2019, p.15)

The Method of Delivery Dilemma

There is a case to be put forward for regular timetabled lessons for PSHE in the main school timetable. Tutor time is usually shorter than an ordinary lesson in most secondary schools, which may result in PSHE content being rushed or solely content-based. This can often be problematic due to a reduced time to cover the PSHE curriculum; therefore limiting opportunities for teachers to include checks for understanding as part of formative assessment. A carefully sequenced curriculum for PSHE can only go so far if implementation is limited and reduced to a drop-down day or a once-a-week tutor time session.

In addition to curriculum planning, the roadmap metaphor can also be applied when thinking about different methods of delivery for PSHE. The variation of PSHE provision between schools is often due to time constraints within the main school curriculum timetable. Whilst some schools are able to deliver PSHE adequately within a short tutor time session each week, the questions to consider would be: is this method of delivery the most impactful? Is it appropriate to deliver sensitive topics during tutor time at the start of the day? To help with selecting the right method of delivery, PSHE leads should ask themselves:

- What will be taught and when?
- How will it be taught?
- Who will teach PSHE?
- What strategies, techniques or pedagogy will be utilized to ensure quality delivery of PSHE and opportunities for learning?
- What resources will be used?
- How will PSHE/RSHE be assessed?
- How will the pedagogy be adapted so that it is accessible and inclusive for all?
- If using a scheme or programme of study – is it sequenced in a way that is suitable and meets the needs of the pupils and school context?

Whether these can be met through a tutor time session will be dependent on each school and the time allocated. Schools which have PSHE embedded within the regular school timetable are more likely to successfully meet the statutory requirements and programme of study as stipulated by the DfE and national curriculum. According to the PSHE Association (2021a para 1), 'the most effective model of delivery for PSHE education is a sequenced, spiral programme that builds on prior learning as pupils progress through school'. They emphasize the importance of parity with other curriculum subjects and recommend PSHE to have regular curriculum time for at least an hour weekly. In an ideal world all schools would have PSHE as part of the regular school timetable; the reality is some schools will need to consider alternative methods of delivery. Often the alternative delivery methods for PSHE are through and not limited to tutor time, off-timetable drop-down days, one-off guest speakers and taught through other curriculum areas. Schools should refer to the DfE which states, 'Schools should seek to use PSHE education to build, where appropriate, on the statutory content already outlined in the national curriculum, the basic school curriculum and in statutory guidance on: drug education, financial education, sex and relationship education (SRE) and the importance of physical activity and diet for a healthy lifestyle' (DfE, 2021). Whichever method of delivery is chosen, it is essential that the statutory requirements are met and that the PSHE curriculum can deliver on its aims.

Here are some of the advantages and disadvantages of each method of delivery:

Table 1.1 Advantages and disadvantages of methods of delivery

Method of delivery	Advantages	Disadvantages
Regular timetabled lessons	• Ensures continuity and progression • Allows for assessment and measurement of progress and impact of PSHE learning • OFSTED and RSHE guidance emphasize the need for effective sequencing which builds on prior learning – this is achievable easily through this method of delivery • Gives the subject status and profile among staff and students • PSHE teaching can be delivered with the same rigour as other curriculum subjects	• Pressure on other subjects for curriculum time due to PSHE being a timetabled lesson
Tutor time/form time	• Staffing is already allocated • No pressure on other subjects for curriculum time as PSHE not a timetabled lesson	• Timing constraint as tutor time is usually 20–30 min or sometimes 15 min • Difficult to sequence content appropriately • Difficult to teach PSHE if the tutor lacks motivation • Easy to replace PSHE learning with administrative tasks and pastoral priorities • Very challenging for PSHE lead and senior team to monitor delivery and impact
Off-timetable drop-down days	• No requirement to timetable PSHE lessons • Can be delivered by external providers for part/whole of school day – although they will need to be quality-assured ahead of the day • Can be a memorable experience for young people	• Students who are absent miss out on the learning which could be their entire provision for RSE • These days usually result in higher absenteeism as students feel it is optional to attend • It is very difficult to ensure effective sequencing, continuity and progression

Method of delivery	Advantages	Disadvantages
One-off lessons and guest speakers	• If selected carefully, speakers are skilled or expert in the chosen content area • Raises awareness of a particular issue	• Difficult to assess learning and impact • Listening passively to a guest speaker does not allow pupils to develop the crucial skills, strategies, and attributes that PSHE education aims to develop • Little or no opportunity for continuity or progression
Other curriculum areas	• It does not require dedicated curriculum time for PSHE lessons • Could increase 'ownership' of PSHE education by all staff and sense of responsibility for it as part of a whole school approach	• Absolute staff 'buy-in' is needed and commitment from the senior team • Difficult to ensure PSHE education learning objectives are achieved as they tend to be secondary to those of the 'main' subject • Often tokenistic when delivered using this method • Nearly impossible to ensure continuity, effective sequencing and progression • Difficult to assess progress • Particularly challenging for young people to draw the PSHE education learning together in a way that makes sense in relation to their own lives

The Department for Education's 2011 research report (Formby et al., 2012, p.4) stated that ' … schools with successful PSHE education are more likely to have the following features: a coherent, progressive curriculum across the full range of elements, core curriculum time, well resourced delivery and CPD opportunities'. Whilst the DfE's 2011 research report (Formby et al., 2012, p.4) recommends PSHE has core curriculum time, PSHE leads are unlikely to have a say over the method of delivery in their school. However, PSHE leads should put forward a compelling argument to the senior leadership team for PSHE education to be delivered as part of the regular school timetable.

Having knowledge about different methods of delivery and knowing the advantages and disadvantages of each provides PSHE leads with a solid starting point for entering this discussion. Secondary school and college PSHE leads are encouraged to browse through the range of different 'programme builders' available on the PSHE Association website. They offer: Cross-phase (KS2-3, Year 3–8 inclusive), Thematic (KS3-4), Competencies-based (KS3-4) and KS5 Programme Builder (including planning tool).

Lesson Planning in PSHE

Planning is critical to effective teaching. Successful PSHE teaching takes place when effective planning has happened, and teachers have the confidence to be responsive in the lesson. There may be times in a PSHE lesson where what you initially planned goes in the complete opposite direction and that is ok! There are some key questions the PSHE Association identifies which teachers can use when planning for PSHE teaching PSHE Association (2021c).

Planning for KS5 Students

In a secondary school with a sixth form attached, it is equally important to ensure the curriculum scope for PSHE includes Key Stage 5. A good way to plan for Key Stage 5 is to plan backwards. Key Stage 5 is the final stage before students are equipped with the knowledge and the skills to lead healthy and happy lives. PSHE leads are encouraged to ask themselves what knowledge and skills a Key Stage 5 student should have after developing these throughout their PSHE education. A carefully sequenced and progressive spiral curriculum would ensure that Key Stage 5 students can build on prior knowledge and start to think about how they can apply acquired knowledge in a range of different settings. For example, a Key Stage 5 student learning about the topic of financial stability should already be familiar with knowledge of saving, borrowing, budgeting and making financial choices. At Key Stage 5, students would build on this knowledge by learning how to plan expenditure and budget for changes in circumstances (e.g. when moving out or going to university).

Working with the Wider Pastoral Team

School context and knowledge of the contextual safeguarding issues are essential when thinking about PSHE curriculum planning. For instance, if a school has numerous incidents of illicit substance misuse affecting its community, this would be known as a contextual safeguarding issue. With this knowledge, a PSHE lead should ensure that sufficient coverage of substance misuse is present in the PSHE curriculum at appropriate times. Furthermore, knowledge of school context and the contextual safeguarding issues will help inform which knowledge needs prioritizing, sequencing of knowledge and the selection of the most appropriate delivery method. PSHE leads should work closely with the safeguarding team or meet regularly with the Designated Safeguarding Lead (DSL) to be aware of issues affecting students. It is good practice for the safeguarding team to work with PSHE leads to ensure that students remain knowledgeable of how to keep themselves safe. For example, students who are taught about child sexual exploitation are more likely to be aware of the signs and take the right steps to report and seek help. It is often the case that students become aware that they have been a victim through learning about it in a PSHE Lesson. Lemov (2018) refers to relational teaching which is the idea that teachers can use the way they teach to build trusting relationships. PSHE teaching provides teachers with more opportunities to continue relationship building with their students. Some schools may find that students feel more comfortable reporting issues affecting them to their PSHE teacher rather than other subject teachers.

Furthermore, working with the wider pastoral team such as the head of year can provide PSHE leads and teachers with insightful and invaluable information which may be affecting their year group. For example, if vaping is taking place among Year 9 students, it might be an opportunity for PSHE teachers to address this within the curriculum. However, it is important to recognize that the PSHE curriculum will not solve every social issue or problem in a school. If a PSHE lead changed the curriculum every time different incidents arose, it would undermine the sequencing and progression within the subject. It is unlikely that the head of department for geography would change their curriculum if suddenly the school had numerous issues with recycling. Therefore, the same consideration should be afforded to the PSHE curriculum.

Inclusivity in the PSHE Curriculum

Pedagogical principles apply in PSHE. It is for this reason the case for specialist teachers of PSHE can be put forward. Often schools feel that the curriculum should be adapted to support students with SEND but actually it is the pedagogy that can be adapted to ensure that all students can access the knowledge. Approaches and strategies used to support SEND students in other curriculum areas can be applied in PSHE too. This is achieved more easily if PSHE education takes place as a regular timetabled lesson as opposed to other methods of delivery. For instance, if an off-timetable drop-down day is taking place for a year group, it could be difficult to maximize the use of learning support assistants. In addition, an off-timetable drop-down day can often present difficulties with student behaviour as the format of the day is usually different to a normal school day. With this in mind, PSHE leads are encouraged to plan ahead for how all students, but especially those with SEND can be supported effectively to ensure that the PSHE curriculum is accessible. Communicating dates in advance with the SENDCo about upcoming drop-down days, PSHE events can be helpful to ensure that the needs of SEND pupils are planned for. Schools should be aware that the DfE stipulates the importance of an inclusive PSHE curriculum in the RSHE Guidance: *124. Lessons should be planned to ensure that pupils of differing abilities, including the most able, are suitably challenged. Teaching should be assessed, and assessments used to identify where pupils need extra support or intervention* (DfE, 2019, p.43). In addition, the PSHE Association has its own planning framework for pupils with SEND to support schools with getting it right. On the PSHE Association (2021 para 13) website it is stated: 'Teachers working with pupils with SEND are acutely aware of the relevance of respectful relationships, online relationships, being safe, mental wellbeing and the changing adolescent body for their pupils – but may wonder how best to approach this curriculum content.' Their solution to this is their planning framework tool, which supports PSHE leads and teachers with developing a comprehensive and bespoke PSHE programme that is accessible for all. Furthermore, it is important to plan for the 'most able' students by ensuring that there is enough stretch and challenge within PSHE. Good examples of this could be extended writing tasks or discussions in response to a scenario or debate. For example, a high-ability student could be given the following discussion statement to evaluate: 'The age for drinking alcohol should be lowered in the UK: Discuss.' This could then be used to form a debate in the class.

Schools and PSHE leads should recognize that there are cases where the statutory content may not be accessible for students with SEND. In these instances, PSHE leads and teachers are encouraged to adapt and differentiate in a way which will still lead to SEND students acquiring the right knowledge from the intended learning outcomes. The PSHE Association planning framework is one way in which PSHE leads can receive support with planning for pupils with SEND. In addition to this, teachers of PSHE are able to apply the same principles they use when providing for SEND students in their own subject areas with PSHE too. For example, if you have students with SEND in your PSHE class, it is good practice to familiarize yourself with their SEND profile and plan to meet their needs. There should be no difference in planning for a student with SEND in your PSHE lesson in comparison to planning in another subject area.

Inclusivity is very much on the agenda for school inspections, particularly with the teaching of protected characteristics. The Equality Act (2010) introduced the following nine protected characteristics: age, disability, gender reassignment, marriage and civil partnership, pregnancy and maternity, race, religion or belief, sex and sexual orientation. The law protects individuals from any form of discrimination and schools should therefore take a zero-tolerance approach to inequalities. The guidance from OFSTED for LGBT teaching is clear when it states: 'Secondary schools could, for example, teach pupils in more detail about sexuality and gender identity as well as the legal rights afforded to LGBT people. As stated in the DfE's statutory guidance, teaching on these matters should be integrated appropriately into the curriculum, rather than addressed separately or in one-off lessons' (Ofsted, 2021). This again supports the case for PSHE being part of the regular school timetable as it avoids one-off lessons taking place which have little (if any) meaningful impact. The emphasis on integration appropriately in the curriculum suggests schools should sequence the teaching of protected characteristics properly. The teaching of protected characteristics can also feature as part of a school's assembly programme or a more holistic school approach to fundamental British Values. Essentially, schools must avoid tokenistic coverage of protected characteristics to ensure students are fully aware of the law and are able to respect differences.

The Case for Specialist Teachers

The release of the RSHE guidance has strengthened the case for specialist teachers of PSHE. With the increasing number of schools refining their PSHE curriculum and ensuring that it is appropriately sequenced, progressive and allows for continuity, the need for better trained PSHE teachers is vast. A starting point for schools could be to train the existing teachers of PSHE internally and/or externally as part of continued professional development. There are countless online training and face-to-face training events offered by credible organizations such as University of Worcester Diploma in PSHE, Chameleon PDE, The National College and the PSHE Association to upskill teachers. With assessment practices developing in PSHE, it is important for schools to factor in time for PSHE leads to train themselves and staff on what effective assessment looks like in PSHE. Chameleon PDE (n.d.) offers straightforward suggestions of what this may look like:

- Discussion
- Questions the pupils ask
- Worksheets
- Video
- Audio
- Written work
- Drama
- Art
- Presentations
- ICT
- Projects
- Pupil reflections

PSHE assessments can easily complement a school's PSHE curriculum and be invaluable in measuring a student's progress with learning. The DfE states: 'Whilst there is no formal examined assessment for these subjects, there are some areas to consider in strengthening quality of provision, and which demonstrate how teachers can assess outcomes. For example, tests, written assignments or self-evaluations, to capture progress' (DfE, Relationships Education, Sex and Relationships Education and Health Education, 2019, p.43). According to the PSHE Association (2021c), 'Effective assessment allows pupils and teachers to reflect on what has been learned, increases motivation for future learning and demonstrates impact.' Furthermore, assessment within PSHE can allow PSHE leads to refine their curriculum and plan for common misconceptions which arise from student responses.

For schools with non-specialist teachers of PSHE, a quick formative assessment technique to use is multiple choice questioning. The Education Endowment Foundation [EEF] states: 'We found well-designed multiple-choice questions (MCQ's) particularly effective for explicitly targeting common misconceptions' (EEF, 2021, p.11). Quick and easy to mark, MCQs increase the time available for responsive teaching within lessons, whilst allowing for next step tasks to be identified and set immediately for individual pupils. Implementing MCQs in PSHE would reveal gaps in knowledge and allow teachers to quickly identify what knowledge needs to be retaught. A case study school included in the EEF strengthens the case for MCQs as a formative assessment. 'By adapting existing formative questions with targeted, diagnostic multiple-choice we reduced the administrative burden on teachers, whilst more efficiently uncovering issues that needed addressing' (EEF, 2021, p.11). This type of formative assessment may prove invaluable in schools which have predominantly non-specialist teachers teaching PSHE. Equally, in schools where PSHE is taught within a shorter time period, the use of MCQs may be a quick check for understanding assessment tool which can happen within a fifteen- to thirty-minute lesson. Nevertheless, schools should have the same high expectations of the quality of pupils' work in PSHE as they would for other curriculum subjects. The DfE states, 'A strong curriculum will build on the knowledge pupils have previously acquired, including in other subjects, with regular feedback provided on pupil progress' (DfE, Relationships Education, Sex and Relationships Education and Health Education, 2019, p.43).

An Example School Leader Who Led an NPQSL Project on Increasing the Capability of PSHE Teaching in a School with Non-Specialists

'I knew that to improve the PSHE offer it would require a dedicated team of PSHE champions. My strategy was to meet with some keen form tutors and train them as PSHE champions and experts. Once I had a PSHE coordinator and PSHE champions in place, it was time to focus on connecting my team to the purpose'. As put clearly by Schmoker (2018) in his book Leading with Focus, "As Daniel Pink (2009) reminds us, knowing what to do isn't enough; people need to also know why it's worth doing' (Schmoker, 2018, p.55). He summarizes this by explaining if teachers are going to accept change, it is essential that they understand they are being asked to change for the better.

'I used Peps McCrea's article on "Expert Teaching" (March 2018) which states, Teaching quality is important. It is arguably the greatest lever at our disposal for improving the life chances of the young people in our care (Hattie, 2015), particularly for those from disadvantaged backgrounds. The power of seeing PSHE as a taught lesson rather than 'form time' was transformational for our school culture. In staff training, we can now use PSHE as a subject example so that teachers are reminded of PSHE being a taught subject rather than a form time filler. Teachers receiving action steps and feedback validates the subject of PSHE as being important and an area which we can still use to develop our teaching quality. Going forward, when teachers receive training for PSHE, it will be designed around the same principles of training and theory we use for CPD. For example, scripting, deliberate practice and cold call will apply in PSHE training sessions. The PSHE lead will attend external PSHE training days and receive coaching on whole school facilitation using my knowledge of teacher educator training.

The findings from the analysis I completed for my NPQSL project have shown that initial CPD training next year will need to be on subject knowledge, and this will take place within departmental co-planning time for PSHE. I am satisfied that the appointment of a PSHE coordinator, team of PSHE champions and protected time for co-planning next year will ensure sustainability of this project.'

Conclusion

This chapter has highlighted the need for schools to have in place a carefully sequenced spiral curriculum for PSHE. There are numerous methods of delivery for PSHE teaching but the case for regular timetabled lessons and specialist teachers of PSHE is strong. Schools and colleges without PSHE as part of the regular school timetable can still achieve these aims, providing PSHE is mapped throughout the school experience and provides opportunities for assessment to ensure progress and impact. Fundamentally, schools should ensure students revisit key concepts and topic areas, each time extending knowledge, deepening understanding and developing skills in order to lead healthy and happy lives.

Reflection Questions for You and Your Setting

- Is PSHE organized, delivered and resourced in a way that ensures it is effective and impactful?
- Have you ensured the PSHE and RSHE curriculum design meets the needs of students and the wider community?
- Is your PSHE curriculum accessible and inclusive for all?
- Do teachers who deliver PSHE have access to training or resources to help with effective teaching of the subject?

Recommended Resources

Chameleon PDE: https://www.chameleonpde.com/
Education Endowment Foundation:
    https://educationendowmentfoundation.org.uk/
Personal, Social, Health and Economic (PSHE) Education: A mapping study
    of the prevalent models of delivery and their effectiveness, Formby et al.,
    DfE, 2011: http://bit.ly/2FyjZE5
Models of Delivery for PSHE Education, PSHE Association resource:
    http://bit.ly/2iq9t6S
Programme of Study for PSHE Education (Key Stages 1–5), PSHE
    Association: http://bit.ly/2qmAdGf
Mary Myatt: https://www.marymyatt.com/blog/some-principles-for-planning
University Of Worcester PSHE Diploma: https://www.worcester.ac.uk/
    courses/university-diploma-in-personal-social-and-health-education

References

Chameleon PDE (n.d.), How do I assess pupil progress in PSHE? *(Personal, Social, Health Education).* Available online: https://www.chameleonpde.com/documents/4-how-do-i-assess-pupil-progress-in-pshe-personal-social-health-education (accessed 1 June 2022).

DfE (2014), Guidance on promoting British values in schools published. Available online: https://www.gov.uk/government/news/guidance-on-promoting-british-values-in-schools-published (accessed 24 June 2022).

DfE (2019), Relationships education, relationships and sex education (RSE) and health education. Available online: https://assets.publishing.service.gov.uk/government/uploads/system/uploads/attachment_data/file/1019542/Relationships_Education__Relationships_and_Sex_Education__RSE__and_Health_Education.pdf (accessed 22 May 2022).

DfE (2021), https://www.gov.uk/government/publications/inspecting-teaching-of-the-protected-characteristics-in-schools/inspecting-teaching-of-the-protected-characteristics-in-schools (accessed 31 Aug 2023).

Education Inspection Framework (2021). Available online: https://www.gov.uk/government/publications/education-inspection-framework/education-inspection-framework (accessed 2 July 2022).

Formby, E. & Wolstenholme, C. (2012), 'If there's going to be a subject that you don't have to do …' Findings from a mapping study of PSHE education in English secondary schools, *Pastoral Care in Education,* 30(1), pp. 5–18. Available at: https://dx.doi.org/10.1080/02643944.2011.651227.

Hattie, J. (2015), What works best in education: The politics of colaborative expertise. Pearson. Available at chrome-extension://efaidnbmnnnibpcajpcglclefindmkaj/h ttps://www.pearson.com/content/dam/corporate/global/pearson-dot-com/files/hattie/150526_ExpertiseWEB_V1.pdf.

Independent Schools Inspectorate (2019). Available online: https://www.isi.net/site/downloads/1.1%20Handbook%20Inspection%20Framework%202019-09.pdf (accessed 2 July 2022).

Inspecting teaching of the protected characteristics in schools (2021). Available online: https://www.gov.uk/government/publications/inspecting-teaching-of-the-protected-characteristics-in-schools/inspecting-teaching-of-the-protected-characteristics-in-schools (accessed 31 May 2022).

Lemov (2018), 'It's the most important tool for building relationships', and other insights about check for understanding. Available online: https://teachlikeachampion.com/blog/important-tool-building-relationships-insights-check-understanding/ (accessed 19 May 2022).

Mccrea, P. (2018), Expert Teaching: What is it, and how might we develop it? *Institute for Teaching,* 1.4 2018.

McLeod, S. A. (11 July 2019), Bruner – learning theory in education. *Simply Psychology.* Available online: www.simplypsychology.org/bruner.html (accessed 25 June 2022).

Myatt, M. (2010), Some principles for planning [Blog] https://www.marymyatt.com/blog/some-principles-for-planning (accessed 8 April 2022).

Ofsted, 2021, https://www.gov.uk/government/publications/inspecting-teaching-of-the-protected-characteristics-in-schools/inspecting-teaching-of-the-protected-characteristics-in-schools.

Personal, Social, Health and Economic (PSHE) Education: A mapping study of the prevalent models of delivery and their effectiveness, Formby et al, DfE, 2011: http://bit.ly/2FyjZE5

PSHE Association (2018b), Preparing for statutory RSE and relationships education within your PSHE curriculum. Available online: https://www.pshe-association.org.uk/curriculum-and-resources/resources/preparing-statutory-rse-and-relationships (accessed 10 March 2020).

PSHE Association (2021a), Build your programme. Available online: https://pshe-association.org.uk/guidance/ks3-5/models-of-delivery (accessed 31 Aug 2023).

PSHE Association (2021b), PSHE education for pupils with SEND. Available online: https://pshe-association.org.uk/guidance/ks1-4/pshe-education-pupils-with-send (accessed 31 May 2022).

PSHE Association (2021c), Writing a PSHE education lesson plan – guidance for teachers and publishers. Available online: https://pshe-association.org.uk/news/news-and-blog/blog-entry/how-plan-pshe-curriculum-pupils-send (accessed 31 Aug 2023).

Schmoker, M. (2018), *Leading with Focus: Elevating the Essentials to Radically Improve Student Learning, 2nd edition,* Alexandria, Virginia US: ASCD.

The EEF Guide to supporting school planning: A tiered approach to 2020-21. Available online: https://educationendowmentfoundation.org.uk/public/files/Publications/Covid-19_Resources/The_EEF_guide_to_supporting_school_planning_-_A_tiered_approach_to_2020-21.pdf (accessed 15 May 2022).

2

Monitoring, Marking, Reporting and Assessment in PSHE

Stephen Lane

Aims of This Chapter

- Consider the need or otherwise for assessment in PSHE.
- Contemplate some of the links between assessment, curriculum and pedagogy.
- Ponder different approaches to assessment, monitoring and reporting in PSHE.

It's data entry time. Again. You have spent several hours clicking on drop-down menus here and selecting grades there. You allow a small smile of relief to creep upon your face as you hit 'submit' on your last pupil. But alas, there is something else. A small slice of red in an otherwise green pie chart of completion glares at you in all its menacing redness. You open the remaining class. It's your form group. You remember, with an intoxicating cocktail of dread and ennui, that your senior leadership team has decided it's going to start collecting assessment data for PSHE. You blink at the screen a little, as your finger gently taps the mouse in what your subconscious deeply hopes is a soothing rhythm. It isn't. Your left eye begins to twitch. There's an inexplicable quivering in the bit of your hand between the thumb and the wrist. Your central executive desperately tries to engage your working memory and trawls the recesses of your long-term memory. The first name of your form group taunts you, much like the child to which it belongs does each morning. Is Barry working at expectation?

Assessment in subject domains is a contested space. In the secondary sector, the death of KS3 SATs and Assessing Pupil Progress left a vacuum that many schools tried to fill with various alternatives (Hunter, 2016; Wynn, 2015), some of which became the source of much debate and derision in the discourses of EduTwitter.

But if subject assessment is problematic, then assessment in the area of PSHE is even more so. Firstly, there are the practical questions that arise in terms of how one might assess PSHE as a subject. Is there a specific body of knowledge that we want children to learn? Are there key facts that they can be asked to recall? Are quizzes the ideal solution? Or is PSHE a more 'skills-based' field? Perhaps students could produce a portfolio of evidence over the course of a term or year. Should assessment be based not on 'testing' at all, but rather on teacher observation? Perhaps pupils could be assessed through oral contributions – class discussions, presentations and so on.

Secondly, and perhaps more profoundly, there are philosophical questions about what PSHE is for and about that ultimately affect the way we might view it as an accessible curriculum artefact. Such questions also lead to pedagogical matters about how to teach PSHE which then also impact upon how it might be assessed.

Thirdly, there are ethical issues around whether PSHE should be assessed at all. Perhaps PSHE should exist as a curriculum space free from the burden of assessment; perhaps its content and subject matter demand more sensitivity than any model of assessment can provide. Perhaps children need to feel safe in PSHE lessons without the anxiety or fear of being assessed – of the possibility of getting an answer wrong, or the humiliation of a low grade. Just imagine being 'below expectations' in PSHE. It is obviously fundamental, therefore, that any model of assessment is designed and implemented in such a way that it can establish learning needs and progress without conveying any sense of failure or judgement. A recent report into the assessment of social and emotional education across the EU highlights the need for assessment to be 'respectful of the rights of the child' (Cefai, Downes, Cavioni, 2021, p.9).

But if PSHE assessment is to be effective, it also must be worthwhile and robust. Back in 2012, Ofsted found that assessment was a weakness of much PSHE provision in schools (Ofsted 2013). And with Ofsted's more recent shift to focusing on intent, implementation and impact (Ofsted 2021), it is clear that schools need to think about how they can assess the impact of any provision in PSHE as part of their curriculum. Furthermore, the DfE makes clear that 'schools should have the same high expectations of the quality of pupils' work in these subjects as for other curriculum areas' and that 'teaching should be assessed' (DfE, 2019, p.43).

It is therefore clear that schools need to have clear and robust methods of assessment in place for PSHE, but what might this look like? Any answer to this question will depend upon what it is you want the assessment to do – what is it for? What is being assessed? What do we want the assessment to tell us? What do we want it to achieve? There are several possible methods of assessment, but they all essentially aim to fulfil one or more of these four purposes:

- Assessment of pupil progress
- Assessment of the curriculum

- Assessment of the teaching
- Pupil assessment of ideas and confidence levels

Any model of assessment will ultimately aim to address one of the above.

The PSHE Association website states that 'assessment is central to effective teaching and learning' and that PSHE education is 'no exception' (PSHE Association, n.d.). They recommend an ipsative model of assessment where a baseline of existing knowledge, understanding or skill is established through 'I can' statements which are then revisited throughout a unit or/and at the end to monitor progress. The baseline assessment identifies strengths and areas of development to inform teaching but also to inform pupils' own awareness of their learning. Such self-reflection can encourage serious engagement with the issues and topics covered in PSHE and can also help children to see the importance of them and the relevance to their own lives of the things that are being explored.

An ipsative model of self-assessment against 'I can' statements could well resolve some of the potential tensions of assessment in PSHE, removing some of the anxiety and fear of failure associated with tests and exams as found in other subjects. However, even self-assessment can have a negative impact upon wellbeing for students, especially for those who perhaps already have a negative self-view. Reflecting upon a bank of statements might lead some children to doubt their own level of knowledge and skill, especially if their peers are scoring themselves more highly. Given the sensitive nature of some aspects of PSHE – particularly the statutory RSE elements – some children may feel they have very limited knowledge indeed. Conversely, some pupils may feel reluctant to respond truthfully if they have experienced traumatic events. Furthermore, the use of self-assessment forms, which are essentially questionnaires, may evoke strong emotional responses in some children who have experienced especially difficult lives outside of school. In a review of the research on student self-assessment, Andrade found that children may have 'unsophisticated understandings' of the purposes of self-assessment that 'might lead to shallow implementation of related processes' (Andrade, 2019, p.8) but that overall self-assessment has positive outcomes.

Further questions arise around what happens with these self-assessment questionnaires once they have been completed. Are they kept in pupil folders? Stored within the classroom? Presumably so if there is to be a comparison with forms completed at a later stage in the unit to demonstrate progress. Given the potentially sensitive nature of these forms, there are ethical and data protection considerations here which teachers and school leaders will need to dedicate serious time to. Schools can overcome these challenges by having a clear strategy that is understood and implemented by all teachers involved.

And then there is the question of recording – how do teachers record the data produced by self-assessment against 'I can' statements; what even are the data that might be produced? Is someone (a teacher?) going to go through children's responses recording the answer to each prompt? Such things could be done electronically, of course, either through some form of machine-readable coding sheets for pupil responses or through a computer-based input programme where children use devices to complete the self-assessments. The latter would have inevitable logistical issues depending upon the availability of such devices.

Another way of thinking about assessment – in any subject, but particularly in PSHE – is to consider it more fully in relation to curriculum. Obviously, 'I can' type statements are generally mapped onto a set of pre-determined curricular objectives. The ipsative model of assessment is intended to measure pupil progress against those objectives so that teachers can claim that progress has been made and everyone is happy. But assessment could be designed to more explicitly identify pupil learning of specific curriculum knowledge. Whilst the obvious way of doing this is a 'test', more pupil friendly methods such as quizzes can be quicker, giving more immediate feedback to the teacher and to the pupil. What's more, they are generally considered more fun and engaging. Such quizzes would test pupils' recall of certain nuggets of knowledge – facts. In the popular education discourses, facts are often derided but there is a growing call for 'knowledge rich' curricula that can give students a secure bedrock. There is no reason why this cannot be the case in PSHE. With the introduction of statutory RSE content, there is perhaps an increased focus on specific things that we want young people to know – issues around the law and consent for example. In this proposition, assessment is intended to show how securely pupils have learnt these specific things and whether or not they need to be re-taught. This approach requires teachers and PSHE leaders to have clearly articulated curricula artefacts – articles of knowledge – that they want their pupils to learn. These then become the basis of the assessment. In her keynote speech at ResearchEd Leicester, Christine Counsell (2022) gave a convincing argument for this approach to assessment, which she summarized as 'Teach them some stuff; check they're secure on it; if not, do something about it'.

This approach to assessment is intertwined with curriculum and there is a strong argument that this should be the case; after all, the overriding purpose of schooling is to equip pupils with knowledge and skills that will enable them to thrive, right? If PSHE is to exist on the timetable, then it demands and deserves a strong and coherent curriculum against which pupil's learning can be assessed and monitored. From this perspective, assessment is a vital tool in ensuring that pupils are competent and confident young people, ready to face the world on their own terms. This is, perhaps, simplistically idealistic. The reality is that schools are expected to assess pupils for the purposes of monitoring their 'progress' which brings us back to the ultimate question of what assessment is actually for. Perhaps one might be convinced that schools are expected to monitor pupil progress only because this in itself will help to ensure good outcomes, but 'outcomes' must be about more than exam results, especially when PSHE is not examined. Perhaps it should be – perhaps there should be a qualification available to students in PSHE. For instance, there is a GCSE in citizenship studies which covers some of the same ground that one might find in a comprehensive PSHE programme. Perhaps an externally validated certification could bring some sharp focus to the study, teaching and assessment of PSHE. Perhaps it would give the subject an added weight in the perception of pupils, parents and, indeed, teachers. Or, perhaps, this is silly. Perhaps PSHE's strength is that it exists outside of these kinds of expectations. As soon as we contemplate any kind of certification in PSHE, we begin to skew the lens through which we view it and, I would argue, pervert the very purpose of PSHE.

I once worked at a school where the entire PSHE curriculum was delivered through drama lessons, and the drama curriculum was driven by PSHE considerations. This novel approach seemed to work well, although I must confess to being unclear on how this was assessed – presumably through drama-based assessment activities.

There is an alternative way of thinking about the curriculum/assessment relationship other than in terms of assessing pupil progress. In a talk at ResearchEDBrum (rEDBrum) in 2022, David Didau gave a convincing argument that assessment should be used to judge the curriculum and the teaching – a point touched upon by one of his recent blog posts where he says, 'If students struggle to answer test items, we should assume the fault is with the curriculum (students across multiple classes struggle) or with instruction (students in a particular class struggle)' (Didau, 2021). Didau argues that the curriculum should be the progression model and gives solid examples of how this can be done in his subject specialism of English (Didau, 2022). However, it could be convincingly argued that such an approach could be applied to PSHE where curriculum-related expectations (CREs) 'help us to specify, teach and assess the knowledge we expect children to acquire' (Didau, 2020). Determining what these CREs should be in PSHE would require school leaders to give time to PSHE leaders to discuss and plan them, but this would be a very worthwhile activity in school.

Any kind of assessment model will raise questions about the interaction between the teacher and the pupil in terms of marking and feedback. As noted above, self-assessment forms raise issues of how teachers might record and monitor the 'answers' or 'scores', but they also raise the difficulty of marking – should self-assessment be marked by a teacher? Perhaps some acknowledgement of having being read might be appreciated by the pupils, but would they like to see teacher annotations or comments on them? Would teachers feel that marking such artefacts is time well spent, yielding a developed understanding of their classes? Or is it far more likely that such an activity would simply (and accurately) be perceived as an unnecessary addition to the workload burden? My advice here would very much err on the side of no 'marking' in these scenarios; I really cannot see the point of it, and we do not want self-assessments to become artefacts of judgement.

Quizzes and multiple-choice-style assessments can, of course, be marked by the teacher but, again, there are fundamental questions about the trade-off between the time spent on doing this and the benefits to be gained in terms of teacher understanding and genuine pupil progress. What does each party gain from this exchange?

Good marking should encourage a meaningful dialogue between the teacher and the pupil that helps the teacher to know where their students are at, and helps the pupil to know what their next steps in learning should be. This is a difficult juggling act in any subject, but even more so in PSHE. Perhaps one response might be to encourage pupils to produce extended pieces of writing in PSHE that enable the teacher to judge their understanding in a fuller way, and marking becomes a richer exchange. However, as Didau (2022) notes, this is not actually particularly helpful in English – where one might expect to find it – and I doubt that teachers, or their pupils, would particularly value essays in PSHE.

A more immediate form of assessment is, of course, through verbal dialogue in class discussions. I imagine that this is the most common approach across schools and it has much to recommend it.

Of course, class discussions can take various forms and shapes. In my experience, the kinds of self-assessment questionnaires discussed above can often lead to some interesting discussions and exchanges of ideas, experiences and points of view. These discussions can be rich, engaging and often entertaining. The tricky bit is to make sure that all pupils have the opportunity to have their voice heard and this raises some questions for pupils who are introverted by nature. Being introverted can often be misread as being shy and these two things are not necessarily synonymous. Whilst children should be given the opportunity to speak, no-one should be made to feel uncomfortable through an expectation of participation in class discussions. One approach might be to allow paired/small group discussions in addition to whole class discussions. There is a rich field of work on dialogic education, most notably that of Robin Alexander (Alexander, 2020), which teachers of PSHE might well be advised to familiarize themselves with.

However, marking and assessment of verbal discourses are notably difficult. As a teacher of English, I am all too familiar with some of the complexities of this. At GCSE, pupils are expected to give a talk which is assessed as pass, merit or distinction against performance criteria provided by the examining body. Whether such an approach could be applied to PSHE is something that teachers would need to discover for themselves, but I can imagine it presenting some difficulties both in terms of logistics and in terms of recording. Furthermore, these kinds of classroom discussions might make a CRE approach to assessment far more difficult. How might one ensure that an individual pupil has securely grasped any or all of the key curriculum artefacts that we want them to know through the medium of class discussion? Teachers might be well advised to develop specific questioning strategies designed to target demonstrable knowledge of such curriculum artefacts. Or, the teacher may consolidate discussion-led learning through quizzes, mini-whiteboards or other such snapshot assessment tools.

Perhaps this 'knowledge' based approach, via curriculum approaches to assessment, is not the best fit for PSHE after all. Perhaps the P4C model points us in another direction where rather than teachers testing pupils' progress against curriculum items, it is pupils themselves doing the testing: testing out ideas, points of view, experiences against those of experts in the field or against test cases. One of the types of self-assessment questions that goes beyond 'I can' statements are those which ask pupils how far they agree with certain statements. These can be plotted on Likert-type responses using 1–5 where 1 denotes 'hard disagree' and 5 denotes 'hard agree'. To make them more appealing to younger pupils, they might be presented as smiley faces or as star ratings and so on. These kinds of questions have two possible advantages. Firstly, any of them could lead to larger discussion in class, or to an extended written response if desired. Secondly, they also provide the possibility for the kind of ipsative assessment noted previously but instead of measuring 'progress' in some kind of numerical sense – as if working towards ever higher scores as a teleological goal – they enable pupils to judge their own shifts in opinion and position. These could be monitored by teachers if this is desired, but I don't think this would really achieve anything. Rather, pupils could monitor their own 'progress' in terms of how their own ideas have developed or changed in the light of materials studied within any given unit. Such an approach might, however, present some difficulties in terms of what it would yield for data collection.

This latter point – the difficulty of assessment in PSHE for the purposes of data – gets right to the heart of an overriding issue with assessment in all subjects, but especially in PSHE: What is it for? In the opening of this chapter, I painted an exaggerated picture of data entry but one that is grounded in reality. My experience of working in a range of schools over a period spanning twenty years is that data entry is largely pointless. Or, rather, the point of data has been to serve managerial purposes rather than those of genuine learning or progress monitoring. A full critique of the uses of assessment data in schools is not within the scope of this chapter and could fill many an academic paper. Suffice to say, pupil assessment data continues to be a problematic arena and this is doubly so in PSHE. Happily, my experience is that most schools do not actually ask teachers to provide any kind of data for pupils in PSHE. Rather, form tutors might be asked to include a comment on PSHE as part of their form tutor reports to parents. Such comments may be based upon the teacher's observations of the pupil's participation in PSHE discussions, their responses to quizzes and self-assessment type forms, or any other form of assessment that may have been employed during the year. But inevitably, such comments are brief and most likely form one element of a form tutor's statement on the pupil. It is highly unlikely that these kinds of comments will make any detailed reference to any kind of performance data, and although the word 'progress' might appear in a statement such as 'Barry has made good progress in PSHE this year', it is likely to be fairly generic and meaningless. The question becomes, then, what would parents most want to know about their child's progress in PSHE? What kind of assessment might be considered meaningful? Do parents even consider PSHE to be an important part of the school curriculum? Hopefully they do, and this will have been fostered by a well-considered approach to PSHE planning that involves communicating the curriculum content to parents and carers; certainly, any statutory RSE components may require parental consent and awareness of their right to withdraw.

Many schools have adopted a model of assessment for the purposes of reporting that describes pupil progress in terms of approaching expectations, working at expectation or working above expectation. This is, like most models, the topic of some debate in the education discourses but it is even more problematic, perhaps, in PSHE. In English, for example, there may be a clear set of criteria against which such judgements are made and, ultimately, there are models of subject assessment which form the basis of external examinations. This is not so in PSHE. Whilst some models of PSHE-specific assessment may have descriptors of performance, or statements of knowledge/skill, there is no general agreed level of performance that can be used for comparison between pupils which is, ultimately, the purpose of examinations such as GCSE and A Level. These exams exist to sort students into hierarchies. To determine whether a pupil is working 'at expectation' it is necessary to determine what such an expectation might be. Often, schools use some form of baseline tests to determine predictors of performance – tools such as the Middle Years Information System (MidYIS) from the Centre for Evaluation and Monitoring (CEM), which uses an adaptive test to establish predictors of performance at GCSE, or Fischer Family Trust (FFT), which uses pupils' prior attainment to make predictions of future performance. These can be used to determine flight paths for students; in secondary this can happen from the outset in Year 7 where schools establish baseline data that ultimately ranks the pupils. It is, perhaps, to be celebrated that this sort of thing does not tend to happen in PSHE. What would 'working at expectation' look like here? How would FFT determine a statistical predictor of performance in a subject such as PSHE?

Thus schools are left with the ongoing pickle of what to do about assessment, monitoring and reporting in PSHE. Whilst no one model is likely to suit all schools, it is reasonable to suggest, I think, that some kind of mixed economy of assessments is the most pragmatic way forward. This would be an approach that combines self-assessment tools, quizzes and tests, and teacher observation. If the school demands progress data, then they would necessarily need to rely on teachers' professional judgement as to whether a pupil is working at, above or below whatever expectation has been agreed. Perhaps the most important aspect of this is for teachers to have conversations about agreed sets of expectations – what might we expect pupils in any given year group to know or understand in relation to each of the topics, and so on. Indeed, teachers working collaboratively to discuss curriculum and assessment in PSHE are to be recommended, but they need to be given the time to do this properly. So often, PSHE is a bolt-on to the school curriculum and is perceived by teachers as an additional workload burden. This narrative needs to be shifted.

Reflection Questions for You and Your Setting

- What do you want the pupils to know in PSHE, and how can you be sure that they know it?
- Do the assessment, marking, monitoring, data recording and reporting models employed in other subjects work for PSHE in your school?
- What do the parents of your pupils want to know about the progress of their children in PSHE?
- Do you want the teachers to assess the pupils, or do you want the pupils to assess themselves? Why?
- What will assessment tell you? How would this affect your teaching of PSHE?

References

Alexander, R. (2020), *A Dialogic Teaching Companion*, Abingdon, Oxon: Routledge.

Andrade (2019), A critical review of research on student self-assessment, *Frontiers in Education*, 4, https://www.frontiersin.org/articles/10.3389/feduc.2019.00087. DOI: 10.3389/feduc.2019.00087 2504-284X.

Cefai, C., Downes, P. and Cavioni, V. (2021), A formative, inclusive, whole-school approach to the assessment of social and emotional education in the EU, NESET Report [online]. Luxembourg: Publications Office of the European Union. Available from: https://doi/org/110.2766/506737.%0Ahttps://doi/org/110.2766/506737

Counsell, C. (2022), Keynote Speech: 'Talking curriculum: how curriculum gets hidden, why this matters and what to do about it.' ResearchED Leicester.

DfE (2019), Relationships education, relationships and sex education (RSE) and health education. Available online: https://assets.publishing.service.gov.uk/government/uploads/system/uploads/attachment_data/file/1019542/Relationships_Education__Relationships_and_Sex_Education__RSE__and_Health_Education.pdf (accessed 22 May 2022).

Didau, D. (2020), Curriculum related expectations: Using the curriculum as a progression model. Available online: https://learningspy.co.uk/assessment/curriculum-related-expectations/ (accessed 26 June 2022).

Didau, D. (2021), The shape of assessment. Available online: https://learningspy.co.uk/assessment/the-shape-of-assessment/ (accessed 26 June 2022).

Didau, D. (2022), Assessing English at KS3. Available online: https://learningspy.co.uk/assessment/assessing-english-at-ks3/ (accessed 26 June 2022).

Hunter, S. (2016), *Life after Levels*, London: Sage.

Ofsted (2013), Not yet good enough: Personal, social, health and economic education in schools. Available online: https://www.gov.uk/government/publications/not-yet-good-enough-personal-social-health-and-economic-education (accessed 31 Aug 2023).

PSHE Association (n.d.), Assessment in PSHE Education. Available online: https://pshe-association.org.uk/guidance/ks1-4/assessment (accessed 26 June 2022).

Wynn, S. (2015), Assessment: Life after levels at Key Stage 3. Available online: https://www.sec-ed.co.uk/best-practice/assessment-life-after-levels-at-key-stage-3/ (accessed 26 June 2022).

3

Parent/Carer Engagement in PSHE

Chris Farman

Aims of This Chapter

- To inform and guide on creating and developing a culture of parent and carer engagement within the subject of Personal, Social, Health and Economic Education.
- To provide an outline and guidance on creating your own strategic direction with engaging your parent body (and more widely with other stakeholders).
- To support readers in considering and reflecting on their current methods of communication with parents and carers, and further developing these.

Introduction

The RSE guidance (DfE, 2021, p.17) states:

> The role of parents in the development of their children's understanding about relationships is vital. Parents are the first teachers of their children. They have the most significant influence in enabling their children to grow and mature and to form healthy relationships.

Ensuring that parents, guardians and carers (referred to as 'parent' from now on) are engaged with the school or college's Personal, Social, Health and Economic (PSHE) Education department is likely to be one of the key components of making sure that the school community fully embraces your department's curriculum and the Government's Relationships & Sex Education (RSE) and Health statutory guidance. However, one key message from me would be this – enjoy it. There are many different ways to keep parents involved (DfE, 2019), and more often than not, parents are delighted that you do so.

Without debate, a successful implementation of your PSHE and RSE curriculum will build a strong partnership and bond between schools, parents and pupils. PSHE programmes which engage with their parents about the programme are a vital aspect of building, improving and providing a high-quality programme (PSHE Association, 2019); I cannot think of a subject that needs to build trusting routes of communication more so than PSHE. I would argue that the future of PSHE and RSE delivery will heavily rely on having open routes of communication to subject leads, with one of those groups being your parent body. From the beginning and/or to improve on your current provision, if you are to create and build an environment where your parent body is fully engaged, culture is absolutely key; if your school community provides resources, time and the respect a high-quality PSHE programme deserves, you will get more back from pupils and their parents. From the outset, if you have a set time for PSHE on a weekly basis with a specialist PSHE teacher, your community will recognize the subject as impactful. Of course, that in itself will not significantly raise the profile of the subject, but it will certainly be a good start.

I will come onto the importance of formalizing PSHE as a subject later; however, as a short anecdote to lead us into the main part of the chapter, we have recently introduced Reporting and Parents' Evening appointments for PSHE to all year groups. During one recent appointment, a parent told me that they were delighted that our school was taking PSHE so seriously because what we had covered during lesson time was helping her child to become more confident at the dinner table and was now prepared to discuss previously sensitive areas openly with parents. This is incredibly powerful qualitative feedback, and if you can get to this point, you are more likely to have parents engaging in your subject.

Strategies to Enhance Parent Engagement

My opening piece of advice here would be to jump on any opportunity to mention PSHE in your school; staff briefings, discussions over lunch, tutor periods, email updates, weekly newsletters home, social media – whatever chance you have – highlight the importance of high-quality PSHE and the themes that have been delivered recently during lesson time. The more that people talk about PSHE, the better: it improves engagement in the classroom, staff begin to use important terms that you have been discussing during lesson time and, in turn, the quality of discussion with parents about the subject begins to improve. The RSE guidance (DfE, 2019) provided by the DfE states:

> Parents should be given every opportunity to understand the purpose and content of Relationships Education and RSE. Good communication and opportunities for

parents to understand and ask questions about the school's approach help increase confidence in the curriculum.

Whilst your school will already have existing mechanisms in place to engage the parent body (and you should fully utilize these), the guidance does state that no additional mechanisms are required. That said, if you are to create an environment where your community is fully engaged, you might need to think outside the box a little, and do something a little different to support the subject in standing out from the crowd.

Regular Communication with Parents

It is important to find any way possible to communicate with parents. You must write to parents (see example letter below) with regards to the right to withdraw as the guidance states:

> All schools should work closely with parents when planning and delivering these subjects. Schools should ensure that parents know what will be taught and when, and clearly communicate the fact that parents have the right to request that their child be withdrawn from some or all of sex education delivered as part of statutory RSE.

I would add here that the official guidance remains unclear on where the line between sex and relationships is with regard to specific content, such as pornography, and I believe it is important within your curriculum that you are clear about where you draw the line before any meeting with parents.

Table 3.1 provides guidance on what parents can and cannot withdraw from.

Table 3.1 Guidance on what parents can and cannot withdraw from

Areas parents can withdraw their child from:	Areas parents cannot withdraw their child from:
Primary school lessons which address sex education, i.e. those that are not within the Relationships Education curriculum.	Relationships education in primary school or secondary school.
At secondary school, parents are able to withdraw their child from sex education (other than the sex education which sits in the National Curriculum as part of science in maintained schools). However, a child will also have a right to opt into sex education from their fifteenth birthday (specifically three academic terms before they turn sixteen).	Maintained primary schools are required to teach National Curriculum science, which includes some elements of sex education. Parents do not have a right to withdraw from this.

Policy and Curriculum Development Example Wording

Parents and carers of (school) pupils have been consulted in the development of this policy, to comply with compulsory requirements from the DfE. On (date), a consultation paper was emailed to all parents with a draft of this policy and all parents were given a four-week window to respond. All (school) staff were invited to respond to the consultation on this policy. The policy is approved by the senior management team.

Engaging Stakeholders Example Wording

We are committed to working with parents and carers by seeking opinion from them at certain times throughout the year, and when particular aspects of RSE are going to be covered, by engaging with parental feedback and responding to questions in advance of lessons with pupils. We work closely with parents to ensure that they are fully aware of what is being taught and provide additional resources, where appropriate. We notify parents in advance when RSE is to be taught, and the legal right of parents to withdraw their children. Parents have the right to request that their child be withdrawn from all or part of the sex education component of the RSE Curriculum, until three terms before their child turns 16. After this point, it is the child's choice: if they choose to be taught the sex education components of the RSE Curriculum, (school) will take all reasonable efforts to ensure that they are. Pupils cannot be legally withdrawn from the aspects of sex education that are taught as part of the national and statutory science curriculum (they may only be withdrawn from the aspects of sex education that are taught as part of the RSE Curriculum). Parents wishing to withdraw their child should write to the Headteacher outlining the reason for withdrawing, along with any further information they would like the school to consider. The Headteacher (or Head of PSHE or Deputy Head Pastoral as delegated by the Headteacher) should discuss the request with parents and, as appropriate, with the child to:

- ensure that their wishes are clear.
- clarify the nature, purpose and intended benefits of the RSE curriculum.
- explain the potential risks of withdrawing a child, including the social and emotional risks of being excluded and the possibility of hearing about sex education elements of the RSE curriculum from other pupils or online, rather than a qualified adult.

These discussions should be noted, and withdrawal requests will be documented on CPOMS (or your school/college's alternative safeguarding reporting mechanism).

When a pupil is withdrawn from the non-statutory areas of sex education, they should be given alternative work which is PSHE-related.

There are, of course, other ways to communicate with parents. This might be as part of a weekly school newsletter, updates on social media, such as X and Facebook, about what is happening during lesson time, being available during parents' evenings or even a weekly PSHE update – we introduced this recently, and is a very short message about what has been addressed during lessons that week and what key terms have been used, to encourage conversation and consolidation of the material covered at home with family and friends. A crucial element of this communication is advice and support on how parents can talk to their child about the lesson content, such as relationships, harassment, sex, abuse, etc. You will see in the below example letter a reference to 'exceptional circumstances'. The guidance does not make clear what could be defined as exceptional circumstances, and I would strongly suggest working closely with your safeguarding team to understand whether this might apply.

Example of a Letter to Send Home

Dear Parents and Guardians,

As a part of your child's education at ********, we promote personal wellbeing and development through a comprehensive Personal, Social, Health and Economic (PSHE) education programme. PSHE education is the curriculum subject that gives young people the knowledge, understanding, attitudes and practical skills to live safe, healthy, productive lives and meet their full potential.

I am writing to let you know that, over the coming academic year, each child will be taking part in lessons which will focus on the relationships and sex education (RSE) aspect of this programme. PSHE education is taught throughout Year 7 to Year 11, and is monitored and reviewed regularly by the staff and governing body. All PSHE teaching takes place in a safe learning environment and is underpinned by our school ethos and values.

You do have a right to withdraw your child from sex education delivered as part of RSE in secondary schools unless there are exceptional circumstances which will be granted up to three terms before your child turns sixteen. At this point, if the child themselves wishes to receive sex education rather than be withdrawn, the school will make arrangements for this to happen in one of the three terms before the child turns sixteen – the legal age of sexual consent. There is no right to withdraw from relationships education at secondary level. However, we are confident you will share our enthusiasm for the successful implementation of our PSHE curriculum, which we feel benefits all of our pupils.

With the above in mind, we would like to invite you to attend a parent information meeting on ********. This will provide you with an opportunity to find out more about what your child will learn, view the materials and resources being used in lessons, and discover how you can best support your child to discuss these topics at home. I will be available during this meeting to answer any questions you might have about our PSHE and RSE provision.

As a school community, we are committed to working in partnership with parents. If you would like to find out more or discuss any concerns, we would urge you to attend the information meeting and look forward to seeing you there.

Yours sincerely,

****

Example of a Newsletter to Send Home

PSHE (inc. RSE) Weekly Department Update
PSHE/RSE events
RSE Parent Online Session: Talking to your child about sexual harassment

Thank you to all that joined the online session last ********. I have received positive feedback in relation to the session, but if you would like to feed back and have not had an opportunity to do so, please do get in touch with me using the email address at the end of this week's weekly update.

If you were unable to attend the session, the recording can be found here: ********

The slides from the session are available via the iSAMS Parent Portal.

RSE Parent Face-to-Face Workshop: Identity
I am very excited to announce that the School of Sex Ed will be visiting the school on ******** to deliver a parent information session on 'Identities'. The session will run from 6.30 pm until 7.30 pm, and will cover themes such as:

- What does LGBTQIA+ stand for?
- Understanding LGBTQIA+ history and context.
- What's the difference between sex and gender?

The session will be in school on this occasion, as it will provide me with an opportunity to meet and say hello to parents and guardians, which has been difficult during the last couple of years due to Covid-19 restrictions. More details will follow as part of next week's PSHE (inc. RSE) Weekly Departmental Update.

This Week's PSHE and RSE Lessons

Year 7

Pupils have been learning about friendships and relationships so far this half-term. Continuing on this theme, we have been discussing coercive friendships this week, discussing what makes a healthy, positive friendship, and identifying traits that would indicate that a friendship is unsafe or coercive.

Key terms to be aware of:

- coercive: pattern of controlling behaviours that create an unequal power dynamic in a friendship or relationship.
- manipulation: the exercise of harmful influence over others.

Year 8:

Pupils have been learning about the risks and consequences of alcohol use. We have been discussing that most young people their age do not use alcohol and that young people's alcohol use is declining, the effects of alcohol misuse and influences on alcohol use.

Key messages that we have discussed:

- Short-term effects include: dehydration, lack of inhibitions and feeling sociable, feeling sick, feeling drowsy, vomiting, headache, diarrhoea, dizziness and lack of coordination, loss of personal possessions, making poor decisions, being at greater risk in certain situations, injuries due to falling over, memory loss, a 'hangover' the following day and alcohol poisoning.
- Long-term effects include: high blood pressure, stroke, cirrhosis/liver disease, effects on mood, fertility issues, cancers including liver, bowel, breast and mouth, alcohol dependency, fallout from unwise actions while drunk including relationship changes and feelings of regret, and serious injuries. There are also sugar-related concerns including obesity, dental health issues and acne.

Year 9

Pupils have been learning about drugs and young people's attitudes and behaviours regarding drug use. We have discussed attitudes and beliefs about the prevalence of drug use amongst young people and the reasons why young people might choose to use or not use drugs.

Key messages that we have discussed:

- Reasons for drug use: makes people feel confident, they think drugs will relax them or give them an interesting experience, to be accepted in a friendship group, peer pressure, to impress someone, they believe everyone else is doing it, they have friends/family members who use drugs, influence of the media, like taking risks, want to escape reality.

- Reasons against drug use: concerns over health risks and short-term effects, e.g. addiction, hangovers and heightened accident risks, valuing a healthy lifestyle in which drugs are not a feature, pre-existing medical condition that means using drugs would be particularly harmful, religious, cultural beliefs or family-based reasons, such as family disapproval, avoid losing control or acting in unwanted ways while under the influence, having a great time without drugs, feeling comfortable making their own choices, worried about breaking the law or getting caught.

Year 10

Pupils have been learning about the impact pornography can have on relationships. We have discussed what pornography is, identified ways in which pornographic material is not representative of real sex and can give misleading information about consent and gender roles in sexual relationships, and considered the possible impact of this on sexual relationships and the expectations people have of relationships.

Key messages that we have discussed:

- Though porn shows actors having real sex, they are not shown as real people with real personalities and feelings.
- Porn only focuses on the body bit of sex, not the feelings bit which for most people is the most important aspect.
- Porn actors are usually paid to do what they do in front of the camera, so they agree to do things which often aren't what most people would agree to do when having sex with their partner.
- Sex in porn is mainly about giving men pleasure and women doing things to instantly turn men on.
- Porn is often violent, especially towards women and often shows women enjoying this. However, they are being paid to do so, and for most people, being hurt, threatened or humiliated is a very bad experience.

Year 11

The 5th Form has been continuing its focus on fertility and pregnancy choices. This week's focus was unplanned pregnancy. Pupils are able to identify the range of options available in the event of an unplanned pregnancy, describe the range of emotions someone might feel in the event of an unplanned or unwanted pregnancy and evaluate the different influences available in the event of an unplanned pregnancy. Pupils have also recognized that miscarriage can occur and where to access support in the event of a miscarriage.

If you would like to discuss anything in relation to our PSHE (inc. RSE) provision, please get in-touch with ********.

Parent Ambassador Groups

There are likely to be parents who are keen to discuss and provide ideas for your PSHE and RSE provision. Provide them with an opportunity to do so, by meeting with a small focus group on a termly basis. Try and hold the meetings at different times though, which will give an opportunity to those unavailable during working hours and also those parents who have more free time during the day. A successful parent group will have representatives from each year group, and gives them an opportunity to provide constructive feedback to the school, whilst also acting as a brainstorming opportunity to impact on future decisions on school policy. Through this group, parents can be consulted on any updates to your school's RSE policy. The RSE guidance states under Point 43 that inviting parents into your school can be 'an important opportunity to talk about how these subjects contribute to wider support in terms of pupil wellbeing and keeping children safe. It is important through such processes to reach out to all parents, recognising that a range of approaches may be needed for doing so'. A PSHE Parent Ambassador Group will provide fantastic opportunities to reach out to your parent body.

Example of the Minutes from a Parent Ambassador Group Meeting

PSHE (inc. RSE) Parent Ambassador Group Meeting Minutes
Attendees: ********

Welcome all to the PSHE Parent Ambassador Group Meeting, including new members to the group.
The objectives of the group were outlined:

- To improve parental engagement in the PSHE curriculum at ********.
- To consider new ideas and approaches for the curriculum and wider school community.
- To discuss any concerns that the parent body of ******** might have in relation to the PSHE and RSE curriculum.
- To discuss and implement ideas in relation to further engagement in PSHE.

The group discussed feedback following the RSE Information Evening:

- Many believed the information evening was an opportunity to ask questions in relation to the delivery of RSE across the school.
- Provided opportunities to see resources, which were being used during lesson time.

- Some members of the group had taken wider feedback from the community; there is a feeling that having the meeting face-to-face meant that attendance was lower than expected, and an online meeting should be considered next time.

Curriculum for 2022/2023:

- There was an agreement around the table that the PSHE curriculum had improved significantly over the last two years.
- One point raised was that some children did feel that the curriculum moved too quickly, and they would prefer to go into more depth with some themes rather than move as quickly through themes.
- There was an appreciation that scenarios during lesson time had been adapted to be more inclusive to the LGBT+ community.
- Two parents noted that the relationships education provided by the school was particularly beneficial.
- Ideas for wider school themes, e.g. LGBT+ History Month/Feb 2023.
- For LGBT+ History Month, the school to buy a pride flag to put onto the flagpole.
- Plaques placed on walls across the school with LGBT+ old pupils.
- Rainbow laces are allowed to be worn by the school community on a certain day.
- LGBT+ charity assembly, including people talking about their experiences/LGBT+ history.
- Parents to lead an LGBT+ evening/event.
- Parents to lead a Pride run/walk to fundraise.
- Each year group could have a colour from the pride flag to represent them.

Items to de discussed during our next meeting:

- The best ways to communicate with parents – a podcast has recently been launched, is this a good way to communicate with the parent body?
- Presentation of the curriculum for 2022/2023.
- Are the reporting systems of the school for PSHE appropriate?

AOB.

Raising the Status of PSHE among Parents

Establishing an environment where it is encouraged for parents to contact and communicate with your school about your PSHE programme and lesson content can encourage parental respect and engagement with the subject in the same way as others. Ultimately, if the subject is going to have maximum impact, parents, pupils and colleagues need to not just see the subject as worthwhile, but as one of the most important subjects taught in your school. With this in mind, ensure that parents are communicating with you as the Head of PSHE/PSHE teacher in the same way they would with other subjects, and ensure as the Head of PSHE that you are liaising with the safeguarding team, adapting the curriculum accordingly for your community.

Arrange regular parent information events, either in-person or online. One of the positives of Covid-19 is that parents are now in the habit of accessing parent events online, and therefore you should ensure you are taking full advantage of this. There are advantages and disadvantages of both in-person and online information events – sometimes it is good to see parents face-to-face and establish a strong connection. It is probably also fair to say that parents are more likely to ask questions if they can catch you one-on-one before or after the event. That said, turnout for your sessions might be better if you host them online, and if you have a visiting speaker, they are likely to be cheaper if you go down the route of an online event. I would suggest you stay flexible and rotate between the two. One of the most powerful activities you can lead as part of the event is to lead part of a lesson; this really gets parents thinking about what their child is doing during a PSHE lesson.

Publish your PSHE education curriculum on your website and as part of your policy: some schools publish their PSHE curriculum as part of their PSHE and RSE policies. This is a real statement of intent in terms of how PSHE and RSE are fully embedded in your school community. Having recently been through an inspection, having your curriculum as part of your policy is a fantastic opportunity to get on the front foot, and demonstrate how well-respected your department is across your community. Do ensure, however, that the policy is regularly updated if the curriculum is changed. Other schools will publish their curriculum on their school website. Either way, publishing the curriculum in this way provides parents with a clear outline as to what is being addressed during lesson time.

Conduct a parent survey once or twice a year to get feedback on the delivery, content and impact of PSHE. This is a really useful way to touch base with a group of parents that perhaps don't attend your information evenings. It provides fantastic evidence too as to how you have adapted your curriculum according to feedback. Furthermore, it is a good way to establish parents' current understanding of RSE and any questions and concerns they may have. This can be used to plan open evenings/information events/communications between school and home.

Create a FAQ of PSHE: The PSHE Association is superb for all things PSHE, and one of the recommendations from them is to create a FAQ of PSHE. I believe this is a superb idea, and a good way to do this is to create a video presented by you (or your pupils). Video-based communication by schools is likely to be the future, and a lovely way to communicate how community-driven your curriculum is would be to have some of your pupils create an introduction to PSHE video which could be on your website.

Written reports and parents' evenings: Write an end-of-year report for each pupil on PSHE. It doesn't have to be particularly in-depth, but once again provides an opportunity to feed back to parents on what has been happening in the classroom and how pupils have been developing their knowledge. Furthermore, ensure that if you teach PSHE, you can be seen by parents at parents' evenings; once again, this sends the right message in saying that PSHE is just as, if not more, important than all other subjects taught across your timetable.

Parent-pupil workshops: One idea that is currently being led by our PSHE pupil voice group is developing greater connections between pupils and their parent/s to support them in improving emotional connection. Get your pupils to lead a mental health workshop to your parent body, ensuring that the parent is working one-on-one with their own child to build better connections. Parent wellbeing is on the decline, and this is a great way to enhance the knowledge of parent mental health, as well as have something delivered by your pupils.

Embrace new media: Finally, as mentioned at the start of the chapter, enjoy finding new ways to engage with your parents. There is no better feeling than creating and leading something new and creative, and it working! Work hard to find different ways to engage – create podcasts, YouTube clips, wellbeing evenings, a school PSHE TikTok account – whatever it might be (within reason), try it. It's fun, and from my experience, parents really respect anything that is a bit different. This, of course, does take time, so try and empower a pupil voice group to lead on aspects of this, with you overseeing.

Creating a Strategy for Parent Engagement

A short word on your development plan for your PSHE department: ensure that parent engagement is an obvious and deliberate theme throughout your strategy. It is important that you communicate and take ideas for your development plan from all stakeholders within your community – governors, SMT, colleagues, pupils and parents. Once you have done so, and started to put together where you are heading on your PSHE journey next, communicate it to all, including your parents. This is something of real substance, and can be presented to them as part of a PSHE Parent Ambassador Group meeting. I've included an example of a two-year whole-school development plan here, and whilst some aspects of this are not directly impacting on parent engagement, I would definitely be ensuring that the whole strategy is presented to parents – once again, this can only be a good thing in raising the profile of your subject across the community.

Here is an example of a development plan that you could use (remember to add in updates as this should be a working document):

Table 3.2 Example of a development plan

Focus area	Objectives	Actions required	Responsibility	Impact date
Inclusive & competence-based curriculum	Continue to focus on personal decision-making within the curriculum, empowering young people to have the knowledge and confidence to make good life decisions	Continued focus on knowledge and strategies within the curriculum.	Head of PSHE	September 2022
	Use drop-down days to host practical RSE-based workshops centred around consent, abuse and sexual health, and work more closely with external agencies	Work with an external provider to provide practical workshops to all pupils at the school. Research possibility of inviting more external agencies into school to enhance provision (e.g. NHS).	Safeguarding Team/ Head of PSHE	January 2023
	Ensure that LGBT+ is fully integrated into the PSHE curriculum	Work with the PSHE Ambassadors group to ensure we provide an inclusive curriculum that all pupils can relate to. Continue to embed LGBT into the whole curriculum, enhancing the knowledge of all pupils.	Head of PSHE/Pupil Voice Group	September 2022
	Continue to provide opportunities for pupils to be part of discussions during lesson time, ensuring all young people have the confidence to speak	Continue to embed 'strong PSHE habits' – respect for others, good listening skills, etc. Increase the number of ways that pupils can communicate their opinions and thoughts.	Head of PSHE/Pupil Voice Group	April 2023

(continued)

Focus area	Objectives	Actions required	Responsibility	Impact date
Subject status	Quality of feedback	Consider what appropriate feedback looks like in PSHE. Work with PSHE Ambassador group to find solutions.	Head of PSHE/ Deputy Head Academic/PSHE Ambassadors	September 2023
	Lesson time, parents' evenings & reporting.	Introduce parents' evenings and reports to increase level of communication home. All pupils across the school to have a weekly timetabled lesson.	Head of PSHE/ Deputy Head Academic	September 2022
	Governor awareness	Ensure that the governing body is kept in-the-loop with regards to developments in PSHE (RSE).	Head of PSHE/ Headteacher	September 2022
	Assessment	Consider how assessment can be developed within the subject. Work with other HoDs.	Head of PSHE	January 2023
	Use of Teams	Continue to develop the use of Teams as a 'hub' for PSHE information and support.	Head of PSHE	September 2022

Focus area	Objectives	Actions required	Responsibility	Impact date
Parent engagement	Develop social media as a communication channel.	Continue to develop social media posts related to PSHE. Use of Instagram/TikTok to engage pupils further. Link to parental support. Consider creativity online to market what we are achieving.	Head of PSHE/ Marketing Department	April 2023
	Opportunities for communication	Ensure that different forms of communication are used to engage with the parent body. Consider introducing a half-termly PSHE coffee morning. Introduce a parental weekly information bulletin. Quick, readable advice based on previous lesson.	Head of PSHE	September 2022
Staff	Staff training	Fully integrate Brook Learn Platform to support the understanding of teaching staff. Evaluate areas of teacher knowledge weakness and arrange attendance at relevant CPD.	Head of PSHE/ Assistant Head (Staff)	January 2023
Pupil voice	Increase status of the PSHE Ambassadors group within the school.	Possible presentations at assemblies. Consider how members can lead within lesson time.	Head of PSHE/Pupil Voice Group	April 2022
	Senior Management Team (SMT)-PSHE Ambassadors Group Relationship	Ambassadors to present at SMT meeting to inform about progress and developments.	Head of PSHE/SMT/ Pupil Voice Group	November 2022
	Ensure all pupils have a voice and are able to contribute to the future of the curriculum	Consider different ways to ensure those who want to contribute and have their say can do so. Online, drop in, in person, safe space, etc.	Head of PSHE	April 2023

Closing Reflections

To have a truly successful PSHE department, the culture across your school is vital. In getting the culture right, you will need to engage and fully embrace all stakeholders of your community, and this includes parents, carers and guardians. If your parent body does not respect your subject for what it is, you may well encounter a few challenges. From my experience, however, more and more parents are getting fully on board with the importance of our wonderful subject, and that can only be a good thing. Remember that your current parents' experiences of PSHE may well be a teacher at the front of a lecture hall waving a condom around in front of a whole year group. Things have changed drastically, and for the better – you're likely to need to communicate how things have changed. This is a really exciting time for the ever-changing PSHE, and one of the only subjects in a school where we can make the subject belong to our communities that we work in – it's everyone's subject, and you are there to allow that to happen.

Reflection Questions for You and Your Setting

- How can a PSHE Lead oversee all stakeholders to ensure maximum interaction, and thus create an environment where PSHE is respected and engaged with as a subject that has significant impact on a young person's future?
- How is PSHE perceived by your community and is it respected in the same way as other subjects?
- How can you spread awareness across your community and make significant differences in a creative way?

Recommended Resources

- The PSHE Association provides numerous considerations for engaging your stakeholders, including parents, about your relationships and sex education education (https://pshe-association.org.uk/guidance/ks1-4/engaging-parents-governors)
- CEOP provide excellent teaching resources, as well as tips on how to engage your parent body, including a sample parent workshop which you could adapt accordingly (https://www.thinkuknow.co.uk/professionals/guidance/relationships-education-and-rse-parental-engagement-guides/)

- The DfE has provided a specific document on engaging parents in relationships education policy (https://www.gov.uk/government/publications/engaging-parents-with-relationships-education-policy)
- The Chartered College of Teaching provides good ideas on how to build relationships with parents, including the following article: In it for the long haul: Building trusting relationships with parents (https://my.chartered.college/impact_article/in-it-for-the-long-haul-building-trusting-relationships-with-parents/)
- Parental Engagement on Relationships Education (DfE, 2019) – although written for primary school practitioners, the guidance is applicable to a secondary context: https://assets.publishing.service.gov.uk/government/uploads/system/uploads/attachment_data/file/884450/Parental_engagement_on_relationships_education.pdf

References

DfE (2019), Relationships education, relationships and sex education (RSE) and health education. Available online: https://assets.publishing.service.gov.uk/government/uploads/system/uploads/attachment_data/file/1019542/Relationships_Education__Relationships_and_Sex_Education__RSE__and_Health_Education.pdf (accessed 22 May 2022).

DfE (2021), Relationships Education, Relationships and Sex Education (RSE) and Health Education Statutory guidance for governing bodies, proprietors, head teachers, principals, senior leadership teams, teachers.

PSHE (2019), Relationships and Sex Education: supporting parental engagement.

4

Meaningful Mental Health and Wellbeing Education

Sophie-Lauren McPhee

Aims of This Chapter

- To ascertain how to deliver messages about mental health and wellbeing impactfully, with safety as the top priority.
- To explore what can and should be covered within the theme of mental health and wellbeing education across the secondary phase.
- To look at ideas for extending mental health and wellbeing education beyond the PSHE classroom.

What Is Wellbeing Education?

PSHE education is synonymous with wellbeing education. Everything which comes under its remit aims to equip children and young people with 'the key skills and attributes … [they] need to thrive both in their childhood and throughout their adult lives' (PSHE Association, 2017). The topics covered in this book are not covered adequately unless they are tied in to wellbeing: We cannot cover the topic of financial capability without discussing the impact of money mismanagement on wellbeing and mental health, we must teach that through active involvement in civic life we can find a sense of achievement and purpose, and emphasize that building strong character attributes in our formative years will help us get through the inevitable tough times in life, to name but a few examples.

Therefore, wellbeing as a concept needs to be woven into all of our PSHE teaching. However, there is a difference between wellbeing and mental health, although the two, of course, overlap. This difference has, helpfully, been elaborated on by Pollard,

Vanderlayden, Alexander, Borkin, & O'Mahony (2021), with wellbeing covering 'flourishing, thriving, satisfaction, self-belief, balance ... emotional, spiritual, social, physical as well as mental dimensions', and mental health defined as 'a spectrum ranging from good mental health to mental illness'.

We have known for some years now that children's mental health is in crisis, but the pandemic, including resulting lockdowns, bereavements, job losses, disruption to education and social lives, has intensified this: the Mental Health of Children and Young People in England 2021 survey found that '39.2% of those aged 6 to 16 years ... had experienced deterioration in mental health since 2017, and ... among those aged 17 to 23 years ... 52.5% experienced deterioration' (NHS Digital, 2021). The same survey found that 'rates of probable mental disorder increased between 2017 and 2021; in 6 to 16 year olds from one in nine (11.6%) to one in six (17.4%), and in 17 to 19 year olds from one in ten (10.1%) to one in six (17.4%)'. Therefore, in every classroom we could now have as many as five pupils with a diagnosable mental health condition. We must start mental health education early, and keep reinforcing key messages in a meaningful way until pupils leave our setting, as 'these illnesses can have a devastating impact on ... physical health, ... relationships and ... future prospects' (Department of Health & Social Care and Department for Education, 2018). Mental health and wellbeing education should not be a stand-alone approach, instead making explicit the links between different areas of life, and how this inevitably leads to fluctuations in overall life satisfaction. This chapter aims to persuade school and college leaders that it is justifiable for mental health and wellbeing education to take up curriculum time, and give PSHE practitioners the confidence and resources they need to teach this topic safely and well.

Getting the Message Right

In their report *Fixing a Failing System: Rethinking Mental Health Support in Schools for the Post-Covid Generation*, The Coalition for Youth Mental Health in Schools stated that 'only a fifth of children [are] able to access support within four weeks ... [and] nearly half ... of young people referred get no access at all' (The Coalition for Youth Mental Health in Schools, 2021). They go on to say that 'school staff are increasingly being expected to deal with more and more children ... who need specialist help and support in school, making it difficult to be proactive around prevention ... as they are so busy firefighting with challenges that they do not and nor should be expected to have the expertise to deal with'. This wholly justifies their demand for weekly timetabled PSHE lessons taught by specialist teachers (The Coalition for Youth Mental Health in Schools, 2021). As we cannot guarantee the speed with which children can access services – if at all – and because, as the Mental Health Foundation says, 'many mental health problems can be prevented with the right approach' (Mental Health Foundation, 2021), this aspect of PSHE education should therefore – as a minimum – encourage children to ensure they get plentiful access to the six components of Dr Steve Ilardi's Therapeutic Lifestyle Change (TLC) Program, namely omega-3 fatty acids, quality sleep, social connection, exercise, sunlight exposure and engaging activity (Ilardi, 2010), which has been proven to have an anti-depressant effect, beneficial to those with and without a mental disorder equally.

This is not to claim that there is a simple, one-size-fits-all solution to our current mental health crisis, and does not take into account the full range of mental health conditions affecting the population, but it is without doubt that PSHE education has a fundamental role to play in educating pupils on daily choices and for new leaders or teachers of the subject, these basic healthy lifestyle components are a good foundation on which to build a sequence of lessons. For some children, additional support from medical or mental health professionals will be necessary, but our aim is to help reduce the number who get to that point, not only to improve the wellbeing of the younger generation overall, but also to reduce the load on already-overstretched school/college pastoral teams and CYPMHS (Children and Young People's Mental Health Services).

Ideally, specialist PSHE teaching will build on basic messages such as the TLC Program and similar approaches such as the NHS's *5 Steps to Mental Wellbeing* (NHS, 2019) or Dr Dan Siegel's *Healthy Mind Platter* (Siegel, 2011), tailoring the curriculum to the needs of individuals in the cohort. One way of ascertaining what pupils need is to assess their mental wellbeing during key points throughout the secondary phase, such as the start of Year 7 and in the lead-up to external examinations. There are pre-prepared questionnaires you can use for this purpose, one prominent example being the Warwick-Edinburgh Mental Wellbeing Scales (WEMWBS), available via the Warwick Medical School website, or Bounce Together, an online mental health and wellbeing survey platform designed for schools. This annual subscription-based website allows you to assign a large number of surveys to pupils for them to complete and submit online, including some related to resilience, life satisfaction and self-esteem, with results available in a variety of formats. Bounce Together is suited for use by various members of the school/college pastoral team, not just the Head of PSHE, and in that case will need a lead member of staff to take strategic oversight of its use.

Local and national data can also be used to inform lesson planning, such as the Joint Strategic Needs Assessment (JSNA) data from your local authority or data from the Association for Young People's Health so that PSHE educators avoid simply using 'off-the-peg' materials, some of which may go out of date quite quickly. Although there are lots of very good 'ready to go' resources, especially those carrying the PSHE Association Quality Mark, these should not be used in isolation, and best practice will always be to combine ready-made resources, one's own experience, consultation with experts and the latest research to create the most engaging, relevant and impactful content for pupils. For a busy member of school/college staff however, this is easier said than done, so do harness the positives of social media platforms like X to share ideas and resources with those in similar roles. It is vital, though, that if accessing materials that do not carry the PSHE Association Quality Mark, you critically evaluate and quality-assure them yourself before delivery.

Do not underestimate, however, the importance of qualitative research, such as pupil and parent focus groups, your own observations around school, in class and from pupils' work and conversations with Heads of Year and the safeguarding team. Teenage life evolves much more quickly than the world of research and education can keep up with, so it is important to adapt your messages to what you find is going on around you – not in an alarmist or reactive way such as by means of an emergency assembly, but by updating your materials regularly in response to your growing teaching experience and understanding of the issue at hand. One recent example of this from my own practice is the realization that pupils need to be taught how to gauge at which point to be concerned about their mental health. As strategic adviser on mental health and wellbeing Gregor Henderson says, 'we are still conflating momentary mental distress with mental illness' (The Coalition for Youth Mental Health in Schools, 2021), despite the statutory guidance for Health Education stating that mental health and wellbeing education should enable pupils to understand 'where normal variations in emotions and physical complaints end and health and wellbeing issues begin' (Department for Education, 2019). One of the downsides to increased mental health awareness is that 'some of the rise in mental health disorders amongst children may be due to over-pathologizing – with normal fluctuations of human emotion being deemed mental health disorders' (The Coalition for Youth Mental Health in Schools, 2021). The Coalition attributes this partly to 'ubiquitous … messaging across social media'.

Certainly, social media, whilst being instrumental in raising awareness and reducing stigma, has also diluted important messages. 'You cannot pour from an empty cup' is an example of this. Whilst absolutely true, we need to find ways of refreshing this message so that it captures the attention of a young audience. Slogans such as the aforementioned are good for your school/college wellbeing department X or Instagram page, but are to be avoided as teaching tools in favour of robust research and expert-led lesson activities from reputable organizations.

Recent experience has also taught me that whilst an increase in school/college-based services, if you're lucky enough to have them, can only be a good thing, we nevertheless need to teach pupils how to tell if their situation calls for independent problem-solving, self-care or help-seeking behaviour. Nowadays, pupils hear time and again 'Tell a trusted adult', but this isn't actually always necessary, and is no doubt contributing to overworked pastoral staff. We must help pupils develop their own toolkit of resources, such as the BLAST approach to managing difficult mental and physical states (signposted in the Recommendations section at the end of this chapter). They can also use the 'HALT' acronym to check if they are hungry, angry, lonely or tired, or whether there is something more deep-rooted at play. In short, a good mental health curriculum will combine static material that never goes out of date, such as how to avoid developing common disorders like depression, with new additions over time that respond to the changing nature of our young people, your setting and issues facing society at large.

It is easy to see how lessons on mental health could be dispiriting, so it is important to emphasize to pupils that in fact, good mental health is the norm: instead of telling them that one in six five- to sixteen-year-olds has a probable mental disorder, we can focus on the fact that 84 per cent do not (NHS Digital, 2020). If we want to avoid over-pathologizing, it is important that even though we should educate about specific disorders, we should also help pupils understand how to improve wellbeing from an already satisfactory or even good starting point. After all, teaching about mental health is not just about how to prevent and treat mental health problems, nor is it just about learning how to support others who are suffering. It is also about teaching pupils how to live their best life, getting the most out of each day and bringing a positive attitude to daily tasks and relationships with others. It is about raising self-awareness and learning how to respond to the needs of one's mind and body.

Mental Health Education across Key Stages 3–5

A key factor when building your curriculum is considering when might be the best time to teach each topic. Topics need to be allocated according to pupils' needs throughout the year, which of course changes from year group to year group. In Year 7 for example, you might want to start teaching about mental health in September as part of the transition process, but in Year 11, this topic would be better placed just before they go on study leave. You may have a particular year group where risk factors for mental illness are particularly prevalent, and so just before the long summer break might be a good time to remind them how to take care of themselves when the structure and support of school or college are not there.

The Coalition for Youth Mental Health in Schools (2021) lists the following groups as being particularly at risk: the socioeconomically disadvantaged; those who identify as LGBTQ+; girls and young women, with Black women in particular; and those with a special educational need or disability. Other possible risk factors cited by the *Mental Health of Children and Young People in England* survey are: having a parent who is experiencing psychological distress, living in a family which has problems with family functioning and having a long-term physical health condition (NHS Digital 2020, 2021), with Public Health Scotland also citing experiencing homelessness, refugee status and involvement in the criminal justice system (Public Health Scotland, 2021). It is interesting to note, however, that NHS Digital (2021) found that rates of probable mental disorder were higher among children and young people in the

White ethnic group than ethnic minority groups. Amongst eleven- to sixteen-year-olds, there was not such a large gap between boys and girls with probable mental health disorders (19.8 per cent of girls as opposed to 15.6 per cent of boys), but this difference widens greatly amongst seventeen- to nineteen-year-olds: 24.8 per cent for girls and 10.3 per cent of boys (NHS Digital, 2021). Given that the same study found that amongst six- to ten-year-olds, the situation is reversed, with 21.9 per cent of boys having a probable mental health disorder compared to 12 per cent of girls, we must not let preconceived ideas about the relationship between race, gender and mental health affect the content or consistency of our provision, although at the same time we need to acknowledge through this and other PSHE topics that there are issues which are more likely to affect the wellbeing of certain groups.

This all adds credence to the idea that we need to really know our pupils in order to create the curriculum for life that they need and not simply deliver lesson plans acquired online with no additions or amendments. As stated in the previous section, it would be easy for us to deliver the same basic content year on year to pupils and overlook the range of aspects to this topic that we can cover at each Key Stage. Here is a snapshot of what we cover in the mental health curriculum in my school in Key Stages 3 and 4:

Year 7:

- Getting to know you
- An introduction to mental health education
- Mindfulness and gratitude
- Neuroplasticity and thinking patterns

Year 8:

- The anti-depressant lifestyle (based on the six components of Dr Steve Ilardi's Therapeutic Lifestyle Change Program)

Year 9:

- The adolescent brain
- Healthy and unhealthy coping strategies (including eating disorders)
- Grief and bereavement

Year 10:

- Stress and stress management
- Mental health disorders

Year 11:

- Mental health and wellbeing at exam time

As you can see, the content changes with pupils' increasing age, covering more challenging aspects from Year 9 onwards, and changes according to different stages in their education journey: in Year 7, it is about establishing healthy thinking patterns to set them up well for secondary school life, and in the GCSE years, the focus is stress and examinations. This is not to say, however, that difficult and sensitive topics should not be covered early in Key Stage 3 and in fact, we must not be under the illusion that younger pupils are immune to serious mental disorders. As Catherine Roche, chief executive at Place2Be, says: 'What we're … seeing is some of the issues that traditionally might have come through in secondary school aged students, we're seeing come in earlier at the top end of primary school. So issues such as eating disorders, self-harm and suicidal ideation … are highlighted again and again as areas of increase' (The Coalition for Youth Mental Health in Schools, 2021). The above is just one example, but as the PSHE lead in your setting, you may use a different model for your mental health curriculum that is equally valid. The important thing is that you have a rationale for doing what you do.

The earlier statistics also show that we must not allow mental health education to fall by the wayside at Key Stage 5, not just because of these concerning insights regarding young women, but because it is a crucial time for helping pupils prepare to live independently. We must have dedicated curriculum time to remind pupils of key messages delivered in earlier years, but also to catch those who are new to our school or college in Year 12 and may not have covered the content to a great extent in their previous setting. There is also content which we will have covered in earlier stages but becomes more relevant and urgent at this age. For example, in 2021, it was found that 13 per cent of eleven- to sixteen-year-olds had an increased likelihood of problems with eating (which does not necessarily mean an eating disorder), yet this increased to an incredible 58.2 per cent of seventeen- to nineteen-year-olds (NHS Digital, 2021). However, we again want to avoid eye-rolling from students by just repeating old content verbatim, but adapting it to where they are at now. For example, we might revisit learning about grief in order to discuss how to cope with the transition from secondary school or college and mourning the life stage and people they are leaving behind. We might expand our discussions on how social media can affect our self-esteem by moving on from simply body image but also managing feelings relating to seeing former classmates seemingly having the time of their lives at university, getting a dream job or meeting a long-term partner. We also need to make them aware of adult mental health services, including those found on the university campus, which is especially important considering that experimental statistics have found in 2021 that 37 per cent of first-year students in England showed moderate to severe symptoms of depression and 39 per cent showed signs of likely having some form of anxiety in the two weeks prior to being surveyed (Office for National Statistics, 2021).

It can be difficult to find a fresh approach to mental health education for sixteen- to nineteen-year-olds, but through membership of the PSHE Association you can access their Scheme of Work planning tool and Programme Builder for Key Stage 5. It may be that you have a personal interest which is relevant and you would like to share with pupils. For example, I am currently studying Transactional Analysis (TA) psychotherapy, and am lucky enough to have the opportunity to pass on this learning to my students. Not only has a case study found that children, young people and teachers with TA skills have better self-awareness, increased understanding of others and as a consequence better relationships (Stuart and Algar, 2011), but I have not yet come across a pupil who has heard of TA, and so this represents a new and unique addition to an already broad wellbeing curriculum.

No matter the age of your pupils, there are some important things to bear in mind when teaching about mental health: do not give them examples of methods of self-harm, suicide or eating disorders, nor use shocking material. Use distancing techniques and be mindful not to use names of pupils in your class if using scenarios. Barksfield (2017) gives excellent further guidance on how to ensure that the PSHE classroom is a psychologically safe space. Pupils need to know what will happen once they access support services, to help reduce any fear associated with help-seeking. Get them to name specific people they can turn to for support, rather than sticking to generic categories such as 'friends', 'teachers' or 'family'. When it comes to family, encourage them to think of people both within and outside of the home. Make sure your pupils can name the specific members of staff responsible for and/or trained in mental health in your setting, too. Be on the lookout during lessons and when reviewing written work for those needing more specialized support – know your reporting and safeguarding procedures, particularly as by teaching about mental health, you are likely to get more pupils coming to you for advice or making disclosures – and possibly staff too. Although the PSHE Association has published guidance on its website about how to deal with mental health disclosures from students, reflect on whether you need to undertake additional training in order to handle any of the above safely and effectively. Finally, as the Department for Education itself recommends, ensure that dialogue about mental health issues is entirely non-judgemental (Department for Education, 2016), as this contributes to the wider aim of all schools and colleges being safe spaces for all who inhabit them, including yourself.

A Wider Approach to Wellbeing and Conclusion

In this chapter, we have looked at an overview of why, what and how to teach lessons about mental health. However, despite campaigning from prominent voices within PSHE, not every school or college is offering the subject on pupils' timetables, particularly at Key Stage 5. This may be beyond your control, but we still need to ensure as far as possible that mental health and wellbeing is on our pupils' radars. One way of doing this in Key Stage 5 is to offer my Change Your Mind ambassador programme, whereby Y12 pupils plan and deliver workshops on health and wellbeing to local primary school pupils. Not only do pupils on this programme learn about mental health through researching their workshops, but also gain work experience, unique opportunities and, hopefully, enjoyment of educating others. By going out to local feeder schools, you yourself can also get an insight into what Key Stage 2 pupils are covering in PSHE, again helping you to personalize your curriculum. With your support, your Change Your Mind team can also help deliver less sensitive content to younger years in your own school, such as how to manage stress around exam time – the feedback I get time and again is that the learning is more impactful coming from pupils not much older than the children whom they are teaching.

Another idea – regardless of whether you already have dedicated timetabled provision or not – is a whole-school Mental Health Awareness Week. We run ours every February to coincide with Place2Be's Children's Mental Health Week and each year have a packed schedule that mixes talks from excellent speakers with those connected to the school community who have lived experience of mental health struggles. During this week, other departments deliver special lessons and activities related to wellbeing, and the school library proudly displays its range of mental health books. Again though, you must quality-assure any speakers, whether internal or external, and have a clear agreement as to the content to be covered, and how it will be covered. In the case of excellent external speakers, ensure that you have endorsements from other schools and organizations for their work.

PSHE educators may sometimes feel the burden of responsibility, but even timetabled lessons on mental health delivered by a specialist are a tick-box exercise if not part of a coordinated whole-school approach that includes all staff and pupils, parents and carers, internal support services such as the safeguarding and pastoral team and external support services such as the local school nursing service. Remember that teachers are not expected to act as therapists, nor solve all of their pupils' problems, nor provide the antidote to the myriad of issues on a domestic, local, national and international scale that threaten the wellbeing of our young people. Nevertheless, it is our duty as compassionate educators to foster the mental health of our children and young people within our resources and capabilities, and that starts at the very basic level of ensuring that our classrooms, regardless of subject, are safe spaces. For pupils to be able to open up in PSHE without judgement, they need to feel able to be vulnerable in front of their peers and teachers in all areas of school or college life without fear of ridicule or shame. Therefore, the wider culture at your establishment will impact what goes on in your classroom. If we don't get the culture right organization-wide, we can do no more than pay lip service to mental health and wellbeing education.

Questions for Reflection for You and Your Setting

- What training do you and your team need to increase confidence with teaching about mental health?
- How will you identify the mental health needs of the pupils in your school/college?
- At which point(s) during the year will you teach about mental health?
- How will you quality-assure the teaching and teaching materials?
- How can your school/college weave mental health awareness into other subjects or areas of school/college life?

Recommended Resources

Anna Freud National Centre for Children and Families (evidence-based support for schools and colleges looking for a whole-school approach to mental health): https://www.annafreud.org/

Association for Young People's Health (national health data for young people in England, Scotland and Wales): https://ayph-youthhealthdata.org.uk/data-for-classroom-teaching/

Beat Eating Disorders (information, support and training about eating disorders, link to the BLAST approach given here): https://www.beateatingdisorders.org.uk/get-information-and-support/about-eating-disorders/downloads-resources/blast-distraction-techniques/

Bounce Together (online mental health and wellbeing survey platform for schools): https://www.bouncetogether.co.uk/

Chameleon PDE (PSHE resources for schools, CPD and training, survey tools for pupil voice): https://www.chameleonpde.com/

Change Your Mind (health and wellbeing ambassador programme training for Y12 and staff): https://qmgschangeyourmind.wordpress.com/

Charlie Waller Trust (mental health charity with resources, training and free webinars for schools/colleges and parents/carers): https://charliewaller.org/

Childline (advice for children and young people about managing feelings): https://www.childline.org.uk/info-advice/your-feelings/

Dr Pooky Knightsmith (mental health educator, speaker, author and advisor): https://www.pookyknightsmith.com/

Kooth (online mental wellbeing community for young people): https://www.kooth.com/

Place2Be (training, workshops and counselling services for schools): https://www.place2be.org.uk/

PSHE Association (national body for PSHE education, providing member schools and colleges with resources, training, guidance, advice, support and research): https://pshe-association.org.uk/

Student Minds (UK mental health charity for students in higher education, providing mental health support and advice, including their 'Know Before You Go' booklet for sixteen- to eighteen-year-olds): https://www.studentminds.org.uk/

The Mix (support website for under 25s on a wide range of issues that affect wellbeing): https://www.themix.org.uk/

Warwick Medical School, *The Warwick-Edinburgh Mental Wellbeing Scales – WEMWBS*. Available online: https://warwick.ac.uk/fac/sci/med/research/platform/wemwbs/

Young Minds (support website for young people, their parents/carers and schools/colleges): https://www.youngminds.org.uk/

References

Barksfield, J. (2017), *Mental Health, Wellbeing and PSHE*. Available online: https://www.sec-ed.co.uk/best-practice/mental-health-wellbeing-and-pshe/ (accessed 21 April 2022).

Department for Education (2016), *Counselling in Schools: A Blueprint for the Future Departmental Advice for School Leaders and Counsellors*. Available online: https://assets.publishing.service.gov.uk/government/uploads/system/uploads/attachment_data/file/497825/Counselling_in_schools.pdf (accessed 19 April 2022).

Department for Education (2019), *Relationships Education, Relationships and Sex Education (RSE) and Health Education: Statutory Guidance for Governing Bodies, Proprietors, Head Teachers, Principals, Senior Leadership Teams, Teachers*. Available online: https://assets.publishing.service.gov.uk/government/uploads/system/uploads/attachment_data/file/1019542/Relationships_Education__Relationships_and_Sex_Education__RSE__and_Health_Education.pdf (accessed 19 April 2022).

Department of Health & Social Care and Department for Education (2018), *Government Response to the Consultation on 'Transforming Children and Young People's Mental Health Provision: a Green Paper' and Next Steps*. Available online: https://assets.publishing.service.gov.uk/government/uploads/system/uploads/attachment_data/file/728892/government-response-to-consultation-on-transforming-children-and-young-peoples-mental-health.pdf (accessed 19 April 2022).

Ilardi, S. (2010), *The Depression Cure: The Six-Step Programme to Beat Depression Without Drugs*, London: Vermilion.

Mental Health Foundation (2021), *Prevention and Mental Health*. Available online: https://www.mentalhealth.org.uk/a-to-z/p/prevention-and-mental-health (accessed 20 April 2022).

NHS (2019), *5 Steps to Mental Wellbeing*. Available online: https://www.nhs.uk/mental-health/self-help/guides-tools-and-activities/five-steps-to-mental-wellbeing/ (accessed 20 April 2022).

NHS Digital (2020), *Mental Health of Children and Young People in England 2020 – Wave 1 Follow up to the 2017 Survey*. Available online: https://digital.nhs.uk/data-and-information/publications/statistical/mental-health-of-children-and-young-people-in-england/2020-wave-1-follow-up (accessed 19 April 2022).

NHS Digital (2021), *Mental Health of Children and Young People in England 2021 – Wave 2 Follow up to the 2017 Survey*. Available online: https://digital.nhs.uk/data-and-information/publications/statistical/mental-health-of-children-and-young-people-in-england/2021-follow-up-to-the-2017-survey (accessed 19 April 2022).

Office for National Statistics (2021), *Coronavirus and First-Year Higher Education Students, England, 4 October to 11 October 2021*. Available online: https://www.ons.gov.uk/peoplepopulationandcommunity/healthandsocialcare/healthandwellbeing/bulletins/coronavirusandfirstyearhighereducationstudentsengland/4octoberto11october2021 (accessed 19 April 2022).

Pollard, E., Vanderlayden, J., Alexander, K., Borkin, H. & O'Mahony, J. (2021), *Student Mental Health and Wellbeing: Insights from Higher Education Providers and Sector Experts*. Available online: https://assets.publishing.service.gov.uk/government/uploads/system/uploads/attachment_data/file/996478/Survey_of_HE_Providers_Student_Mental_Health.pdf (accessed 19 April 2022).

PSHE Association (2017), *A Curriculum for Life: The Case for Statutory Personal, Social, Health and Economic (PSHE) Education*. Available online: https://pshe-association.org.uk/evidence-and-research/a-curriculum-for-life-case-statutory-pshe-education?hsCtaTracking=5f5b7918-ae74-44da-bd80-869f8b4a992c%-7Cadaeef48-1689-4524-99c1-ea0e7ff7c528 (accessed 20 April 2022).

Public Health Scotland (2021), *Children and Young People's Mental Health*. Available online: http://www.healthscotland.scot/health-topics/mental-health-and-wellbeing/children-and-young-peoples-mental-health (accessed 21 April 2022).

Siegel, D. (2011), *The Healthy Mind Platter for Optimum Brain Matter*. Available online: https://drdansiegel.com/healthy-mind-platter/ (accessed 20 April 2022).

Stuart, K. & Algar, A. (2011), The use of transactional analysis in secondary education: A case study, *Teacher Education Advancement Network Journal (TEAN)*, 3(1). Available online: https://insight.cumbria.ac.uk/id/eprint/1368/1/89-423-1-PB.pdf (accessed 21 April 2022).

The Coalition for Youth Mental Health in Schools (2021), *Fixing a Failing System: Rethinking Mental Health Support in Schools for the Post-Covid Generation*. Available online: https://www.publicfirst.co.uk/wp-content/uploads/2021/10/MHC-Report.pdf (accessed 19 April 2022).

5

Making Informed Choices for Physical Health

Charlotte Ross, Kimberley Hibbert-Mayne and Dave Woodward

Aims of This Chapter

- To consider how we present the notion of health in education.
- To suggest a content structure for health, physical activity and sleep across Key Stages 3, 4 and 5.
- To explore ideas regarding positive pedagogy when teaching health education to encourage pupils to understand how to change/maintain healthy behaviours over time.

What Is Health Education?

Comprehensive and thoughtful health education allows pupils to approach decision-making from an informed perspective and understand the impact of such decisions. Although health education as a concept is vast and difficult to define due to its meaning for each individual, the PSHE statutory guidance (Department for Education (DfE), 2021b) offers key principles and content that will support pupils in and beyond their school years.

The World Health Organization (WHO) recognizes that there is a 'sense of urgency' required to respond to the ever-changing needs of our young people (WHO, 2017, p.25). This is compounded by concerning data published by the National Health Service (NHS) demonstrating the decline in children and young people's mental health and quality of sleep, school days missed and an increase in eating problems between 2017 and 2021 (NHS, 2021).

The place of education is pivotal as part of the broader Public Health Framework (Public Health England (PHE), 2015). Understanding how to present health education is constantly changing. However, there may be some pedagogical choices that can engage our pupils of creativity, pupil voice and choice are employed. Strömmer et al. (2021) suggest that adolescents do not prioritize being healthy, and Youth Sport Trust (2021) found that over half of secondary-age girls do not take part in any sport at school outside of PE lessons, citing their period, self-consciousness and lack of confidence among other things as key reasons; therefore, traditional methods of information giving with health as the only motivator are met with poor outcomes. Interventions should allow pupils to have multiple opportunities that are easy to access and achieve and incorporate their peers. Physical activity guidelines from the Department of Health and Social Care (2019) reinforce this message by ensuring that we communicate beyond the guidelines and highlight to our pupils that health benefits are irrespective of how much exercise is completed, there is 'no absolute threshold' (p. 14). This could help pupils to feel empowered to reach achievable goals with strong links to motivational processes.

Table 5.1 Suggested content structure for health, physical activity and sleep

Health	
Key Stage 3*	• Consider what might influence decisions regarding health choices; for example, diet • Nutritional information on food packaging; advertising and marketing of food • The possible impact of unhealthy choices on physical and mental health • How to keep oneself safe in the sun and how to monitor moles on the skin • First Aid – how to assess a casualty; how to make a call to the emergency services; CPR (as a minimum) • Menstrual health and wellbeing
Key Stage 4	• How to conduct a testicular and breast self-examination • How to decide which mode of support is needed: 999, a visit to A&E, a visit to the GP, a visit to the pharmacist, self-care at home • First Aid – taking care of injuries, allergic reactions, asthma (as a minimum) • Health supplements, such as vitamins and protein shakes
Key Stage 5	• How to recognize illnesses that are particularly associated with young adults • First Aid – particularly in the context of where the casualty has consumed drugs and/or alcohol; the recovery position (as a minimum) • How to access health services when living away from home • Body modifications and the potential impact on health, such as tattoos, cosmetic surgery and other procedures

Health	
Statutory health education objectives	'Pupils should know … the characteristics and evidence of what constitutes a healthy lifestyle, maintaining a healthy weight, including the links between an inactive lifestyle and ill health, including cancer and cardiovascular ill-health. … about the science relating to blood, organ and stem cell donation' (DfE, 2021).

*It is important to note that the design and technology national curriculum in England states that pupils should 'understand and apply the principles of nutrition and health' (DfE, 2013). PSHE education can clearly help meet this objective.

Physical activity	
Key Stage 3	• Addressing gaps in post-pandemic physical literacy • Encouraging pupils to find physical activity that they enjoy • Introduce the wider benefits of physical activity, for example, the effect on self-esteem, motivation and confidence, plus the cultivation of character attributes.
Key Stage 4	• How physical activity might aid stress management, such as through the effect on brain chemicals • The importance of balance in physical activity between cardiovascular exercise and strength-building activities • 'Quick wins' for building more physical activity into the day
Key Stage 5	• How to maintain physical activity on a budget when living away from home • The impact of yoga on mental health • The advantages and disadvantages of fitness trackers
Statutory health education objectives	'Pupils should know … the positive associations between physical activity and promotion of mental wellbeing, including as an approach to combat stress' (DfE, 2021).

Sleep	
Key Stage 3	• Benefits of sleep: improved memory, creativity, mood, physical performance and productivity • Basic sleep hygiene
Key Stage 4	• The importance of sleep: that insufficient sleep causes illness (e.g. high blood sugar levels, cardiovascular strokes, depression, anxiety) • The unique challenges for teenagers, who experience a temporary body clock shift in adolescence • Tools and strategies for successful sleep habits • The impact of sleep habits on learning capacity
Key Stage 5	• Embedding positive sleep habits and well-informed decisions • The symbiotic relationship between poor sleep and mental health • The different stages and types of sleep and their benefits
Statutory health education objectives	'Pupils should know … the importance of sufficient good quality sleep for good health and how a lack of sleep can affect weight, mood and ability to learn' (DfE, 2021).

Health

Health can be personal and emotive for pupils, teachers and families; therefore, sensitivity is required. The PHE (2015, p.6) framework states that relationships are 'central to young people's health and wellbeing', with an approach that recognizes the intricacies and links between physical and mental health. The paper also notes that positivity and building resilience are imperative to a holistic approach. Signposting where pupils can access support within and outside of the school community drives this notion of pupils being able to take responsibility for health and associated decisions.

The PSHE Association provides lesson plans and PowerPoints that look at the influence of others, potential barriers and strategies in relation to healthy eating and physical health choices in Key Stage 3 and 4. The PHE focus on whole-school ideas (https://campaignresources.phe.gov.uk/schools/topics/healthy-eating/whole-school-ideas) for healthy eating has some suggestions for supporting pupils; however, the resources are very much tailored to primary education. Creating a pupil voice forum has the potential to set up similar infrastructures more relevant to secondary schools and drive healthy eating options.

In addition to pupil voice, encouraging a wider perspective could include the involvement of parents/carers and use celebrities as role models. Harnessing the power of social media may help pupils align health decisions with their own values (Strömmer et al., (2021). The manner in which this involvement is integrated and planned for should be mindful and have clear intentions. Carefully choosing potential celebrities to support discussions whilst incorporating the criticality of what makes a positive role model may help pupils work through distanced scenario work, particularly if this is underpinned by values-based education (Menon, Kar and Padhy, 2021).

Pupils may have lived experiences of ill health. There must be a balance between information and support. Staff pre-reading on ill health such as cancer and cardiovascular diseases might help understanding; for example, by using World Health Organization factsheets (https://www.who.int/news-room/fact-sheets). Charities such as Cancer Research UK (https://www.cancerresearchuk.org/about-cancer/causes-of-cancer) and the British Heart Foundation (https://www.bhf.org.uk/) have information pages about how to reduce risk; however, it is important to note that these are often not specifically targeted at school-age pupils.

One area of the curriculum that has potential for emotive reactions to be displayed can be around the broad area of donation. Delivery of this topic would encompass not only health but value-driven education, with pupils learning how their values, cultural and religious beliefs can influence decisions. Possible areas of discussion would be the change in the law regarding organ donation in 2020 or the ethical implications of donating or receiving blood. We can also engage pupils with facts about the willingness of people to donate versus the actual amount of people that do and the type of donations needed (for example, the need for more blood donors from Black, Asian and minority ethnic backgrounds).

Inequalities exist in health outcomes, such as Black maternal health (The Guardian, 2021), and access to health and leisure services through disability and financial circumstances. Engaging pupils in such information may go some way to empowering them to understand their own experiences and futures. To present and discuss health inequalities with pupils should be through considerate and clear language, talking about the wider life of pupils and recognizing pupils' 'sense of personal identity' (McKeown, 2022, p.12). There is a clear link here to the topic of diversity, covered in Chapter 9 of this book.

Physical Activity

The relationship between physical activity and mental wellbeing is cemented and steadfast; however, the statistics present an uninspiring picture. In the academic year 2020/21, only 44.6 per cent of children and young people met the Department of Health and Social Care (2019) Physical Activity Guidelines of an average of 60+ minutes of sport and physical activity per day, which is 94,000 less than in pre-pandemic data (Sport England, 2021). Understanding possible barriers and interventions across the Key Stages should support pupils in moving to a more consistent motivation to sustain physical activity. How we frame physical activity will ultimately affect pupil perceptions. The Youth Sport Trust 2022–2035 Strategy (2022a) includes empowering young people as 'changemakers' who build relationships and co-create opportunities within sport and physical activity with the ability to lead their peers. Research from Sweden also corroborates the notion of pupils having a voice in decision-making processes about physical activity. This research also suggests that praising pupils for effort and providing opportunities to become more competent will improve self-efficacy (Mikaelsson et al., 2020).

As per the above table, physical literacy can underpin pupils' confidence by acknowledging motivation, understanding, participation and fundamental movement skills. This is particularly important as 'higher physical literacy in children is associated with favourable health indicators' (Caldwell et al., 2020, p.1). Benefits have also been found when pupils volunteer in sport (Sport England, 2021). Allowing pupils time to explore physical activity through choice, relating to peers and providing ample opportunities within school to gain improved competence is key. If learning activities are focused on the local area or school community, such as by leading sports clubs with younger pupils at their own school or a feeder primary school, pupils might feel there is more meaning and engage with the content further.

Delving deeper into the wider benefits of physical activity across the Key Stages naturally coincides with stress management for examinations and helps to address additional concerns, such as the legacy of Covid-19 and resultant negative impact on social and mental wellbeing. The Youth Sport Trust Annual Research Report (2022b) notes the wider benefits of PE, physical activity and school sport as physical health, brain function, social wellbeing and mental health. As pupils move through secondary education, developing skills to make autonomous informed decisions about their physical activity should permeate the curriculum.

New messages and a personalized approach to teaching about physical activity would be more effective if embedded within the entire school culture beyond PSHE and PE. This is based on the simple fact that 'unhappy, unhealthy children don't learn effectively' (Youth Sport Trust, 2022a, p.9). Although difficult to organize in a busy school, the short-term output would be worth the long-term gains. Schemes such as Bikeability have the dual benefit of encouraging more pupils to be physically active by cycling to school whilst simultaneously reducing the burden on the environment.

Sleep

Sleep is just as important for our wellbeing as physical activity, diet or any other of our fundamental needs. Research has proven that a lack of sleep can cause illness, compromise our safety, ability to learn and our overall quality of life (Pandi-Perumal, 2018). As the statutory guidance 'Physical health and mental wellbeing: Secondary', content about the importance of good-quality sleep should be introduced positively and at age- and stage-appropriate points (DfE, 2021a). This is especially important as the sleeping patterns and cycles of secondary-aged students are likely to change for various reasons during that time, but particularly because, as Walker (2018, p.93) writes, due to biological reasons, 'the sixteen-year-old will usually have no interest in sleeping at nine p.m'.

We suggest that during Key Stage 3 pupils should know the importance of sleep and how our bodily organs, including our brains, revitalize with sleep, leading to better physical health, improved mood, memory and creativity (Pandi-Perumal, 2018). The following basics of good 'sleep hygiene' could be introduced:

- getting plenty of daylight
- being physically active
- having a tidy bedroom
- keeping to regular betimes
- switching off screens thirty minutes before sleep

(Firth, 2016)

By the time pupils get to Key Stage 4, they have heavy homework burdens, increased extra-curricular and social activities and bigger weekday-to-weekend differences in sleep timings (Sun et al., 2019). It is important to educate pupils on the complex effects that these, as well as innate changes in teenagers' circadian rhythm, can have on sleep. Pupils should be taught how to recognize these changes and be equipped with tools and strategies to develop sleep and protect their health and wellbeing. As many as 50 per cent of teenagers in the UK are reported to be sleeping less than the recommended hours (Singh, 2021). As previous sections in this chapter have already emphasized, pupils need to become autonomous decision makers so that by the time they leave Key Stage 5, they are not within the 25 per cent of adults who are sleeping for fewer than the recommended hours (Singh, 2021). As pupils can't practise sleep in school, communication with parents and carers about what is taught (e.g. by sharing the resources below) is of great benefit and importance.

Conclusion

A key component of health education is to avoid generic goals, too-basic guidelines and normative statistics as the focal point of lessons. Whilst important that pupils are armed with information, a whole school culture of reflective health, individual awareness and future targets should support and motivate pupils and avoid idealistic impressions of life-long health. A non-judgemental approach to health education could also provide a platform in which pupils feel more confident to discuss concerns, barriers and possible strategies to embed healthy behaviours.

Questions for Reflection for You and Your Setting

- How might you gather information regarding the needs of your pupils? How can you build your curriculum plan to meet these?
- Can pupils be involved in the food served in school? How might this work logistically?
- Could QR codes be used to signpost external support to enable pupils' easier access to health support?
- Are learning materials up-to-date with current research? Who is responsible for this?
- How do you communicate the intentions of your curriculum plans with all key stakeholders?
- How can you develop the health education content as a thread across departments?
- How are pupils assessed on their knowledge and understanding of health? How are they praised for individual health progress/goals met?

Recommended Resources

- Activity Alliance and Disability Rights UK (an everyday guide for people living with an impairment or health condition): https://www.activityalliance.org.uk/assets/000/000/149/2518_BeingActiveReport_A4_FINAL(1)_original.pdf?1461165840
- Bikeability (training courses for people of all ages to cycle confidently on the road): https://www.bikeability.org.uk/
- CoppaFeel! (information and guidance on breast and chest self-examination): https://coppafeel.org/
- 'Food and Mood' video from Mind, the mental health charity: https://www.mind.org.uk/information-support/tips-for-everyday-living/food-and-mood/about-food-and-mood/
- Movember (resources and information about men's health): https://uk.movember.com/
- NHS Better Health, Every mind matters: https://www.nhs.uk/every-mind-matters/mental-health-issues/sleep/
- NHS Blood and Transplant (Donation teaching resources: KS3 and KS4: Curriculum-linked resources to help teachers in England educate their students about blood, organ and stem cell donation): https://www.nhsbt.nhs.uk/how-you-can-help/get-involved/download-digital-materials/donation-teaching-resources/
- NHS school resources including Change4Life and Rise Above lesson plans: https://www.england.nhs.uk/get-involved/learning/schools-resources/
- PSHE Association: pshe-association.org.uk
- Sport England (resources for secondary schools – whole school approach, inclusion of SEND students in PE and teacher training): https://www.sportengland.org/how-we-can-help/secondary-teacher-training-programme#contactus-12758
- Teen Sleep Hub (tips and resources for teenagers, schools and parents/carers): https://teensleephub.org.uk/
- This Girl Can (resources that are free to download and a 'studio you' for secondary PE teachers): https://www.thisgirlcan.co.uk/resources-for-schools/
- Your Privates (testicular cancer awareness and resources): https://www.yourprivates.org.uk/

References

Caldwell, H., Di Cristofaro, N. A., Cairney, J., Bray, S. R., MacDonald, M. J. & Timmons, B. W. (2020), Physical literacy, physical activity, and health indicators in school-age children, *International Journal of Environmental Research and Public Health*, 17(15), pp. 5367. https://doi.org/10.3390/ijerph17155367

Department for Education (DfE) (2013), *National Curriculum in England: Design and Technology Programmes of Study*. Available online: https://www.gov.uk/government/publications/national-curriculum-in-england-design-and-technology-programmes-of-study/national-curriculum-in-england-design-and-technology-programmes-of-study#cooking-and-nutrition (accessed 2 July 2022).

Department for Education (DfE) (2021a), *Physical Health and Mental Wellbeing (Primary and Secondary)*. Available online: https://www.gov.uk/government/publications/relationships-education-relationships-and-sex-education-rse-and-health-education/physical-health-and-mental-wellbeing-primary-and-secondary (accessed 1 July 2022).

Department for Education (DfE) (2021b), *Relationships Education, Relationships and Sex Education (RSE) and Health Education*. Available online: https://assets.publishing.service.gov.uk/government/uploads/system/uploads/attachment_data/file/1019542/Relationships_Education__Relationships_and_Sex_Education__RSE__and_Health_Education.pdf (accessed 2 July 2022).

Department of Health and Social Care (2019), *UK Chief Medical Officer's Physical Activity Guidelines*. Available online: https://www.gov.uk/government/publications/physical-activity-guidelines-uk-chief-medical-officers-report (accessed 1 July 2022).

Firth, J. (2016), Getting a better night's sleep, a guide for students, *Medium*, 16 June. Available online: https://medium.com/@jwfirth/getting-a-better-nights-sleep-8594bfe69113 (accessed 1 July 2022). https://campaignresources.phe.gov.uk/schools/topics/healthy-eating/whole-school-ideas

McKeown, R. (2022), *Language Matters: How to Talk about "Health Inequalities" in the Context of Young People*, London: AYPH.

Menon, V., Kar, S. K. & Padhy, S. K. (2021), Celebrity role models and their impact on mental health of children and adolescents: Implications and suggestions, *Journal of Indian Association for Child and Adolescent Mental Health-ISSN 0973–1342*, 17(2), pp. 210–5.

Mikaelsson, K., Rutberg, S., Lindqvist, A. K. & Michaelson, P. (2020), Physically inactive adolescents' experiences of engaging in physical activity, *European Journal of Physiotherapy*, 22(4), pp. 191–6. DOI: 10.1080/21679169.2019.1567808

NHS (2021), *Mental Health of Children and Young People in England 2021 – Wave 2 Follow up to the 2017 Survey*. Available online: https://digital.nhs.uk/data-and-information/publications/statistical/mental-health-of-children-and-young-people-in-england/2021-follow-up-to-the-2017-survey (accessed 1 July 2022).

Pandi-Perumal, S. (2018), 'Why we sleep: The new science of sleep and dreams by Matthew Walker, Ph.D.', *Sleep and Vigilance*, 2, pp. 93–4. https://doi-org.apollo.worc.ac.uk/10.1007/s41782-018-0034-0

Public Health England (2015), *Improving Young People's Health and Wellbeing: A Framework for Public Health*. Available online: https://www.gov.uk/government/publications/improving-young-peoples-health-and-wellbeing-a-framework-for-public-health (accessed 1 July 2022).

Singh, T. (2021), "Sleep health: A meaningful measure of relationship between sleep and our health", *Sleep and Vigilance*, 6(1), pp. 243–5.

Sport England (2021), *Coronavirus Challenges Highlight Importance of Physical Activity and Sport for Children*. Available online: https://www.sportengland.org/news/coronavirus-challenges-highlight-importance-physical-activity-and-sport-children (accessed 1 July 2022).

Strommer, S., Shaw, S., Jenner, S., Vogel (nee Black), C., Lawrence, W., Woods-Townsend, K., Farrell, D., Inskip, H., Baird, J., Morrison, L. & Barker, M. (2021), How do we harness adolescent values in designing health behaviour change interventions? A qualitative study, *British Journal of Health Psychology*, 26. DOI: 10.1111/bjhp.12526.

Sun, W., Ling, J., Zhu, X., Lee, T. & Li, S. (2019), Association between weekday-weekend sleep discrepancy and academic performance: systematic review and meta-analysis, *Sleep Medicine*, 40, pp. e318–e319.

The Guardian, *Black Women in UK Four Times More Likely to Die in Pregnancy and Childbirth*. Available online: https://www.theguardian.com/society/2021/nov/11/black-women-uk-maternal-mortality-rates (accessed 2 July 2022).

Walker, M. (2018), *Why We Sleep*, London: Penguin.

World Health Organization (2017), *Global Accelerated Action for the Health of Adolescents (AA-HA!) Guidance to Support Country Implementation*. Available online: https://www.who.int/publications/i/item/9789241512343 (accessed 1 July 2022).

Youth Sport Trust (2021), *YST Girls Active National Report for Girls' Data June 2021*. Available online: https://www.youthsporttrust.org/media/mhid4zje/girls-active-secondary-national-report-2020-21.pdf (accessed 2 July 2022).

Youth Sport Trust (2022a), *Inspiring Changemakers, Building Belonging*. Available online: https://www.youthsporttrust.org/media/nu1dxzz3/yst_strategy_2022-35.pdf (accessed 1 July 2022).

Youth Sport Trust (2022b), *PE and School Sport in England: Annual Report 2022*. Available online: https://www.youthsporttrust.org/media/enwncbsg/yst-pe-school-sport-report-2022.pdf (accessed 1 July 2022).

6

Let's Talk about Puberty

Annie O'Neill

Aims of This Chapter

- To increase your knowledge and confidence to deliver lessons about puberty to pupils.
- To explore how to build on pupil knowledge and know what to include.
- To share some practical ideas to support your teaching.

Getting puberty education 'right' is crucial. Elyssa Rider (Brook, 2021) is clear about how important teaching puberty is for young people. She states, 'Puberty education is arguably foundational to most other sex and relationships topics.' Hopefully within a secondary setting you will be building on a foundation already laid during primary school years, and there really is no right or wrong way to do it. However, there are some basics that it is vital all children know, about how their own bodies work and about how the bodies of others work as well. It is a dictum that is used constantly within health: 'If you don't know what is "normal" for your body, how will you ever know when something goes wrong?' It may be important to state now that this chapter may well take a slightly different tack to other chapters in this book, as it has been written by a nurse and not an educationalist, a nurse who is passionate about education and specifically, Relationships, Sex and Health Education (RSHE), passionate about empowering children and young people to understand their own bodies and make informed decisions and choices about what they do with that body and how to keep themselves safe.

The Department for Education (2019) expects that by the end of secondary school, pupils should know the 'key facts about puberty, the changing adolescent body and menstrual wellbeing' plus know about the 'main changes which take place in males and females, and the implications for emotional and physical health'. This is a huge topic that needs to be carefully planned and sensitively implemented – the physical changes are relatively straightforward, but it is worth thinking about separating aspects of puberty education to deliver them effectively to students, e.g. emotions, the impact of hormones and then a different session about the physical changes.

Even before delivering your first session, it is important to consider your own starting point as this intrinsically impacts how we teach, as do your own personal values, religious and cultural beliefs, plus personal experiences and relationships. Doing a little bit of preparation can be invaluable and thinking in advance about your ground rules for RSE lessons, both for the class and for you personally and professionally. Having something about sharing information (other people's and your own) is a good start – nobody's mum wants the whole class to know about her periods, plus preparing a response should you be asked a personal question. Your own experience of learning about puberty will also affect your teaching, so thinking about what it was like for you, and also what the best and worst bits were, is often worth reflecting upon before you deliver your own sessions to pupils.

Teaching about Physical Changes

Never assume that they know the basics – always check that everyone has the relevant and appropriate knowledge and then fill in the gaps as needed.

An effective starting point with the basics is, when does puberty start? How long does it last? Check and build on existing knowledge and correct any misunderstandings. Then, ask pupils to think about the physical changes that happen during puberty; using a series of physical change statements and asking small groups to discuss whether the change is one that happens to girls and boys, just girls or just boys, encourages the idea that puberty is not solely linked to one particular sex! It is interesting how often pupils think that mood swings are often only associated with girls and underarm hair only associated with boys. A good idea can be to link some of the changes to the importance of hygiene; for instance: you sweat more, your skin changes and you get spots and your hair may get more greasy – always worth emphasizing that having a bath, shower or wash every day is imperative, as is regularly changing underwear and socks. Discussing the use of deodorant, and general personal hygiene, including teeth brushing at this point may be useful.

Ensuring that pupils are aware of the correct names for the male and female reproductive organs using a diagram that they have to label works well. There is a body of research which suggests that 'adults have a poor understanding of external female genitalia' (Vollans, 2022), and when adults feel uncomfortable saying something or talking about something they avoid it or make up pet names to hide or avoid their embarrassment. As educators we need to ensure that our pupils are aware of the anatomy of both male and female genitalia and their differences plus feel confident to name it correctly and confidently.

Include a section which explains the menstrual cycle and talks about what a period is, have a selection of sanitary products to demonstrate how they are used, how often they might be changed, and also allay any fears about school having a supply of products should they start their period in school. Recommending that menstruating pupils keep a spare pencil case or small makeup bag with emergency supplies (sanitary towel, spare pants, wet wipes and a small plastic bag for any soiled underwear) in their school bag can go a long way to reassuring girls that they will be able to cope should their period start at school.

Making Your Lessons as Inclusive as Possible

Whilst there is a lot of debate about whether classes should be taught separately to boys and girls, Ramoya Randall from Brook Education suggests that lessons that are mixed 'create a safer and much more inclusive environment particularly when considering the needs of intersex and young people of trans experience' (Brook, 2021). However, consideration must be given to the individual cohort – some young people may feel more comfortable and able to explore the topic and ask more questions in a single sex lesson. Certainly, in some faith schools, lessons are taught to single sex classes. Whatever the decision, everyone should be taught that puberty happens to all genders and not just their own. We do need to consider how we talk about 'boys' and 'girls' and how this could be troublesome if you have a child in your lesson who is struggling with their gender identity. Using language like: 'changes also ensures that happen to biological boys, and to biological girls' ensures that everyone is included. 'This also means that young people in a broader context are more aware and tolerable of their peers and the changes they may be experiencing' (Brook, 2020, p.3).

Teaching about Emotional Changes

The psychological impact of puberty and reaching adolescence for both boys and girls should not be underestimated. Everything is changing, not just physically: the way they view the world and themselves alters, they grow more independent, more sensitive to how others see them, they become more self-conscious and are more influenced by their peers rather than their parents (Krause, 2022). As well as hormones involved in puberty playing a part in the emotional turmoil, the way that the adolescent brain develops also has a bearing – it is a time of significant growth, unused connections within the brain are being pruned and at the same time other connections are strengthened, as Blakemore (2006) suggests: 'Adolescents develop the capacity to hold in mind more multidimensional concepts and are thus able to think more strategically.' However as this is coupled with increasing self-awareness, this can be a time when there is a dip in self-confidence and self-esteem. It has been estimated that up to half of adolescents will struggle with low confidence levels during their early teenage years, so educating them about the emotional rollercoaster that is a normal part of puberty is vital to help them understand and weather the puberty storm.

Getting pupils to think about their own emotions and also realize that their peers are experiencing very similar emotions can be very helpful; they understand that they are not alone and it helps to normalize some of the feelings that they are having. Ask pupils about the emotions that they have experienced, get them to share with each other. One way to facilitate this is by asking pupils to answer a series of questions by standing up: stand up if you have a sister, stand up if you like peas, stand up if you have a pet – at this point not everyone will have stood up together, but if you ask them to stand up if they have ever felt angry everyone in the class will stand up. Get them to understand that it's normal for them to have these feelings, to feel angry, sad and upset in the space of five minutes, or to feel sad for a few days, and understand that this does not necessarily signify anything more than normal puberty emotions.

Emotional regulation is often one of the hardest aspects for young people to understand and master during puberty and well into adolescence, and as educators we need to ensure that they have a range of tools available to help with this. Teaching simple breathing techniques, giving help and advice around friendship difficulties and guidance to negotiate relationships will all prepare and set the foundation for future success.

What Else Do We Need to Talk about?

During conversations and lessons about puberty it is important to recognize that a normal part of child development means that young people become interested in their own bodies, other people's bodies and sex: 'Normal child development involves some degree of behaviour focused on sexual body parts and curiosity about sexual behaviour' (National Center on the Sexual Behavior of Youth, 2022). As adults it is important that we do not shy away from having those frank discussions about sex, masturbation and pornography. Most young people, by age ten, have a basic understanding of how babies are made, pregnancy and childbirth – hopefully in primary school they have covered conception to birth. They are naturally curious, and we need to equip them with the correct information and give them the opportunity to talk to an adult that they trust about these topics. If we do not, they will inevitably turn to the internet to answer their questions. Over 60 per cent of children eleven to thirteen have seen pornography, albeit accidentally, with some stumbling across it even earlier – in some cases as young as seven or eight (bbfc, 2019). We need to talk to young people, as latest research tells us that young people are turning to pornography to learn about sex and have their questions and curiosity answered; we need to have open and honest conversations to ensure that they are not consuming this content and believing that this is what sex is like in an intimate relationship. Learning about your own body and what you like is a vital step in a fulfilling sex life and part of learning this includes experimenting with masturbation and self-stimulation – both of which are natural. A 2009 study indicated that adolescent girls felt that masturbation was more acceptable for boys than girls (Hogarth & Ingham, 2009), and these ideas perpetuate into adulthood. As Hogarth suggests, 'there is more than a lingering historical perception that, in many cultures, masturbation is a shameful and problematic activity' (Hogarth & Ingham, 2009), as a result there is a reluctance to talk about the topic. As long ago as 1994 it was suggested that 'adults, particularly parents and carers, should be talking to young people about pleasure and desire' (Hogarth & Ingham, 2009), but it would appear that even today, some thirty years later, this idea has still not permeated the sex education agenda, in fact the results of a word search in the statutory guidance for schools for teaching sex and relationships show that pleasure is not mentioned at all, and neither is masturbation. However as educators these conversations need to happen with both sexes and be fully inclusive. Obviously full consideration needs to be given to the religious and cultural beliefs within your school community. In the Catholic faith masturbation is seen as a sin, so there needs to be careful thought about how this is tackled within an RSE lesson, if at all. In some faith schools various aspects, including masturbation, are simply omitted. However, when masturbation is part of the lesson it needs to be made very clear that this is something that is only experienced in private places.

Key Stages 4 and 5

Hopefully by the time pupils reach Key Stages 4 and 5, they already have a good knowledge of puberty and everything from this point is building on the foundations previously laid. Conversations about consent and healthy relationships should continue, including your relationship with yourself, plus discussions about the impact of pornography on relationships.

If you have a young person who has not yet started puberty as they reach Key Stage 4 or 5 (the average age for girls is between nine and thirteen, and boys eleven and fourteen), consideration needs to be given about any extra support that the individual may need – signposting to GP being the starting point. Teachers also need to be sensitive about any bullying or 'banter' around the subject that may occur. As adolescence is reached peers become increasingly important, and fitting in and being part of the group becomes a big focus. If you stand out from your peers because you are different in any way – including because you have not started puberty yet, it can cause a lot of distress. School and college staff play a vital role in making it clear that any harassment or bullying is not acceptable and taking action to tackle it.

Environmental Considerations

In today's world where climate change and environmental consciousness are an ongoing concern, we need to ensure that this is tackled when talking about sanitary products. Sanitary towels are always recommended for younger girls when they first start their periods; however, there are environmentally sustainable alternatives which should also be considered and educated about. There is 'growing recognition of the ruinous environmental impact of single-use menstrual products. The Women's Environmental Network estimates that up to 2bn menstrual items are flushed down Britain's toilets each year and in 2020 15 per cent of menstruating women opted for environmentally friendly products (Kale, 2021).

Using 'period pants' mitigates the need for sanitary towels or tampons; they are being increasingly used especially as they are more readily available at reasonable prices; a well-known chemist introduced period underwear at the beginning of the month and reported that, over that month, sales increased by 319 per cent (Kale, 2021). Reusable tampon applicators are now available and are certainly more environmentally friendly, although tampons without applicators are kinder to the environment, younger girls may be reluctant to use them as it involves inserting their own finger into their vagina. Certainly, in Key Stages 4 and 5 their use could be encouraged, as well as the use of a reusable menstrual cup which is inserted into the vagina, collects the menstrual blood, and is then removed, rinsed and replaced.

Conclusion

As the title of this chapter states, puberty happens to everyone, so because you have already been through it yourself, that almost makes you the expert here! Half the battle has already been won – you have lived experience. Being confident in your delivery, knowing your stuff and being prepared, goes a long way to ensuring success when delivering sessions about puberty and the associated topics. Pupils will take their lead from you: If you are embarrassed, they will be embarrassed, and this perpetuates the idea that the whole topic is taboo. Creating a safe and inclusive environment for pupils to be able to learn about their changing bodies and discuss, with an adult that they trust, all that is happening with them as they try to negotiate their way through puberty and into adolescence is essential.

Reflection Questions for You and Your Setting

- How inclusive are your resources on puberty?
- Have you got a range of products available when talking about menstruation, including environmentally friendly products?
- How do you make your learning environment a safe space for young people to feel empowered to ask questions?

Recommended Resources

- www.amaze.org – age-appropriate information on puberty with some great videos which tackle sensitive subjects with humour
- Brook Learn – FREE e-learning modules for professionals on a wide range of topics.
- OM Health & Wellbeing Consultancy Ltd – a private company who deliver RSE in schools – www.omhwc.org.uk
- PSHE Association has training resources and toolkits available for download
- School Nurse – liaising with the in-school nurse or local school nursing service can offer an expert approach to health education

References

Blakemore, S.- J. & Choudhury, S. (2006), 'Development of the adolescent brain: Implications for executive function and social cognition', *Journal of Child Psychology and Psychiatry*, 47(3–4), pp. 296–312.

British Board of Film Classification (BBFC) (2019), *Research into Children and Pornography*. Available online: www.bbfc.co.uk (accessed 14 May 2022).

Brook – Healthy lives for young people (2021), *Why Teaching Young People about Puberty Is Essential*. Available online: www.brook.org.uk/brookblog (accessed 20 April 2022).

Brook – Healthy lives for young people (2020), *5 Top Tips for Teaching about Puberty*. Available online: www.brook.org.uk/brookblog (accessed 20 April 2022).

Brook – Healthy lives for young people (2021), *10 Top Tips for Your First Time Teaching RSE*. Available online: www.brook.org.uk/brookblog (accessed 25 May 2022).

Department for Education (2019), *Relationships Education, Relationships and Sex Education (RSE) and Health Education.* Available online: www.gov/uk/government/RSE (accessed 20 April 2022).

Hogarth, H. & Ingham, R. (2009), 'Masturbation among young women and associations with sexual health: An exploratory study', *Journal of Sex Research*, 46, pp. 558–67. (accessed 14 June 2022).

Kale, S. (2021), The rise of period pants: are they the answer to menstrual landfill – and women's prayers? *The Guardian Wednesday 1st September 2021* (accessed 14 June 2022).

Krause, N. (2022), *Don't Panic about Puberty.* Available online: www.always.co.uk (accessed 10 May 2022).

Manchester Evening News (2019), *It's Not a Cookie, It's a Vagina – Social Worker Warns Using Pet Names for Body Parts Puts Children at Risk.* Emma Gill 9.10.2019. Available online: https://www.manchestereveningnews.co.uk/news/parenting/vagina-penis-names-sexual-abuse-17057579 (accessed 9 May 2022).

Maisie Darling (2019), *Teaching Children about Their Private Parts.* Available online: https://www.pacey.org.uk/news-and-views/pacey-blog/2019/october-2019/teaching-children-about-their-private-parts/ (accessed 9 May 2022).

National Center on the Sexual Behavior of Youth (2022), https://learning.nspcc.org.uk/child-health-development/sexual-behaviour

NSPCC – PANTS Rule and Pantosaurus (n.d.). Available online: https://www.nspcc.org.uk/keeping-children-safe/support-for-parents/pants-underwear-rule/ (accessed 9 May 2022).

Vollans (2022), *Good Practice: Anatomy – The 'V' Word.* Caroline Vollans 4.1.2022. Available online: https://www.nurseryworld.co.uk/features/article/good-practice-anatomy-the-v-word (Accessed 9 May 2022). www.ncsby.org *Childhood Sexual Development* (accessed 14 May 2022).

7

Young People, Drugs and Decisions

Fiona Spargo-Mabbs

Aims of This Chapter

- To examine the evidence-base for effective drug education, in order to enable teachers to follow best practice principles in their planning and delivery.
- To outline appropriate content across year groups and Key Stages to ensure learning is relevant and timely, and builds on, reinforces and extends what has been covered before.
- To consider potential issues and challenges specific to drug education and propose approaches to address and respond to these.

[Note: I refer generally to drugs and drug education throughout, but this also (generally) includes alcohol].

Introduction

Drug education has to be done. This is not just because it is a mandatory part of Relationships, Sex and Health Education, but because it matters. Alcohol and other drugs are an unavoidable part of the world most young people inhabit, whether online, in real life or both, and schools are key players in enabling them to gain the knowledge and skills they need to navigate that world safely. People who use drugs usually begin to do so in late childhood and adolescence. Most recent government data shows that 59 per cent of fifteen-year-olds in England have been offered illegal drugs, and 38 per cent have tried them at least once,[1] and by the time they reach the end of their teens almost all will have had to make a decision about drugs. Most will say no, most of the time, but some will say yes, some more than others, and some of these will come to harm. Evidence shows that universal drug education, done correctly, and embedded within a whole-school programme of PSHE, can prevent or reduce harm from drugs to young people, and the school community, environment, policies and wider practices can also all play a protective role.

As well as examining the evidence-base, we'll also explore specific considerations relating to making the classroom, and school, a safe place for students, a little more complex with drugs than it is for many other areas of PSHE. We'll also consider ways to ensure lessons are accessible, not only in relation to SEND, but also to cultural and religious differences within your student community. And before we begin, we need to be clear about where we want to get to. Reaching consensus across the wider school community on an appropriate and achievable aim for drug education can be more tricky than it might at first appear, and again, more complicated than for some other areas of PSHE.

What Do They Need, and How Do You Know?

Before beginning to plan and deliver drug education, it is important to know what your students need to gain from it, to ensure it is relevant and useful for them. This is best sought both in relation to current national data and local needs assessments. It might include the extent of substance use, types of substances being used, the context, means and frequency of use, and any common characteristics of young people using substances, including age of onset. It can be valuable alongside this to look at other related health information, such as young people's mental health data. It is also useful, especially by Key Stage 5, to ask students what they would find most beneficial themselves from drug education, and what they think would be useful for their younger peers.

Designing and deploying a student survey for your school will provide the most relevant information, but these have to be approached with some caution. Honesty is important, so anonymity has to be genuine and guaranteed, and student trust secured. Questions also have to be thought through carefully. They need to be age-appropriate, to avoid normalizing use and increasing risk for younger students, and direct questions about drug use may bring anonymous disclosures that can't then be dealt with. There can be significant differences in preferences and levels of substances used across schools within one local area, however, and across year groups within one school, and this is invaluable information.

Finding data

The following government and local authority reports provide data on smoking, alcohol and drug use of secondary school-aged children across the UK.

England: Smoking, Drinking and Drug Use in Young People in England (11–15s)

Wales: Student Health and Wellbeing Survey (11–16s)

Scotland: Scottish Schools Adolescent Lifestyle and Substance Use Survey (13–15s)

Northern Ireland: Young Persons' Behaviour & Attitudes Survey 2019: Substance Use (11–16s)

England and Wales: Drug Misuse Statistics (16–59s, including 16–24s)

Association for Young People's Health – Key Data on Young People: Brings together key data from a wide range of data sets, including smoking, drinking and drug use and other related health data.

Public Health England (PHE) – Public Health Profiles: Local health profiles that include data on under eighteen alcohol-related hospital admissions. (PHE is now the Office for Health Inequalities and Disparities (OHID)).

Joint Strategic Needs Assessments (JSNA): Conducted by local authorities to examine specific issues in detail, which may include young people's drug and alcohol use.

What Do You Want to Achieve?

Deciding and defining an overall aim and specific outcomes for your students, and being clear about these from the outset, is key to planning a whole school programme, and to measuring its impact and evaluating its effectiveness. Abstinence will of course be the safest option for students, but the complex factors involved in decision-making relating to substance use mean this will be an unrealistic ambition for the whole student community. The European Prevention Curriculum states: 'Substance use prevention has a broader intent: to keep people healthy and safe and to help them to realise their talents and potential.'[2] If the overall focus is too narrow, students can miss important learning which could limit potential risk and harm, and schools can miss capturing broader but also positive outcomes. These can include reduced intention to use, delayed initiation of use (which evidence shows reduces the risk of longer-term harm), reduction of risky behaviour and the prevention of the transition from experimental use to addiction.

How Can You Make It Safe?

Along with all that creates a safe and effective PSHE learning environment – establishing ground rules, using distancing techniques, responding safely to students' questions – there are also specific considerations for drug education. In the average secondary school around forty children will live with a parent with a substance use disorder, many more will have extended family members who do, and in either case schools will often not know. Depending on the age of your class, some of your students may have used, or be currently using drugs themselves, and for some this could be problematic. Approaching all lessons with the assumption that at least one of your students is likely to be personally affected by what you are teaching will make sure it is safe not just for them but for all of the class. That includes the language used and any attitudes expressed. Drug use and addiction remain heavily stigmatized across society, and stereotypes and assumptions will inevitably be present in your classroom, including possibly your own, and these need to be appropriately addressed.

Signposting to support is an essential component of drug education. Before you begin, make sure you know what support students can access in the school and the local area. Make sure you let relevant pastoral and safeguarding staff know you are teaching this topic, so they are alerted for students they may be supporting, and aware that others might need their support. It's also possible that those delivering drug education have had experiences that could make teaching this subject challenging. Where this is the case, being able to talk honestly to a line manager about this is important, as is getting any support that is needed.

How Can You Make It Inclusive?

Materials, and their delivery, need to be sensitive to, and respectful of, cultural and religious differences in attitudes to alcohol and drugs, while recognizing that for most young people they will be present in their world, and they will present potential risks, whatever their background. Drug education also needs to be made accessible to SEND in the ways and means in which it is delivered, to allow all students to access core knowledge, and practise key skills, recognizing the additional vulnerabilities some neurodiverse young people have to substance-use, especially those with autism and ADHD. For those with an education, health and care (EHC) plan lesson outcomes can be linked to statutory 'preparing for adulthood' outcomes.

What about Sanctions?

Familiarity with your school's drug and alcohol policy is important, both for you and your class, as you begin doing drug education together. What happens if a student discloses drug use, or concerns for a friend, or for a parent? You all need to know what sanctions and support are in place. Students will often assume that letting on to a teacher they've used drugs will result in exclusion, and it may, but the response will probably be personalized and dependent on individual circumstances. Schools have a tricky balance to find when it comes to drugs between pastoral and safeguarding responsibilities for individuals at risk, and for the wider school community. However, students ideally need to know they can ask questions openly, and that they'll be listened to, taken seriously and not judged, if they do make a disclosure. Policies may not have been recently updated, or they may solely fall within safeguarding and/or behaviour policies, and if this is the case there's an opportunity for positive change if it is needed.

What Works in Drug Education?

Doing drug education well is important for reducing risk to your students, but not doing it badly is equally vital, because unlike most other areas of learning, drug education has the potential to increase risk and cause actual harm to its recipients. Thankfully, the evidence-base for what works and what does not is well established.

There are two common assumptions about approaches to drug education we need to rule out right at the start, though to do so with both is somewhat counter-intuitive. The first of these is the 'Just Say No' approach, championed by US First Lady Nancy Reagan back in the 1980s. Robust evaluation of the drug education programmes that came in its wake demonstrated not only were they ineffective in reducing drug use, for some young people they actually increased risk. Saying no will always be their safest option, but most of the time it's not quite so simple, and students need more than just this as a strategy. The second of these is the use of shock and fear arousal tactics, whether in stories, images or visible, real-life drug-related wounds. These worst-case scenarios have been shown to be ineffective overall in changing perceptions of possible consequences of drug use, and moreover can be harmful. They can be triggering for those who have experienced a related trauma; they can be inspiring for those who love the thrill of a high-risk experience, and they rapidly become discordant with the reality of students' own experiences, or encounters with drug use amongst their peers, and then all credibility is lost.

Firstly, drug education needs to be delivered by teachers who are trained to do so, and whose training is regularly refreshed. The issues as well as the substances causing them change over time, and confidence to deliver drug education well can often begin quite low, and can quickly falter. Lessons also need to be interactive to be effective, with the teacher adopting the role of facilitator rather than lecturer, which can be unfamiliar and uncomfortable for some subject teachers, and so additional training in modes of delivery can also be useful.

Secondly, drug education needs to be planned as a spiral curriculum of structured, age-appropriate sessions, delivered as a regular series of lessons throughout secondary education, and integrated coherently into the overall planning for PSHE.

One-off, stand-alone sessions, however effective, on their own lack the lasting impact and value that can be gained through planned, prolonged opportunities to explore, discuss, reflect and re-evaluate. The information drug education provides needs to be realistic and relevant to your students, and it needs to be accurate and current. This is why good training, up-to-date and evidence-based resources, and knowledge of student needs are all so important.

In providing information about drugs, care needs to be taken not to make their use seem attractive, for example when describing their effects. Teachers can also unintentionally provide instruction in substance use, including through images of drugs being used in materials, which can also add to the risk of normalizing behaviours. Drug education needs to challenge myths and misconceptions about the risks and consequences of drug use. It also needs to challenge social norms and assumptions, and importantly not to reinforce false normative beliefs about substance use. The more prevalent any of us believe a behaviour to be, the more likely we are to engage in it ourselves, and young people often significantly over-estimate the numbers of their peers who are using drugs and drinking to excess.

Knowledge is important, and the Department for Education curriculum for Health Education lists what this is for secondary schools in England,[3] which includes facts about legal as well as illegal drugs and their risks, with legal including prescribed medication. However, knowledge alone is far from enough, and information-only approaches to drug education have been shown to be ineffective. While increasing what students know, they can fail to give them the skills to apply that knowledge in the complex social context of adolescent substance use. As well as understanding the effects, risks and possible consequences of drug use, students need drug education to improve their personal and interpersonal skills, including problem-solving and decision-making contextualized to drugs. They need the opportunity to develop and practise skills for increasing self-control and improving self-esteem, and for coping with challenging life situations in healthy ways, again contextualized to drugs. They need to acquire substance and peer refusal competencies to counter the social pressures that reach a pitch of intensity in adolescence. They also need drug education to provide them with opportunities to reflect on their own views and values, and to scrutinize and question the influences that can shift and direct these, and shape their perceptions of risk or harm associated with substance use. These can come from a broad spectrum of media and social media, as well as their family and, importantly in adolescence of course, their friends. Older students also need harm reduction advice and strategies, and to know what to do in a drug-related emergency.

Specialist external speakers can add enormous value to the drug education work being done in the classroom, bringing expertise, experience, and a fresh face and voice, but their input needs to be embedded within the whole school plan for drug education. Outside speakers also need to be chosen with some care. They need to be trained and experienced in the delivery of interactive and engaging sessions, they need to know and follow best practice in evidence-based drug education, and they need to follow your guidance so their session can best be integrated into your overall aims and outcomes for drug education. They need a teacher to be present throughout (unless for a planned and agreed purpose), who can model engagement, manage any behavioural issues, and be alert to any issues arising for individuals that need following up.

Evidence cautions against the use of police officers and ex-addicts to deliver drug education, for different reasons. Police officers who are trained to deliver drug education, who follow best practice, and who have a positive and trusted relationship with the school and its students can bring valuable expertise in drugs and the law, but for some students their presence can create hostility which is counter-productive. People with lived experience of substance use disorders can unintentionally normalize, or even glamorize, drug use and risky behaviours. Their stories can be very moving and powerful, but they can also traumatize, or trigger past traumas for students. Moreover, their life trajectory is often a world away from the experiences of the average adolescent sitting before them. There may be little students can take away and apply to their own decisions about drugs, and the types and patterns of substance use they describe can minimize risks students may be taking themselves.

What to Do When?

Drug education needs to begin early enough to be preventative – the transition from primary to secondary is the best time to start – and it needs to continue consistently to the end of Key Stage 5, when pupils' exposure to drugs will be reaching its heights for many. It needs to build on prior learning, and develop as young people mature and encounter different drug-related scenarios, and the knowledge and skills they need to manage these situations evolve.

The majority of pupils will arrive at secondary school with some understanding of the risks of alcohol and tobacco, and the generic risks of medicines, and some will know more. Most will not yet have encountered illegal drugs directly (though some will), but by the age of fourteen almost half (41 per cent) will have got drunk, one in eight (13 per cent) will have tried cannabis and one in five (21 per cent) will have vaped. Drug education in Key Stage 3 can begin to provide opportunities for students to develop positive attitudes and values that do not support drug use, and to build their personal and interpersonal skills as outlined above, including understanding social and societal influences on decision-making about drugs. Tackling myths, misconceptions and false social norms can increase through these year groups as their awareness grows. Substance-specific learning will lean on your local information-gathering about what drugs are around for your students, but generally should focus on the short- and long-term effects and risks of alcohol, caffeine, smoking and vaping, and volatile substances, adding cannabis by Year 8 or 9. Students should also learn about the social and legal consequences of drugs.

In Key Stage 4, pupils can build on this to learn more about the impact of drug use on themselves and on others, including on other risk-taking behaviour and their personal safety. As well as revisiting alcohol, nicotine and cannabis, individual substances they need to be aware of at this stage may also include nitrous oxide and MDMA, but again your local knowledge will be useful here. Learning about legal risks needs to be relevant to situations in which they may find themselves, including 'social supply'. This practice, whereby one person gets the drugs in for the group and shares them out, is the most common route of access for young people. Government data shows 57 per cent of eleven- to fifteen-year-olds who had used illegal drugs had got them from a friend. It's also a criminal offence, however, even if no money is exchanged, and it is one that can carry serious penalties and lasting consequences.

Along with continuing to strengthen the personal and interpersonal skills described above, understanding motivation and adolescent brain development in relation to decision-making, peer influence and risk management is important at this stage. Developing strategies based on this to make safer choices in scenarios involving drugs can encompass house parties, gatherings and first music festivals and gigs, where drug use is generally more widespread than in other environments. Practical safety advice and general harm reduction information can begin to be included during Key Stage 4, but the latter needs to be handled with care in a universal setting, to avoid implicitly giving 'permission' to use drugs, or to imply it is possible to make drug use entirely safe. This can be avoided by coming at it sideways, talking in terms of how they might advise or take care of a friend, including in an emergency.

The complex relationship between mental ill health and substance use should be highlighted, along with exploring healthy coping strategies and sources of support, especially at stressful times such as assessments and exams, particularly GCSEs and final assessments. Students also need to know about and understand addiction, but it is important to challenge any preconceptions that a binary state exists in which people are either addicted or not, because this can create barriers to students identifying that they may be taking risks, or may need help and support. They also need to know how and where to find this support, for themselves or others.

Drugs are likely to be an increasing part of pupils' social environment online and offline by Key Stage 5, including a wider range of substances and a more diverse variety of social situations in which they might come across them. All the elements of drug education covered in Key Stage 4 should be reinforced and built on in these last two years of formal education, contextualized to these later teenage years and growing independence, and drawing on feedback from students. Legal risks, for example, should encompass issues such as consent, drink and drug driving and drug use abroad. Preparing for the vulnerabilities transition from school or college brings in relation to alcohol and drugs is important, especially if students are moving on to university, where they may encounter different drugs, new modes of use and more commonplace exposure. More specific harm reduction advice is important, as is practical advice including drugs and alcohol first aid.

Drug Education and Higher-Risk Students

In every class, in every year group, there will be students who are more vulnerable to using drugs, and/or those who are already using them. The most recent NICE guideline identifies specific groups at greater risk, many of whom will already be on your pastoral radars, including looked-after children, those who are homeless or have unsettled housing, those who have parents who use drugs, or who are being, or have been, sexually exploited or assaulted. It includes those with behavioural conduct disorders, those who have involvement with the criminal justice system and those who have been excluded from school or who regularly truant. It also includes LGBTQ+ young people, for whom drug use is statistically higher, as it is for those who have mental ill health. And the guidance broadens out to encompass those who go to festivals and clubs, where drug use is more normalized, and those who use drugs occasionally or regularly, who are taking risks. Schools might not know about many of these, but discussions during drug education lessons may highlight concerns to follow up. Evidence shows that even the most vulnerable young people will benefit just as well as others from universal approaches, but there is also a case for providing drug-specific prevention interventions. These are often delivered by local young people's drug and alcohol services, who can then also build relationships and trust with individual students, and create valuable connections to external sources of support. However, beware of targeted interventions stigmatizing and potentially isolating already-vulnerable students.

Cross-Curricular Connections

Drugs and alcohol can and do appear across the curriculum – in Science, PE, RS, English, media studies, psychology, citizenship and of course extensively across PSHE. For young people, the important issues PSHE encompasses never sit as separate, discrete elements in their lives, but interact and overlap continually, and what helps one will help and enrich another, and all of that will help them. Understanding what makes for a healthy friendship, and how the complexities of the social dynamic can influence perceptions of risk, and decisions about drugs, can strengthen social resilience. Multiple sexual risks can be taken when drugs and alcohol are involved, including legal risks around consent. Online safety skills are of vital importance when it comes to managing the risks from exposure to drugs on social media. Mental health challenges can lead people to use drugs to cope, as well as their use potentially triggering, exacerbating and prolonging mental illnesses. Making sure these connections are made continually, and not just to content but also to all the transferable personal and interpersonal skills gained across all these areas of PSHE, is so important in supporting young people to make safer choices all round.

Involving Parents and Carers in Drug Education

The evidence-base for what works in drug education reinforces the importance of parents' roles. Multisectoral programmes with multiple components, including the school and community (and community includes parents), show benefit in preventing and reducing smoking, drinking and drug use. Parents are the most sought-after source of 'helpful information about drug use' at home, according to their eleven- to fifteen–year old offspring, and the same is true for alcohol. They can and do play a much more fundamental role, however, providing many of the protective factors that can reduce risky behaviour and prevent harm from drugs. Parents are a vital and valuable resource not only to their children, but to their children's schools and colleges, but the world is a very different place to what it was when they were at school themselves. All you can do in your role at school to support them in theirs at home, and involve them in doing drug education together, will benefit the young people about whom you both care, and make what you do so much more effective.

How Do You Know What Difference It Has Made?

As always, we need to end where we began, and before we start the next cycle, with the aims and outcomes agreed at the outset, and the extent to which these have been achieved. Knowledge is important, but there's no evidence that knowledge itself has an impact on drug use, and so measuring knowledge isn't enough. More important is behaviour change, both actual and intended, along with changed perceptions of risk and consequence. With drug education it's also especially important to allow scope to identify unintended outcomes, whether positive or negative, knowing that drug education has potential to cause harm as well as do good. Deciding what to measure, and how and when to measure it, is something to integrate into your planning, and within your overall PSHE programme.

A Personal Note

As you'll no doubt have read, I started this drug education journey when my sixteen-year-old son Dan died taking MDMA. Dan, I found out, had received no drug education, and neither had the friends he was with that last night – and neither, we learned, had so many other young people across the country. Whether it would have helped in that moment of decision I can't of course ever know, but I'm sure the odds of him getting to come home would have been improved. Dan's was the worst-case scenario, but good drug education has the potential to prevent avoidable harm in all its shades and varieties. Schools can improve the odds for so many young people of getting to go home in one piece.

Questions for Reflection for You and Your Setting

- What do you and your school want to achieve for your students through drug education?
- In what ways do current planning, resources and delivery meet evidence-based standards, and where and how do improvements need to be made?
- How do the school's drug and alcohol policies support effective drug education?
- How can you engage and involve parents and carers in drug education?
- Where is support for students available in the school and within the wider community?

Recommended Resources

DSM Foundation is a drug and alcohol education charity providing evidence-based drug education to young people, parents, teachers and professionals, through workshops for students and parents, training for teachers and other professionals, and a spiral curriculum of planning and resources available for teachers to deliver drug education from Key Stages 3 to 5 in lessons or shorter form time sessions. The verbatim play the charity commissioned Mark Wheeller to write that tells the story of Dan, *I Love You, Mum – I Promise I Won't Die*, is a GCSE Drama set text on the Eduqas syllabus, and tours schools annually as a professional Theatre in Education production and workshop. See www.dsmfoundation.org.uk

PSHE Association has developed planning and resources for drug and alcohol lessons for Key Stages 1 to 4, and planning and resources for students with SEND from Key Stages 2 to 4. Planning is available free to download from the website; PowerPoints are available free to PSHE Association members. They also provide a range of resources and training for schools to support PSHE. See www.pshe-association.org.uk

It Happens Education is an RSHE provider working in schools across the UK. Their team of professionals provide evidence-based drug and alcohol education talks, workshops and training sessions for students, teachers and parents, working in both primary and secondary settings. Email info@ithappens.education

'I Wish I'd Known: Young People, Drugs and Decisions – A Guide for Parents and Carers' Fiona Spargo-Mabbs (Sheldon Press, 2021)

'Schools, Colleges, Drugs and Decisions – A Pack for Teachers' to accompany 'I Wish I'd Known', Fiona Spargo-Mabbs (Sheldon Press, 2022)

'Drugs, Decisions and Difference – Neurodiversity and Drug Use in Young People' to accompany 'I Wish I'd Known', Fiona Spargo-Mabbs (Sheldon Press, 2022)

'Teen substance use, mental health and body image', Ian MacDonald (Jessica Kingsley Press, 2019)

'Say Why to Drugs', Dr Suzi Gage (Hodder & Stoughton, 2020)

Note: This chapter is based on the following publications which pull together the most robust and rigorous research and evidence, and the most effective policy and practice, in prevention and education globally:

- *International Standards on Drug Use Prevention (UNODC, 2018), developed by UNODC and WHO*
- *European Drug Prevention Quality Standards (EMCDDA, 2011)*
- *European Prevention Curriculum (EMCDDA, 2019)*
- *'What works' in drug education and prevention? (Scottish Government, 2016)*

References

CHLDRN – Local and national data on childhood vulnerability, Children's Commissioner (2019), Available online: https://www.childrenscommissioner.gov.uk/chldrn/

Department for Education and Department of Health (2015), *Special Educational Needs and Disability Code of Practice: 0 to 25 Years*. Available online: https://www.gov.uk/government/publications/send-code-of-practice-0-to-25 (accessed 1 June 2022).

DfE (2019), *Relationships Education, Relationships and Sex Education (RSE) and Health Education.* Available online: https://assets.publishing.service.gov.uk/government/uploads/system/uploads/attachment_data/fi le/805781/Relationships_Education__Relationships_and_Sex_Education__RSE__and_Health_Education.pdf (accessed 6. May 2022).

EMCDDA (2019a), *European Prevention Curriculum (EUPC): A Handbook for Decision-Makers, Opinion-Makers and Policy-Makers in Science-Based Prevention of Substance Use. European Monitoring Centre for Drugs and Drug Addiction.* Luxembourg: Publications Office of the European Union. Available online: https://www.emcdda.europa.eu/publications/manuals/europeanprevention-curriculum_en (accessed 4 May 2022).

Lillenfield, S. & Arkowitz, H. (2014), *Why "Just Say No" Doesn't Work*, Scientific America, 1 January. Available online: https://www.scientificamerican.com/article/why-just-say-no-doesnt-work/ (accessed 2 July 2022).

National Statistics, NHS digital (2019), *Smoking, Drinking and Drug Use among Young People in England 2018 (NHS Digital).* Available online: https://digital.nhs.uk/data-and-information/publications/statistical/smoking-drinking-and-drug-use-among-young-people-in-england/2018 (accessed 2 June 2022).

Warren, F. (2016), *'What Works' in Drug Education and Prevention?* Available online: https://www.gov.scot/publications/works-drug-education-prevention/ (accessed 6 June 2022).

Notes

1. Smoking, Drinking and Drug Use among Young People in England 2018 (NHS Digital): https://digital.nhs.uk/data-and-information/publications/statistical/smoking-drinking-and-drug-use-among-young-people-in-england/2018
2. EMCDDA European Prevention Curriculum: https://www.emcdda.europa.eu/publications/manuals/european-prevention-curriculum_en
3. https://www.gov.uk/government/publications/relationships-education-relationships-and-sex-education-rse-and-health-education

8

Building a Foundation for Healthy Relationships

Victoria-Marie Pugh and Sophie-Lauren McPhee

Aims of This Chapter

- To consider the importance of relationships education for young people.
- To highlight different complexities which young people may face within their relationships and the skills and attributes needed to successfully navigate these.
- To explore the importance of a whole-school approach to relationships education and how this can be integrated into the whole-school culture.

Introduction

Good relationships are the foundation upon which stable, happy and healthy lives are built. We have the same genes biologically as our hunter-gatherer ancestors from many thousands of years ago, whose very survival was built on forging strong relationships with others, but whilst thanks to online networks our social net is cast wider, relationships nowadays are rich in breadth, but not depth. This increasing isolation and lack of true connection nowadays has become enough of a problem within UK society that the theme of Mental Health Awareness Week 2022 was loneliness, and even before the pandemic and its resultant lockdowns a You Gov (2019) survey found that 88 per cent of young adults feel lonely to some degree, making eighteen to twenty-four years the age group that feels lonely the most. The year before, the UK government under Prime Minister Theresa May launched its loneliness strategy, and the country's first 'Minister for Loneliness', Tracey Crouch, told *Time* magazine that even with her own support network of family and friends, she has at times felt cut off from the world. Since then, our young people have missed out on literally hundreds of days of missed opportunities to practise social interaction in different contexts by making mistakes, repairing relationships and forming bonds, so it is even more important that we explicitly teach the relationship skills that some young people may be missing due to not only their lives being lived increasingly online, but also due to being confined to their homes for extended periods.

To enable pupils to have successful interactions with others, however, they need to cultivate a healthy self-concept, i.e. a healthy set of beliefs about themselves. After all, ' … the most important relationship they will have in life is with themselves as it "sets the tone for every other relationship" they have' (Holden, 2020, in *Proactive Pastoral Care*, by Maria O'Neill, 2021, p.118). Therefore, foundation teaching on self-esteem should have already been taking place pre-Key Stage 3, with exploration of one's own values forming part of wider self-awareness and self-reflection training. Opportunities must also be taken during the transition to the secondary phase to identify and nurture those children whose self-belief needs strengthening.

The attachments formed in early childhood have a profound effect on an individual's view of not only themselves, but about others and the world at large, and all of these beliefs inform the quality of our connections to others and therefore impact on life satisfaction and perceived life success. 'If our view of the world is that people are good, then we will anticipate good things from people. We project that expectation in our interactions with others and thereby actually elicit good from them' (Perry and Winfrey, 2021, p.51). Again, it is crucial to identify at an early-stage pupils who are lacking significant adult connection but in general, all pupils should learn that 'you get what you give'. Even more crucial is to identify children who have suffered severe early neglect and/or trauma, because, as Perry and Szalavitz (2017, p.229) write, 'Reactive Attachment Disorder (RAD) … is marked by a lack of empathy and an inability to connect with others … The regions of their brains that help them form relationships … do not develop properly, and they grow up with faulty relational neurobiology, including an inability to derive pleasure from healthy human interactions.'

If you have ever worked with a group of children, you will probably know that the classroom environment provides ample evidence that human beings naturally mirror one another. Many of us will have been in the situation where we have led a class in a less-than-good mood, only to find that the pupils reflect this right back at us. The opposite, of course, is also true. So, successful relationships education goes hand-in-hand with high-quality wellbeing education and is best led by example. It is not enough to teach how to have peaceful, productive, clear and respectful interactions with others – we have to model it.

Hopefully, you will already be doing this through your regular routines of greeting pupils as they come into the room to set the tone for the lesson, by communicating with them in a manner that asserts authority but does not imply superiority, and so on, but recognition of each individual's right to emotional safety, a vital component of building healthy relationships with others, can be modelled through your approach to safeguarding in PSHE lessons. The importance and nature of co-constructed ground rules are covered elsewhere in the book, but sensitivity is the *modus operandi* for a PSHE teacher, and for every difficult or uncomfortable topic we cover, we must teach about it as if at least one of the pupils in front of us has first-hand experience of it. As a school, we may indeed not know if they have.

Nevertheless, it is a good idea to alert key pastoral and safeguarding staff at the start of each half-term to the topics being covered, and ask them to let you know of particular pupils who might feel vulnerable. In this instance, if it is deemed okay for you to do so, you can invite the pupil to look through the lesson plans and materials with you so that they know what to expect, or a trusted member of the pastoral team can. However, this is not to suggest that relationships education is all about danger – on the contrary, it should mainly be focused on appreciating the joy that is gained from connecting with other human beings and navigating the inevitable turbulent times. For pupils in the early years of secondary school, who are suddenly being exposed to a much larger number and wider range of people, the topic of friendships provides the most engaging context through which they can access the overarching theme of human relationships.

Friendships

For any teacher in school, it goes without saying that you will have experienced pupil friendship issues. School and educational settings can be complex emotional environments for pupils; however, as educators we can support the development of social and emotional skills and awareness through relationships education as part of a whole-school approach. According to Bezzina and Camilleri (2021, p.48), 'Positive and supportive interpersonal relationships are key to the development of social and emotional competencies which are conducive to learning, personal growth and overall well-being.'

Goodenow (1993, p.80) supports the use of a whole-school approach and promotes school connectedness which they state is 'the extent to which students. feel personally accepted, respected, included, and supported by others in the school social environment'.

During adolescent development, young people can often find themselves wanting to spend more time with their peers than their parents/carers or siblings. Therefore, peer friendships form an important and influential part of their lives (Healey, n.d.). It is important that the characteristics of a healthy relationship are explored and that time is taken to look at a range of aspects over time rather than through a standalone lesson on friendships, or a drop-down day.

If we consider pupil transition from primary to secondary school, or to middle school depending on the geographical area, it would seem pertinent to consider the significant changes which this might bring for some pupils and their friendships. There may be pupils who are not in the same classes as best friends from primary school, or friendships which change and grow apart and sadly, for some, a feeling of loneliness or isolation if they have not found a friendship group to become a part of. Therefore, lessons which explore changes in friendships and how to make friends may be supportive in KS3. Giving pupils the language and skills to be able to join a group of other pupils or to ask to become part of a game or discussion can be life changing for a young person. Research demonstrates that good-quality friendships can provide emotional support through changing times such as school transitions (Berndt, 1989; Berndt & Murphy, 2002; Poulin & Chan, 2010); this was echoed by Ng-Knight et al. (2019) whose research concluded that having a quality friend continue into secondary school can increase stability in friendships and may impact attainment and positive behaviours.

Conflict Resolution

It is inevitable that at some point throughout a friendship there will be some sort of conflict no matter how small. Chrispino (2007) suggests that conflict is a divergent opinion or difference in perception to a particular event which can arise from a difference in interests or background. Quality relationships education can support pupils to navigate these incidents through the development of listening and communication skills, practising assertion rather than aggression when solving or reducing the impact of conflict. However, these are not skills which are learnt overnight or within one lesson which reinforces the need for a spiral curriculum throughout KS3, 4 and 5.

To begin with, conflict resolution skills can focus on scenarios to pull apart what is happening between characters and how each of them may be feeling. It is a great opportunity to explore secondary emotions such as – is a character displaying behaviours of anger when they are actually jealous or anxious when they may be feeling frustrated? Using scenarios not only allows for a supportive critique of the situation but supports the students to be able to look at the situation as an outsider. Using these types of 'distancing' techniques ensures that no personal or individual pupil situations are used, allowing for a more objective perspective and response to them (PSHE, 2018).

It could be argued that for pupils to be able to navigate the ups and downs of friendships that they must be able to understand their own emotions, be able to regulate these and understand the emotions and/or perspectives of others. It is also important for young people to recognize and accept that 'relationships never provide you with *everything*. They provide you with *some* things ... It's only in the movies that you find someone who gives you all of those things'. Yanagihara (2015, p.565, italics author's own). However, this doesn't mean accepting behaviours which are neglectful but being realistic about what people can offer and knowing that no-one is perfect.

Social media can often exacerbate this 'fairytale' idea of friendships and relationships by neglecting to show the whole story and instead present only the good bits to followers. Lessons around what's real and what's not online and developing digital criticality can be useful for pupils in their approach to processing this information. This does not mean, however, that we should downplay the importance of friendships and relationships online as these can form an important part of life for some pupils and provide them with connections they may not have formed elsewhere. It would be trite to say that life online is not real but instead provide an understanding for pupils that parts of relationships might be more easily edited than in their offline relationships.

One aspect of relationship education that can support the development and nurturing of healthy friendships is the promotion of emotional literacy skills. Emotional literacy was first defined by Steiner and Perry (1997) as the ability to be able:

(a)   to understand the emotions of others;
(b)   to better understand one's own emotions;
(c)   to have the ability to empathize with others; and
(d)   to express emotions more appropriately and efficiently.

In Key Stage 3, this can take the form of exploring what they do to be a good friend. This supports them to recognize that friendship is a mutual exchange and that they must exhibit behaviours of a good friend if they wish to receive these behaviours in return. However, it also supports their own understanding of what is important to them in a friendship. For example for some pupils they may value having shared interests over them being humorous or valuing trust over good listening skills. Becoming more self-aware and being able to identify what is important to them and being able to communicate this can help to prevent misunderstandings and low-level annoyances between friends. A study by Duval and Silva (2002) concluded that people who have higher levels of self-awareness tend to have higher levels of self-confidence and self-worth. Developing empathy for others and understanding how others feel is a vital life skill; however, we can understand how someone feels but do nothing about it; therefore, empathy must be combined with compassion in order to be truly effective. This distinction between cognitive empathy and the ability to demonstrate empathy skills can be developed throughout KS3–5 through the use of self-reflection, discussing what strategies for compromise can be made and noticing the body language and dialogue of others.

According to Kerr-Gaffney et al. (2019, p.102), 'Cognitive empathy refers to the ability to recognize and understand another's mental state, while affective empathy is the ability to share the feelings of others, without any direct emotional stimulation to oneself.' Therefore, work around volunteering is a great way to promote empathy skills as well as supporting the work of wider citizenship.

Exploring what makes an unhealthy friendship and considering toxic friendship can also be helpful for pupils in learning to recognize behaviours such as jealousy, exclusion and manipulation. Toxic friendships or 'frenemies' can take a multitude of forms, such as expecting the pupil not to socialize with anyone else, never being happy for them or celebrating their achievements and exerting power over them and asking them to do things they don't want to. Being able to identify these behaviours can empower pupils and allow them to refocus power dynamics within friendships or make decisions to end the friendship respectfully.

In Key Stage 4, this can be explored by considering how a friendship might make them feel – if they are made to feel guilty or unhappy within the relationship it may need to be reflected upon honestly by the pupil and for them to be reminded that it is ok to end a friendship which is not healthy for them. Berkman et al. (2000) and Tome et al. (2012) suggest how friendships and social connections can affect mental health as well as behaviour focusing particularly on social influence by creating social norms such as smoking, drug taking and alcohol consumption as well as other risky behaviours. Pupils who feel influenced to take part in behaviours they do not feel comfortable with or that they feel pressured into undertaking may benefit from evaluating their friendships and the power dynamics within them. Having a solid understanding of what coercion, manipulation and lack of respect within friendships are can support them to identify and address these relationship issues. Teaching how to step away from a friendship or to end a relationship respectfully is also a key skill to develop going into KS5 and beyond as well. The PSHE Association Key Stage 5 programme of study includes specific objectives such as 'to manage the ending of relationships safely and respectfully, including online'.

It can often be the case that pupils in Key Stage 5 no longer receive PSHE education or RSHE; however, navigating the complex world of changing friendships, education settings and possibly workplaces calls for further development of relationships education. Sessions focusing on professional relationships within the workplace are a supportive element within relationships education and can provide pupils with a better understanding of workplace norms and expectations so that they are able to enter the workforce with the communication skills and tools necessary.

Bullying

The concept of bullying is much more complex than putting up posters around school for anti-bullying week. Although we may associate this word with a problem experienced only by children, it is a topic which should be revisited at all Key Stages, changing the vocabulary to suit the context being discussed and the age of the pupils.

At Key Stage 3, we would normally discuss bullying in the context of friendships, but actually, there may be a wider conversation to be had about bullying by adults towards children if you are confident enough to handle this discussion sensitively using the distancing technique, such as by creating TV storylines or putting pupils in the role of agony aunt or uncle (Deacon, 2015). This would support other learning about healthy family relationships, healthy parenting techniques and in the context of teacher-pupil relationships, healthy workplace relationships. If exploring this aspect of power dynamics, it is crucial not to allow the conversation to descend into sharing stories about when a member of staff 'picked on me cos she hates me', so the Head of PSHE should ensure that teachers in their department (if a specialist department) are suitably trained to handle sensitive topics correctly. This would not be recommended for a quick form tutor session delivered by a non-specialist with no prior training.

Pupils at this age use 'bullying' as a catch-all term to denote any unkind behaviour, so it is important to clarify the difference between isolated acts of unkindness – which of course are not okay either – and 'the repetitive, intentional hurting of one person or group by another person or group, where the relationship involves an imbalance of power' (Anti-Bullying Alliance, 2022). We need to make fully clear to pupils what bullying is and isn't, explore different bullying tactics such as baiting, threats and coercion, and at which point pressure crosses over into bullying.

We must ensure that our PSHE lessons are not all doom and gloom, as is always the risk. Rather than always focusing on negative behaviours, we must make space to be 'pro-kindness' as well as 'anti-bullying', which we can link to the concept of neuroplasticity and strengthening pathways in our brain so that pro-social behaviours become our norm. Dan Siegel, great champion of adolescents and an expert in child and teen brain development, talks about this in his book *Brainstorm* (2019), which is recommended reading for not just PSHE teachers, but anyone working with this age group.

As pupils progress into Key Stage 4, one main focus point needs to be on adolescents' need for peer acceptance and the implications of this for risk-taking behaviour and interpersonal relationships. Blakemore (2019) cites a study where unlike ten- to thirteen-year-olds, those aged thirteen to seventeen felt that what their friends thought of them 'affected their feelings of social or personal worth', something which will not come as a surprise to many people, but do we take the time to explore the science behind this and link it to how, as a result, pupils might be more susceptible to being a victim or even a perpetrator of bullying? After all, knowledge is power, and some pupils will need an academic slant to their PSHE lessons to be convinced of their value.

Another angle to take in order to avoid superficial coverage of this topic is to look at power dynamics not only in terms of relative roles within society but the influence of unconscious biases, intersectionality, the concept of privilege and how all of these impact on relationships. Depending on the ability of your cohort to grasp and discuss these issues, you may choose to cover this at Key Stage 4 or Key Stage 5, but either way, if you have the time and space to do so, there can be incredibly interesting conversations to have about the messages we are fed from lots of different sources (family, friends, the media, the government, etc.) and how these influence our behaviour.

Of course, one key source for discussion when looking at the interplay of power, intersectionality and the influence of media is the impact of pornography on real-life relationships. Clinical psychologist Dr Elly Hanson has found that free online pornography normalizes the assertion of power in relationships where there should be equal agency, often depicting 'violence, exploitation, humiliation and denigration, in most part towards women' (Hanson, 2020). With pornography's influence on sexual scripts and such scripts' correlation with 'more permissive attitudes towards sexual coercion and aggression' (Tomaszewksa & Krahe, 2016, 2018, cited in Hanson, 2020), it is clear that no comprehensive approach to the topic of bullying can be complete without reference to this issue.

Coercion and control within relationships aren't solely due to pornography consumption, of course, and needs curriculum time in and of itself. As PSHE educators we have an important role to play in the UK government's Violence against Women and Girls (VAWG) strategy, which seeks to eliminate 'crimes such as rape, female genital mutilation, stalking, harassment and digital crimes such as cyber-flashing, "revenge porn" and "up-skirting"' (Home Office, 2021), all of which involve the acquisition of power through immoral means and therefore constitute some of the more severe forms of bullying. Here, we will want to not only discuss how such crimes contravene human rights, but what penalties perpetrators can expect to receive under UK law. However, educators should be careful in their use of language so that boys do not feel alienated from the discussion as potential perpetrators. It is important to include reference to the fact that all forms of bullying can happen between two individuals belonging to any combination of identity groups under the Equality Act 2010, but those with certain protected characteristics are more likely to be victims than others.

At Key Stage 5, you could choose to put more emphasis on bullying behaviours in the workplace, as well as reiterating messages about key issues explored in the younger years. Stalking can be explored as another means by which someone might exert power and control within a real or perceived relationship, and the Alice Ruggles Trust has very good resources for this, and for relationship safety in general, that are suited to sixteen- to eighteen-year-olds. Within the lesson activities, pupils are encouraged to reflect on what they consider acceptable relationship behaviour, from seemingly relatively benign behaviours such as giving someone a gift every one-month anniversary, to switching between compliments and criticism to try to win a partner back. These resources are excellent because they help pupils understand how certain relationship behaviours can be seen as harmless, when in fact they are attempts at control, and therefore how a person may miss the 'red flags'. Through such lessons, pupils are invited to consider where their own boundaries lie, which underpins the teaching of consent.

Consent and Boundaries

When we think of consent in PSHE we very often go straight to sexual consent. In Chapter 11, we look in depth at a spiral curriculum example of consent education. But what about consent and boundaries within non-sexual relationships? This can be as little as 'No thanks, I don't want to talk about it at the moment' or 'You have an eyelash on your cheek, would you like me to wipe it away or do you want to do it?' Just like how two people can be in a healthy relationship yet come into conflict from time to time, pupils need reminding that just because a friend says no thank you doesn't mean they are no longer friends, it just means that they are voicing what is right for them and in fact, they are more likely to be respected by those around them, personally and professionally, if they are able to articulate their needs and boundaries.

The PSHE Association provides a consent lesson pack for its members which covers Key Stages 1–4, yet this teaching will be most effective if supported by opportunities outside of the classroom to develop the personal attributes which make asserting boundaries possible, such as self-esteem and confidence. In addition, it is no good if we promote the notion of consent in our teaching, but don't give pupils opportunities to give or withdraw consent in reality. These need not be grand or artificial gestures, but just as simple as asking pupils if they are happy to have their photograph taken for the school's social media page, regardless of whether their parent signed a slip at the beginning of Year 7 which allows it, or giving them the option to 'pass' when asked a question in PSHE. Our classroom cannot be a bubble, however – it needs to be part of a whole-school commitment to respectful, equal relationships as the bedrock of a healthy school culture.

A Whole-School Community Approach to Relationships Education

The skills and attributes needed for pupils to successfully navigate their relationships cannot solely be taught through the statutory RSHE objectives or indeed through a wider PSHE curriculum but should be embedded through tutor time, assemblies and wider school experiences to give pupils a variety of opportunities to experience and practise these skills. However, even this is not enough if we as school staff are not modelling the principles we are advocating. After all, as a young person's counsellor said to Joe Hayman while interviewing for his book *British Voices*, 'You don't teach empathy, you imbibe it from those around you.' Empathy is often touted as the ultimate virtue, but Bregman (2021) tells us that 'a better world doesn't start with more empathy', quoting Shaw's (1903) Platinum Rule: 'Do *not* do unto others as you would that they should do unto you. Their tastes may be different.' Anyhow, the point is that if we are not demonstrating these and other valued attributes in our day-to-day interactions with students, our teaching will seem hypocritical and will certainly be ineffective. This does not mean that we have to be perfect; on the contrary, there is a lot of value in leading by example on how to deal with mistakes, how to apologise and make amends.

Secondary schools and colleges, being where hundreds of people spend their working day, provide ample opportunity to practise these skills. Many places are choosing to implement restorative practice as part of their pastoral care, focusing on repairing relationships when ruptures occur rather than a simply punitive system. This is PSHE in action – applying the knowledge and skills acquired in your conflict resolution sessions to a real-life situation – and an opportunity to demonstrate the impact of your curriculum.

This chapter has considered the need for quality relationships within schools as colleges and both the positive and negative impacts that friendships can have on pupils' sense of belonging, healthy life choices as well as self-confidence and esteem. As well as needing the skills to be able to form healthy relationships, young people also need the skills to be able to maintain them and recognize when these relationships are no longer balanced or supportive. These skills will not only serve them in navigating the complexities of school and social life but in the workplace, with their own families and within their intimate relationships.

Questions for Reflection for You and Your Setting

- Are you communicating clearly with stakeholders about what is being covered in your lessons on relationships, and are you inviting consultation and collaboration?
- How are you safeguarding pupils within your class who have experience of the issues you are covering?
- Are the messages from your PSHE lessons on relationships modelled in the wider school/college culture?

Recommended Resources

The Alice Ruggles Trust Relationship Safety resources: https://aliceruggletrust.org/relationship-safety-resource

Anti-Bullying Alliance: https://anti-bullyingalliance.org.uk/

British Values Project: https://britishvaluesproject.uk/

Chameleon PDE

Childline: https://www.childline.org.uk/info-advice/your-feelings/feelings-emotions/being-assertive/

CRESST Curious About Conflict? Resources

Eberhardt, J. (2019), *Biased: The New Science of Race and Inequality*, London: Penguin Random House.

Finnis, M. (2021), *Restorative Practice: Building Relationships, Improving Behaviour and Creating Stronger Communities*. Carmarthen: Independent Thinking Press.

Great RSE by Alice Hoyle and Ester McGeeney

Jubilee Centre for Character and Virtues https://www.jubileecentre.ac.uk/

PSHE Association for Schemes of Work, Consent lesson pack, Family Life lesson pack, Managing Healthy and Unhealthy Relationship Behaviours lesson pack, Relationship Safety, Recognising and Making Disclosures about Abuse, Disrespect NoBody, FASTN: Commitment, Working out Relationships

Siegel, D. (2014), *Brainstorm: The Power and Purpose of the Teenage Brain*. London: Scribe UK.

https://assets.publishing.service.gov.uk/government/uploads/system/uploads/attachment_data/file/1019542/Relationships_Education__Relationships_and_Sex_Education__RSE__and_Health_Education.pdf

References

Anti-Bullying Alliance, *Our Definition of Bullying*. Available online: https://anti-bullyingalliance.org.uk/tools-information/all-about-bullying/understanding-bullying/definition (accessed 3 July 2022).

Bergin, C. & Bergin, D. (2009), Attachment in the classroom, *Educational Psychology Review*, 21(2), pp. 141–70. https://doi-org.apollo.worc.ac.uk/10.1007/s10648-009-9104-0 [Crossref], [Web of Science ®]

Berkman, L. F., Glass, T., Brissette, I. & Seeman, T. E. (2000), From social integration to health: Durkheim in the new millennium, *Social Science and Medicine*, 6, pp. 843–57.

Berndt, T. J. (1989), Obtaining support from friends during childhood and adolescence, in D. Belle (Ed.), *Children's Social Networks and Social Supports* (pp. 308–31). New York: Wiley.

Berndt, T. J. & Murphy, L. M. (2002), Influences of friends and friendships: Myths, truths, and research recommendations, in R. K. Kail (Ed.), *Advances in Child Development and Behavior*, vol. 30 (pp. 275–310). USA: Elsevier.

Bezzina, A. & Camilleri, S (2021), Happy Children: A project that has the aim of developing emotional literacy and conflict resolution skills. A Maltese Case Study, *Pastoral Care in Education*, 39(1), pp. 48–66. DOI: 10.1080/02643944.2020.1774633

Blakemore, S. (2019), *Inventing Ourselves: The Secret Life of the Teenage Brain*. London: Black Swan.

Bregman, R. (2021), *Humankind: A Hopeful History*. London: Bloomsbury.

Chrispino, Á. (2007), Gestão do conflito escolar: da classificação dos conflitos aos modelos de mediação, *Ensaio: Avaliação e Políticas Públicas em Educação*, 15, pp. 11–28. Doi: 10.1590/s0104-40362007000100002

Deacon, L. (2015), *Using Distancing Techniques in PSHE*. Available online: https://www.creativeeducation.co.uk/blog/using-distancing-techniques-in-pshe/ (accessed 21 May 2022).

Duval, T. S. & Silvia, P. J. (2002), Self-awareness, probability of improvement, and the self-serving bias, *Journal of Personality and Social Psychology*, 82(1), pp. 49–61.

Goodenow, C. & Grady, K. E. (1993), The relationship of school belonging and friends' values to academic motivation among urban adolescent students, *The Journal of Experimental Education*, 62(1), pp. 60–71. http://www.jstor.org/stable/20152398

Hanson, E. (2020), *What Is the Impact of Pornography on Young People? A Research Briefing for Educators*, London: PSHE Association.

Hayman, J. (2012), *British Voices*. Leicestershire: Matador, p.13

Healy, S. https://www.walkinmyshoes.ie/library/blogs-and-articles/2017/september/adolescents-and-the-importance-of-friendships-in-the-school-setting

Home Office (2021), *Tackling Violence against Women and Girls Strategy*. Available online: https://www.gov.uk/government/publications/tackling-violence-against-women-and-girls-strategy/tackling-violence-against-women-and-girls-strategy#contents (accessed 21 May 2022).

James, Park (1999), Emotional literacy: Education for meaning, *International Journal of Children's Spirituality*, 4(1), pp. 19–28. DOI: 10.1080/1364436990040103 To link to this article: https://doi.org/10.1080/1364436990040103 Published online: 18 May 2010.Submit your article to this journal Article views: 904 View related articles Citing articles: 4 View citing articles.

Kelley, J. (2006, September 12). When belonging matters most: Making friends at school can be tough. *Arizona Republic*. Available online: https://www.proquest.com/newspapers/when-belonging-matters-most/docview/238746432/se-2?accountid=15133

Kerr-Gaffney, J., Harrison, A. & Tchanturia, K. (2019), Cognitive and affective empathy in eating disorders: A systematic review and meta-analysis, *Frontiers in Psychiatry*, 10, p. 102. https://doi.org/10.3389/fpsyt.2019.00102

Mental Health Foundation (2022), *Mental Health Awareness Week 9–15 May 2022 – Loneliness*. Available online: https://www.mentalhealth.org.uk/campaigns/mental-health-awareness-week (accessed 20 May 2022).

Ng-Knight, T., Shelton KH., Riglin, L., Frederickson, N., McManus, IC. & Rice, F. (2019), 'Best friends forever'? Friendship stability across school transition and associations with mental health and educational attainment, *Br J Educ Psychol*, 2019 Dec; 89(4), pp. 585–99. doi: 10.1111/bjep.12246. Epub 2018 Sep 27. PMID: 30259513.

O'Neill, M. (2021), *Proactive Pastoral Care*. London: Bloomsbury.

Perry, B., & Szalavitz, M. (2017), *The Boy Who Was Raised as a Dog*. New York: Basic Books.

Perry, B. & Winfrey, O. (2021), *What Happened to You? Conversations on Trauma, Resilience and Healing*. London: Bluebird.

Poulin, F. & Chan, A. (2010), Friendship stability and change in childhood and adolescence, *Developmental Review*, 30, pp. 257–72. https://doi.org/10.1016/j.dr.2009.01.001

PSHE Association (2018), Handling complex issues safely in the PSHE education classroom. https://pshe-association.org.uk/guidance/ks1-5/handling-complex-issues-safely-classroom (accessed 10 July 2023).

Steiner, C. & Perry, P. (1997), *Achieving Emotional Literacy: A Program to Increase Your Emotional Intelligence*. Avon: Bloomsbury.

Tomé, G., et al. (2012), How can peer group influence the behavior of adolescents: Explanatory model, *Global Journal of Health Science*, 4, pp. 26–35. https://doi.org/10.5539/gjhs.v4n2p26

Time (2018), *How the World's First Loneliness Minister Will Tackle the 'Sad Reality of Modern Life'*. Available online: https://time.com/5248016/tracey-crouch-uk-loneliness-minister/ (accessed 20 May 2022).

Yanagihara, H. (2015), *A Little Life*. London: Picador.

You Gov (2019), *Who Are the Most Lonely People in the UK?* Available online: https://yougov.co.uk/topics/lifestyle/articles-reports/2019/10/03/young-britons-are-most-lonely (accessed 20 May 2022).

9

Diversity and Discrimination

Zahara Chowdhury, Holly Parker-Guest, Katja Pavlona, Victoria-Marie Pugh, Kit Marie Rackley, Elizabeth Swan and Hannah Wilson

Aims of This Chapter

- To explore the possible barriers and opportunities to ensuring quality diversity, equality and inclusion within PSHE education.
- To highlight the ways in which safe spaces can be developed so that all pupils feel included and safe in PSHE education.
- To consider the importance of representation in PSHE education.

Introduction

Personal, social, health and economic (PSHE) education is an important aspect of the secondary curriculum that can often be squeezed out and diluted at the expense of core subjects. The hidden or, as Hawkes (2018) calls it, the 'inner' curriculum is more important now, than ever before, as we ground ourselves post-Brexit, post-Covid and in the wake of increased hate crimes (see Figure 9.1)

We are two years on from George Floyd's murder, a moment of awakening for the school system, which jumped to attention to commit to diversity, equity and inclusion (DEI) approaches. DEI starts with the culture and the ethos of our schools, spanning throughout the curriculum and underpinning every policy and practice. DEI needs

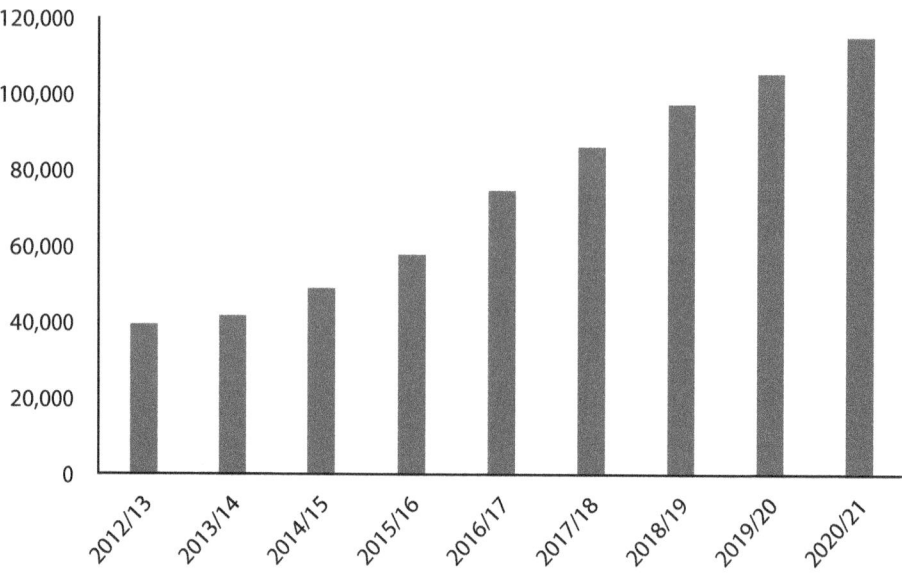

Figure 9.1 Official Statistics – Hate Crime England and Wales 2020–21 (Excluding Greater Manchester Police).

to be a whole-school strategic approach – we need strategies for being inclusive, for nurturing belonging, for creating psychological safety. The strategic vision needs to include an awareness of the Equality Act (2010) which raises consciousness, develops confidence and builds competence across all of the stakeholders to lean into courageous conversations about identity and representation. The Equality Act (2010) specifically states that it is against the law to discriminate against anyone because of:

- age
- gender reassignment
- being married or in a civil partnership
- being pregnant or on maternity leave
- disability
- race including colour, nationality, ethnic or national origin
- religion or belief
- sex
- sexual orientation

All staff need to be aware of all of the protected characteristics and to be empathetic to the diverse lived experiences of different individuals. A DEI commitment starts with meaningful and authentic conversations about who we are, our values and our place in the community. The foundation for this work lies in the PSHE curriculum.

Identifying and Removing the Potential Barriers to This Work

Delivering high-quality PSHE is essential to developing students in a holistic way in this ever-changing world to shape them into productive and moral citizens. However when committing to this there are many barriers that leaders and teachers of PSHE can face. Fear being the first and foremost: fear of content, fear of student reactions, fear of parental complaints (Fine-Davies and Faas, 2014). There are several ways these barriers can be broken down and overcome.

It is important to remember as educators that we have a duty under the Public Sector Equality Duty (2011) to:

(a)   eliminate discrimination, harassment, victimization;
(b)   advance equality of opportunity between persons who share a relevant protected characteristic and persons who do not share it;
(c)   foster good relations between persons who share a relevant protected characteristic and persons who do not share it.

Therefore, sitting alongside statutory guidance and the Equality Act (2010), it is difficult to separate PSHE from DEI: teaching students about personal, social, health and economic education (and more) has to be diverse in its approach, accessible and inclusive for all students and equitable in its outcomes in order to prepare students to navigate their futures in the twenty-first century.

Addressing Contemporary Issues and Hot Topics

Generation Z and Generation Alpha are set to be the most diverse generations yet (Fry & Parker, 2018). We might also say they are the most globally connected generations, consuming fast news before the school day begins, thanks to social media. Therefore, navigating discussions about contemporary issues and global awareness is becoming a fundamental teaching skill for the profession. As much as contemporary issues and hot topics are easily accessible through the media, managing a diverse range of responses poses several challenges for teachers. In order to overcome these challenges, it is useful for teachers and schools to use the principles of *culturally responsive teaching* (CRT) to guide their teaching of DEI in PSHE. Put quite simply, CRT is authentically tailoring lessons to the diverse learning styles of your students using lived experiences, storytelling, analogies and more that make the lessons culturally relatable and relevant (Will & Najarro, 2022).

CRT strategies make teaching and learning equitable and accessible for all students. They help overcome barriers to learning, including implicit and explicit bias. In order to teach contemporary issues in a safe, inclusive and enjoyable environment, it is helpful to consider the cultural lived experiences of your students (without making assumptions), to share these experiences in a safe and secure manner and to establish a culture of respect in the classroom to manage diverse responses to contemporary issues.

Social Media

Research suggests that a child's moral cognition, empathy and understanding of justice are influenced by their parents and care environment too (Cowell & Decety, 2015). Social media has become a very influential source of education on contemporary topics for students; however, its binary and unregulated form can be problematic for schools. It has also been liberating, enabling peaceful online protest, awareness and understanding for so many – it is social media awareness that has led to so many watershed moments including following the murders of George Floyd, Sarah Everard and during the occupation of Palestine and the war in Ukraine. PSHE lessons can help students navigate these topics so that they feel confident and able to manage sensitive issues. As well as following the school or college setting's safeguarding policy and precursing every PSHE session with rules grounded in respect, empathy, listening and safety, the following guidelines will ensure PSHE lessons about contemporary issues have a positive impact on all students:

- Acknowledge their emotions. Often, responding to 'hot topics' needs to be proactive and in the moment; therefore, can lead to heated feelings. Acknowledge these feelings from the outset, but explain to students that your discussions are not personal and will help everyone navigate a critical understanding of the event or issue.
- Start with the facts: a range of credible news sources can help provide a skeleton for your discussion, remembering, however, that publications do often come with their own bias, however unintentional. Provide students with a range of factual evidence about hate crime and assault so that they can evaluate the social, moral and economic impact of these issues. When discussing sensitive and triggering topics, factual evidence followed by lived experiences can help navigate emotive responses. Remind students we all have the equal right to live in a fair, safe and just society and we must work together to overcome any obstacles that prevent this.
- Take a solutions-based approach. Consider the impact of contemporary issues on different groups in society: is it possible to create a truly equitable world?

What problems do we address first? What skills are needed in the twenty-first century to solve the global mental health crises, climate change, for example? Are there any marginalized groups which might be more vulnerable?

- Explore the pros and cons of social media. Encourage students to critically consider the role of influencers and unregulated information on social media platforms. To do this, it is important for students to think empathetically: how might their trust and belief in a particular influencer or online news source impact those with protected characteristics in their class? What is the impact (and value) of a thirty-second TikTok story about transgender rights, compared to reading and exploring a research paper or other sources of information about LGBT+ experiences?

Most importantly, giving students a medium to express their thoughts and views in a way that feels safe for them. This might be art, blogging, podcasting or something else. The term 'intersectionality' was 'originally coined by American scholar and lawyer Kimberle Crenshaw, who drew inspiration from Black feminist movements in the US, and highlights how race, gender, class, and other factors are interconnected' (El Gharib, 2022: para 12). Enabling individual expression when teaching sensitive topics can help students explore their own intersectionality and therefore strengthen their knowledge and understanding about the range of topics too. The key is to encourage empathy and diverse thinking, two key leadership skills students will inevitably need in their future.

Creating Safety for Staff and Students to Embed DEI

Creating safe spaces within the curriculum does not refer to the physical safety of learners, but instead describes creating a space free from psychological or emotional harm (Holly & Steiner, 2005). 'A safe classroom space is one in which students are able to openly express their individuality, even if it differs dramatically from the norms' (Holly & Steiner, 2005, p.50). As educators, we must not confuse being safe with being comfortable, providing a structured space for children to confront issues that make them uncomfortable and 'force them to struggle with who they are and what they believe' (Holly & Steiner 2005).

As teachers of PSHE, it is important to create safe spaces to empower learners to share their voices and listen to their peers. The benefits of having diverse voices heard should not be outweighed by the negatives, such as feeling ashamed or ostracized. With students perceiving that they learn more in a safe space (Holly & Steiner, 2005), how can we create safe spaces in our schools?

1 Establish ground rules: Ground rules, aligned to the school values and the Equality Act 2010, support inclusive and respectful discussions where many children learn turn-taking, respect the views and privacy of others, become aware of body language and how to assert themselves respectfully in discussions. Ground rules also reference the school's safeguarding policy in relation to disclosures that may occur in the lesson. Although the Equality Act provides the legal framework schools need to follow, it can be good practice for schools to develop a DEI policy and have a staff lead who co-creates an action plan to support the creation of safe spaces and a culture of inclusion (see the references at the end of this chapter for further guidance on resources to help schools create a DEI policy and framework).

2 Create a non-judgemental approach: Great PSHE lessons stimulate thought and discussion. In a safe space, 'safe' does not mean avoiding conflict. Children should be supported to scrutinize and struggle with their values and explore their ideologies without recrimination for expressing different opinions from their peers. 'A classroom in which "safe" means no conflict, and that no-one is ever feeling challenged is likely to be a classroom in which little learning and growth are occurring' (Holly & Steiner, 2005, p.52). The anonymous PSHE question box can support in exploring sensitive questions, enabling children to ask questions and provide teachers with time to research or prepare responses.

3 Know your pupils' names: This is the first step to knowing and acknowledging your pupils as individuals (O'Brien et al., 2014). Taking the time to learn and correctly pronounce a child's name does not only make them feel valued, but also provides an opportunity to model inclusive behaviour and create a positive classroom climate.

4 Use micro-affirmations: Rowe (2008, p.46) identifies apparently tiny acts which can have a huge impact in helping others be successful, 'opening doors to opportunity, gestures of inclusion and caring, and graceful acts of listening.' Weaving opportunities to scaffold micro-affirmations for children defines your safe space: model active listening with older children; demonstrate the impact of body language on the listener; staff and older children can use scripted prompts to support responses that validate feelings, emotions and opinions.

5 Use storytelling as a medium to create a common understanding between children. Stories can reinforce the concept of the safe space and normalize children's feelings by allowing them to share experiences. Within PSHE lessons, using 'no real names,' the third person or an alias creates a space between the child and an experience.

Ensuring Representation in PSHE and RSHE

Thomas (2022) recounts the story of one Black prisoner she mentored who tells her that had she been his teacher (or someone else that looked like him), he may not be in prison. The same prisoner explained to her that all he had seen were white people in power and only 'seeing himself in sport, media and crime' (Thomas, 2022, p.2). This powerful story explains why diverse and equitable representation in PSHE is so important – representation has the ability to change the narrative and path of every student we teach.

One of the best tools in our PSHE planning toolkit is the use of diverse and intersectional case studies and scenarios to explain ideas, issues and solutions. For all secondary key stages, a variety of diverse case studies and lived experiences can be used. It is important to offer trigger warnings where necessary and, with reference to CRT, to ensure the use of case studies and resources is appropriate for your students.

Nurturing Global Citizenship through 'British Values'

'British values' of democracy, the rule of law, individual liberty, and mutual respect and tolerance of those with different faiths and beliefs are split into several objectives in non-statutory guidance to promote spiritual, moral, social and cultural (SMSC) development in maintained schools (gov.uk 2014).

However, 'British values' are not exclusively British. They are values of human rights shared across the globe (e.g. the United Nations Universal Declaration of Human Rights). Additionally, we are all global citizens. Our world has shrunk due to the spread and influence of popular culture and branding; we are more connected whether physically through extensive transportation networks or digitally through the internet. The Covid-19 pandemic perfectly demonstrated the former through its means of spreading across the globe, and the latter as we shifted towards remote schooling, working and socializing.

The killing of George Floyd in 2020 caused a global resurgence of empowerment. In the UK, it enabled focus on DEI and decolonizing curricula to become more prominent, organized and influential. Teaching and learning materials increasingly contain perspectives outside normative spheres, and those which do not, or misrepresent groups and places, are called out. This aligns with the 'British values' of *mutual respect and tolerance of those with different faiths and beliefs.*

While our young people are the most globally minded generation, there is a notable political trend towards nationalism and isolationism. Influential figures and elements of the popular press have pushed back against progress towards DEI, often using terms such as 'woke' in a derogatory fashion. Some politicians have warned against teaching students about issues such as privilege and colonialism, and fly a false flag under the guise of championing freedom of expression in Higher Education. These attitudes are contradictory to 'British values'. How can we empower our young people to embrace the fundamental principles of 'British values' through PSHE in the face of this hostility?

Whether it be on social media or in the popular press, you can find examples of how being progressive based on principles aligned with 'British values' are attacked. For example, in December 2017 a Conservative minister claimed via X that 'left wing snowflakes are killing comedy, tearing down historic statues, removing books from universities, dumbing down panto, removing Christ from Christmas and suppressing free speech' [verbat]. PSHE topics such as free speech, historical events, religious holidays, etc. can utilize such claims as a stimulus for discussion and critical thinking; for example, is there evidence that comedy is 'dying'? How do we differentiate between comedy and hate speech? Once explored, students can be in a position to decide whether this is 'woke-ness gone mad' or actual applications of 'British values'.

Curriculum Resources

Perhaps one of the wider challenges teachers face is how to practically make DEI teaching and learning accessible in PSHE lessons. Every school structures and teaches PSHE in a variety of manners and access to resources is always a teacher's first question, especially if the subject is being taught by non-specialists. Having a strong DEI ethos is about creating a culture of belonging in the school setting. It is about creating safe spaces to enable diverse conversations where every voice matters and a variety of views can be discussed. Below are a range of resources and methods teachers can use to implement DEI teaching in PSHE at every key stage.

A Consistent Approach

Begin DEI PSHE lessons with ground rules as mentioned above, and defining what 'diversity', 'equity' and 'inclusion' mean. To do this, it is advised to inform students about the Equality Act, protected characteristics and the expectation of political impartiality in the classroom. Lessons which explore the Universal Declaration of Human Rights (1948) and The UN Convention on the Rights of the Child (UNCRC, 1992) can also be supportive when exploring social inequalities.

The resources below are diverse and therefore teachers may find they complement other subject areas too. They can be differentiated to use across the key stages as, effectively, DEI in PSHE is about an understanding of the Equality Act, protected characteristics and how to have uncomfortable conversations in a safe space. We highly recommend a complementary and consistent approach to teaching DEI: when students see patterns, overlap and ideas being reinforced across different subject areas, it will enrich their learning experiences and provide a relevant and engaging approach to teaching PSHE too.

It is clear that effective, diverse, equitable and inclusive PSHE education is everyone's responsibility within a school community and must be a golden thread running through the vision and mission of every school. It is this collective consciousness in the school community, from students, staff, parents and carers, governors and all stakeholders that will ensure young people leave school equipped to stay healthy, safe and prepared for life and work within diverse Britain and beyond.

When considering diversity in the PSHE curriculum the PSHE lead and teaching team need to invest time in doing the inner work before starting the outer work – teachers need to understand themselves, their personal belief systems, unconscious biases and how their worldview has been shaped. This may feel uncomfortable and take longer than a CPD session; however, it is necessary if DEI is to be taught in PSHE in a culturally responsive and empathetic manner. The beauty of teaching and learning about DEI is that it is personal, relevant and necessary for every individual – therefore every individual is somewhat triggered, passionate or keen to create an equitable society. It is important to nurture the passion, anger, love and empathy you will find in your students to create a healthy culture of belonging and safety for all. And, as it should, DEI will go beyond the PSHE classroom, preparing our students to be valuable citizens in a globally diverse arena.

Questions for Reflection for You and Your Setting

- Who is teaching PSHE and how diverse is their individual and collective identity?
- What is your privilege(s)? What opportunities do you have that others do not? What barriers do you face that others do not?
- Explore your discomfort around teaching DEI. Where does this come from? What support do you need to overcome it?

- How do we identify and close the gaps in our own lived experiences to navigate any unconscious biases that we hold?
- What are the visible identities of the learners and their community, and how do we ensure they are represented?
- How will you address the bias and barriers faced by LGBTQ+, religious, racial, neurodivergent, disabled (and more) communities at your school? Sit with the discomfort this causes in order to develop resources and actions to create an inclusive school community.
- How do we create a space to unpack the potential conflict between some of the protected characteristics?

Recommended Resources

Decolonizing Geography: A great website designed by geography educators to decolonize the geography curriculum. Although geography-specific, the topics can be explored in PSHE lessons, from global governance to migration. There are schemes of work for all key stages. The blogs can be used in KS5 lessons to discuss and explore current global issues. www.decolonisegeography.com

Diverse Educators: An excellent platform with a range of blog posts, resource recommendations and DEI toolkits to help develop your PSHE curriculum. The toolkits are easily accessible to KS4 and KS5 students. They can almost be used as self-directed study and can help support independent learning too. They may also inspire schools and students to create your own DEI charters and resources for your school stakeholders. www. diverseeducators.co.uk

End Sexism: A great campaign to explore sexism in literature. This campaign is currently specific to the Key Stage Three curriculum and using their resources, blogs and research in PSHE lessons for KS3 can complement diversifying the English curriculum at school too. www.endsexisminschools. org.uk

Equality and Human Rights Commission: Comprehensive lesson plans and resources for all key stages to support teaching and learning in PSHE about protected characteristics, bullying and DEI in schools. https://www. equalityhumanrights.com/en/secondary-education-resources

Facing History: A wide range of blogs, lessons and resources for Key Stages 3 to 5, which explore a diverse range of historical events to challenge prejudice, discrimination and bigotry. Facing History also provides an excellent range of CPD seminars for PSHE and other subject areas too, which can help weave DEI into a curriculum-wide strategy. https://www.facinghistory.org/

Gal-Dem: Recommended for KS4 and KS5, this was an excellent diverse, online publication exploring intersectional experiences. Although publication has now ceased, previously published material has been archived and is still accessible on the website. It will encourage students to explore DEI in a range of mediums, from writing to speaking, to further engage students in the subject area. https://gal-dem.com/

Generation Feminist: A comprehensive, thought-provoking and engaging set of resources and podcasts about feminism in the twenty-first century. Authentic and organic, the resources can support lesson planning and the podcasts themselves can be used for discussion and independent learning too. www.genfem.co.uk

Global Equality Collective: The first DEI app for schools. A fantastic resource filled with playbooks and engaging videos that can be used to help develop DEI lessons for all key stages and for staff training too. www.thegec.org

MA Consultancy: Founded by Dr Muna Abdi and recommended for staff training, KS5 resources and KS5 workshops, MA consultancy can support the PSHE curriculum with racial equity and inclusion. www.ma-consultancy.co.uk

School Should Be: An authentic blog and podcast which explores a range of diverse topics aimed at students in KS4 and above. Schools and students are encouraged to contribute to the blog and podcast about diverse topics and issues they wish to talk about and write about. www.schoolshouldbe.com

Split Banana: An excellent set of resources for all key stages to support the RSE curriculum and diversity and inclusion in RSE too. Split Banana also provides 1:1 consultancy, training and development for PSHE leads looking to make RSE safe and inclusive for all students. www.splitbanana.co.uk

The Conversationalist: An American-based platform for Generation Z (KS4 and above) to encourage and support the ability to have open and inclusive conversations. The Conversationalist provides blogs and YouTube videos to explore a range of contemporary issues which will help teach students how to have critical and challenging conversations. https://www.theconversationalist.com/

You Be You: A great set of lessons, workshops and resources for KS3 on gender equality in schools. www.youbeyou.co.uk

Zenarations: An American-based platform founded by High School students during the pandemic to teach students about a range of global, diverse issues. The blogs and infographics are lessons in themselves and Zenarations support schools to create their own Zenarations branches – a great way to get KS3 and KS4 students actively involved in DEI education. https://zenarations.wordpress.com/

References

Arshad, F. (2021), Why representation matters in the primary curriculum, *Twinkl*, 21st September. Available online: https://www.twinkl.co.uk/twinkl-digest/ks2-news-digest/why-representation-matters-in-the-primary-curriculum (accessed 6 June 2022).

BBC News. (2022), Available online: https://www.bbc.co.uk/news/uk-england-leicestershire-57350735 (accessed 3 June 2022).

Brown, B. (2018), *Dare to Lead*. London, England: Vermillion.

Coleman, A. (2019), *What's Intersectionality? Let These Scholars Explain the Theory and Its History*, 29th March, Available online: https://time.com/5560575/intersectionality-theory/ (accessed 23 June 2019).

Cowell, J. M., & Decety, J. (2015), Precursors to morality in development as a complex interplay between neural, socio environmental, and behavioral facets, *Proceedings of the National Academy of Sciences – PNAS*, 112(41), pp. 12657–62.

DfE (2019), Parental Engagement on Relationships Education. Available online: https://assets.publishing.service.gov.uk/government/uploads/system/uploads/attachment_data/file/884450/Parental_engagement_on_relationships_education.pdf.

Department for Education (DfE) (2019), *Statutory Guidance on RSE for Schools in England*, London: DfE. Available online: https://www.gov.uk/government/publications/relationships-education-relationships-and-sex-education-rse-and-health-education

El Gharib, S. (2022), What Is Intersectionality and Why Is It Important?, Global Citizen; para12. Available https://www.globalcitizen.org/en/content/what-is-intersectionality-explained/ (accessed 10 July 2022)

Fine-Davis, Margret & Faas, Daniel (2014), Equality and diversity in the classroom: A comparison of students' and teachers' attitudes in six European countries, *Social Indicators Research*, 119, pp. 1319–34. DOI: 10.1007/s11205-013-0547-9.

Fry, R. & Parker, K. (2018), Early Benchmarks Show 'Post-Millennials' on Track to Be Most Diverse, Best-Educated Generation Yet. Available online: https://www.pewresearch.org/social-trends/2018/11/15/early-benchmarks-show-post-millennials-on-track-to-be-most-diverse-best-educated-generation-yet/

Gibbs, R. (2021), Why representation matters in primary schools, *Foundation Stage Forum*. Available online: https://eyfs.info/articles.html/primary/why-representation-matters-in-primary-schools-r366/#:~:text=It%20provides%20hope%20and%20something,beauty%20of%20diversity%20for%20themselves (accessed 3 6 2022).

Gov.uk (2014), Promoting fundamental British values as part of SMSC in schools. Available online: https://www.gov.uk/government/publications/promoting-fundamental-british-values-through-smsc (accessed 3 June 2022).

Gov.uk (2011), The Public Sector Equality Duty. https://www.gov.uk/government/publications/public-sector-equality-duty.

Gov.uk (2013), *Equality Act 2010: Guidance*. [online] Gov.uk. Available online: https://www.gov.uk/guidance/equality-act-2010-guidance (accessed 6 June 2022)

Gov.uk (2022), Political Impartiality in Schools. Available online: https://www.gov.uk/government/publications/political-impartiality-in-schools/political-impartiality-in-schools

Hawkes, N. & Hawkes, J. (2018), The inner curriculum: How to develop Wellbeing, resilience & self-leadership, John Catt Educational Ltd.

Hickel, J. (2018), *The Divide: A Brief Guide to Global Inequality and Its Solutions*. London: William Heinemann.

Holley, L. C. & Steiner, S. (2005), Safe space: Student perspectives on classroom environment, *Journal of Social Work Education*, 41(1), pp. 49–64.

Home Office (2021), Hate Crime; England and Wales 2020–2021. Available online: https://www.gov.uk/government/statistics/hate-crime-england-and-wales-2020-to-2021/hate-crime-england-and-wales-2020-to-2021 (accessed 2 July 2022).

O'Brien, M.T., Leiman, T. & Duffy, J. (2014), The power of naming: The multifaceted value of learning students' names. *QUT Law Review*, 14. 101.5204/qutlr.v14i1.544.

Rowe, Mary (2008), Micro-affirmations & micro-inequities, *Journal of the International Ombudsman Association*, 1(1), pp. 45–48.

Thomas, A. (2018), From a Whisper to a Shout, representation matters, *The Bristol Magazine*. Available online: https://thebristolmag.co.uk/from-a-whisper-to-a-shout-representation-matters/ (accessed 3 June 2022).

Thomas, A. (2022), *Representation Matters*. London, England: Bloomsbury Education.

Will & Najarro (2022) Available online: https://www.edweek.org/teaching-learning/culturally-responsive-teaching-culturally-responsive-pedagogy/2022/04 (accessed 26 June 2022).

Yabut Nadal, K. L. (2021), Why representation matters and why it's still not enough: Reflections on growing up brown, queer, and Asian American, *Psychology Today*, 27th December. Available online: https://www.psychologytoday.com/gb/blog/psychology-the-people/202112/why-representation-matters-and-why-it-s-still-not-enough#:~:text=Positive%20media%20representation%20can%20be,reducing%20stereotypes%20of%20underrepresented%20groups (accessed 3 June 2022).

10

Teaching Relationships and Sex Education

Victoria-Marie Pugh and Sophie King-Hill

Aims of This Chapter

- To explore the ways in which safe spaces can be developed for quality relationships and sex education to take place.
- To identify the benefits of planning using a spiral curriculum.
- To recognize how relationships and sex education can inform consent and support pupils' rights and safety.

Introduction

This chapter will aim to explore the classroom environment needed to deliver meaningful sex education lessons, the need for a spiral curriculum which builds upon skills, values and content, as well as some of the ways in which complex questions around sex can be answered in a respectful but informative way.

Relationships and sex education (RSE) is often perceived as a difficult topic to teach. It can cause fear and discomfort in teachers and giggles amongst pupils, which both impact upon the education received. RSE education in schools has a complex history, unlike other subjects such as English or Maths. We have to ask ourselves why this is, why RSE and the issues around it are so contentious. In relation to the curriculum, RSE has only become statutory since 2020, and schools must have an up-to-date policy on this, yet this still has caveats. This is due to be reviewed in 2023. At the time of writing, parents and carers can choose to withdraw their child from sex education at secondary school (except sex education within the National Curriculum as part of science in maintained schools). However, a pupil also has the right to opt into sex education from their fifteenth birthday (specifically three academic terms before they turn sixteen). Although there are no statutory requirements for RSE at

KS5, the PSHE Association provides clear KS5 objectives within their programme of study so that quality provision can be continued into sixth form or college education.

Prior to this, for some schools it has been purely scientific in nature set within biology lessons, for others it may have been a video wheeled out by an embarrassed looking form tutor or subject teacher. The experiences of RSE are individual. However, there is still have a long way to go in relation to RSE and needless to say, our young people deserve more. There is a plethora of reasons why robust and carefully planned RSE is vital for children and young people (CYP). These link to keeping themselves safe, providing safe space for exploration of concepts and experiences, imparting information, adequate assessment of sexual behaviours and allowing them to make informed choices when it comes to their relationships and sexual experiences (King-Hill, 2021, 2022; King-Hill and Woolley, 2017). In addition to this there is a wealth of research that suggests that CYP are more likely to delay sex if they have access to robust and clear information on all aspects of RSE (Sex Education Forum, 2015).

The Need for Quality Sex Education

According to research from the Sex Education Forum (2020), young people who receive high-quality sex education are:

- more likely to report sexual abuse
- more likely to delay first sex until they are ready
- more likely to have first sex that is consensual
- more likely to use contraception and condoms
- less likely to have an unplanned teenage pregnancy or sexually transmitted infection.

These findings make the case for quality, context dependent, RSE and supporting teachers to teach these topics and concepts effectively and confidently is a priority.

Sex and Shame

It is important to explore where the feelings of shame and regulation around sex come from before exploring what can be done in contemporary education. In terms of historical influences, in the times of the hunter-gatherers sex was celebrated, was for procreation and regulated by extended breast feeding (Buss, 2002). Then with the rise in agriculture and more organized societal groups the shifts in sexuality changed. Paternity became an issue due to the accumulation of resources. Gendered ideologies emerged and with that came the control of sexuality and the perception of the woman as the child-bearer. Then with the Industrial Revolution children were needed in the workforce, extended breastfeeding rates went down and birth rates went up.

Then from the Industrial Revolution children were not needed in relation to the labour market and keeping childbearing regulated became an important factor in rising society and a focus upon sex as a means to procreation only within the confines of marriage was introduced, and with this came age-related restrictions. Economic productivity was the focus and time wasted on sexual matters was frowned upon.

Alongside this, and this is a key point, there was a distinct shift in the ideologies surrounding children, changing from a useful commodity to the labour market, to innocent representations of the future society. Running alongside the practical matter of history and childbearing were the emerging matters of sex and morality. Influential perspectives of universal rights and wrongs in relation to sex were being consolidated into wider society and any variation from the static ethical code was seen to be immoral behaviour.

This was reinforced by dominant Christian ideologies in Western culture which bolstered this thinking, with lust and sex outside marriage being seen as a mortal sin. These ideas embedded themselves into wider society with the condemnation of any sexual variance outside heterosexual marriage as an assault on morality. Whilst the Christian Church's influences are diminishing in contemporary society, there are still remnants of the perception that sexuality is a fixed system of right or wrong and that any divergence from this is seen as a direct offence to public virtue (Stewart, 1995).

The stones were being laid for the demonization of sexuality. Masturbation is a key example – many still shudder at the thought of any public discussion on this topic. Even as far back as the 1700s the physical consequences of masturbation were widely published, and were often associated with the young.

'fits, epilepsy, im-potence, and in woman, fluor albus, hysteric fits, consumption, and barrenness' (Fishman, 1982)

Sexual intercourse in accordance with the law, via marriage, was reinforced to protect the reasoning capacity of an individual and ensure equality and morality. Then Foucault, a French philosopher known for his commentary on sexuality, put forward ideas stating that the normalization of sexuality through marriage and religion has resulted in repressed attitude towards sex in contemporary culture by wider society, linking it to social regulation and cultural control. He also implied that the sexuality in children and young people is held as something dangerous that needs to be monitored and controlled (Foucault, 1990, 1992a, 1992b).

The Perception of the Child

Contemporary perceptions of children also contribute to the discomfort that many people have when talking about children and RSE. Sex and children are concepts that are seen as mutually exclusive, and this then inhibits the education that they receive. It is useful to explore how we define a child. Just think for a second, how do you define a child and childhood? Where does it begin? Where does childhood end? Why? Is this different for different individuals?

Childhood is a social construction. It is not a prescribed state of being but rather an idea. Whereas infancy is a biological category, childhood is not. Yet childhood is a social idea rather than a social fact and they did not exist until around the 1700s. Prior to this the concept of the child was different to what we have now – they were infants and then young adults.

The emergence of childhood as a recognized state is only relatively recent and with this came the emerging perception of innocence and need for regulation which resulted in the perception of the modern-day child that is firmly embedded in a society that is focused upon achievement and career rather than child-bearing, with sexual behaviour posing a risk to this ideology.

Relationships and Sex Education: What to Teach and How

Many teachers and schools are concerned with what they should teach and how they should teach it. The statutory RSE guidance DfE (2019) sets out the requirements for statutory relationships, sex and health education which includes elements such as positive one-to-one relationships, reproductive health, identifying sexual pressure and Female Genital Mutilation (FGM).

Creating Safe Spaces

Creating a safe space for young people to learn in is not a new concept in education. It could be argued, however, that it is imperative within RSE where pupils will come to lessons with a range of experiences, values and cultural or religious backgrounds.

It is important that an environment is established where pupils can make mistakes, ask questions and feel comfortable to challenge ideas. Ground rules and group agreements are an essential element to encourage a safe and supportive learning environment. Even if we teach through a trauma-informed approach, it would be impossible for teachers to know everything that every young person we teach has gone through or currently manages. Therefore, setting boundaries and creating safe spaces can help to keep everyone feeling secure.

Ground rules allow for a co-constructed, agreed way to approach discussions, disagreements and curiosity within topics. Historically, ground rules have been designed devoid of pupil voice and have little function other than to exist as an A4 page on a class display. In order to fully embrace inclusive, informative and relevant sex education, it is imperative that these agreed ways of working are created, discussed and clarified rather than being a list of 'do not' statements which leave little room for questions or to seek clarity (Childnet, 2019).

Here are some examples of ground rules which have been co-constructed and discussed with pupils. The ground rules need to be constructed with pupils and as such will be different for each class.

- No put-downs
- Show respect by listening, not interrupting and only one person talking at a time
- Don't make assumptions about people
- Use scientific names for body parts
- You don't have to say things about yourself if you don't want to
- Keep other people's stuff confidential
- Tell the story without giving identifying details away
- It's okay to get things wrong
- Have fun!

These can be designed in Year 7 and act as a working document, being continually revisited and developed throughout the years. As well as designing the agreed ground rules it is important to discuss them to ensure that the meaning is understood by all. It is easy to say that discussion needs to remain confidential but the practicalities of this are not always understood by children and young people. To support this, reinforcing safeguarding procedures and specifically sharing key information about how pupils can contact the Designated Safeguarding Lead (DSL), specifically name those members of staff and options for communication such as email, face-to-face meetings or anonymous platforms which might be available. Identifying key members of staff such as pastoral support, mental health first-aid-trained staff and any external agencies such as school counsellors can also provide support and signposting for pupils.

According to Ashcraft and Murray (2017, p.305), 'There is increasing evidence that using anatomically correct words – such as penis, scrotum, vagina, and vulva – is beneficial to children's early development of body confidence, self-empowerment, and safety.' Sometimes pupils may find humour when the word penis, vulva or vagina is mentioned, but this is okay and relates to the taboo and shame that surrounds sex as previously discussed. This may eventually subside as statutory RSE filters through the academic years, but culture shifts take time. Often, we can assume that pupils understand vocabulary or concepts which they may be unsure about or have some misconceptions which have developed. This is where creating a space in which they can make mistakes is paramount. Research by Metcalfe (2017) highlights the importance of encouraging mistakes. This can be due to worries around using the wrong terminology or ways to identify people or concepts; however, having a classroom in which they can say 'I'm not sure what the right term to use here is' or 'I don't really understand this' can be beneficial for all as it models being honest than using a term which may offend others.

In order to develop this safe space, teacher response is crucial. Pupils have questions which may seem tricky or that some teachers might find awkward to answer. It may be that a pupil does not know how to phrase a question appropriately or is not sure of the vocabulary to use and it is important to facilitate these questions. Some ways of being able to do this are by having an 'ask-it basket' per class, where pupils can write questions anonymously and you can then read it, change the language if necessary and then respond. By asking all pupils to write something on a piece of paper and putting it in the basket (they can doodle instead) take the emphasis off who has written a question and allow the focus to be on the discussion of the question instead. By having ground rules boundaries will be clear. Having a question which pupils work in groups to write the answer to can also be a powerful way to facilitate discussion and to check for meaning in the vocabulary being used, as often pupils use phrases or words they do not fully understand. As educators, we often feel as though we have to know all of the answers. This is simply not true. If a question is asked which is not in the planning for that year group or that you do not know the answer to, it is okay to say, 'Thanks for that question, I'm not sure how to answer it right now, but I am going to find out and get back to you.' This approach is also led by the young people and sessions can then be tailored to their needs. Listening to young people, and working with them to establish what they need, is a key component of robust and valuable RSE sessions. This has been outlined in the recent research published by the NSPCC (Renold et al., 2023) and also can be seen in the guide for teachers co-produced with King-Hill (2023) and young people.

Developing a Spiral Sex Education Curriculum

Although some schools or senior leaders may consider it the only option for delivery within their settings, teaching RSE on a drop-down day can inhibit learning. It is essential that the skills and content are developed and built upon throughout the key stages. Given parent/carers' right to withdraw their child from sex education lessons, any lessons which are solely sex-related and not linked to the statutory relationship objectives will need to be clearly set out with the school RSE or wider PSHE policy.

The PSHE Association states that 'the most effective model of delivery for personal, social, health and economic (PSHE) education is a sequenced, spiral programme that builds on prior learning as pupils progress through school'. By creating a spiral curriculum for sex education, you can ensure that pupils revisit topics, facts and concepts building upon what they already know and use this knowledge to make sense of new learning and skills. This spiral curriculum needs to be co-constructed with pupils and pupil voice is a crucial component of RSE as they know where their needs lie. Encouraging pupil voice through surveys, steering groups, online spaces and discussions within class offers opportunity for pupils to share what they want to know, what they need to know and how best this information can be delivered. It is often useful to ask pupils in KS4 what they wish they'd been taught in KS3 and so on. This can open up key discussions around what is age and stage relevant. Valuing and utilizing pupil voice not only increases pupil engagement but can improve relationships between pupils and teachers and support better communication between pupils and the school (Rudduck et al., 2003).

Creating a spiral curriculum means that topics and skills can be revisited and built upon each year and Key Stage. For example, research by Martellozzo et al. (2020) tells of 'a growing number of young people accessing pornography, and at a younger age, with children as young as seven accidentally encountering pornography online'. This does not mean that pupils have actively sought out porn, but it can be accidental or something which they access through social media unintentionally. To support this, information about pornography can be integrated within the KS3 sex education programme, concentrating on what to do if they access material online that they do not feel comfortable with or that they don't think is appropriate. This can then be developed across KS4 and 5 lessons by looking at how pornography can influence how people perceive their bodies, conduct relationships, view healthy or unhealthy relationships, etc. Critiquing the impact of porn in KS4 and 5 can be a powerful way to explore how and why pornography exists and the impacts it can have on young people, societal norms and expectations of sexual actively.

Key Stage 3

In Year 7, schools may choose to revisit the area of puberty education. Although this sits in the health education guidance, it does provide a starting point for pupils to ensure they have a solid understanding of scientific terms for body parts, changes to the body and why these changes occur (see Chapter 7, which explores the need for an understanding of body parts). Given that many pupils will come from a range of primary or previous settings, a recap supports a shared understanding of the topics and can act as a baseline set of lessons. This then allows for pupils to engage with other areas such as sexual intercourse, consent, contraception, FGM and attitudes towards sex across KS3.

In Key Stage 3, exploring peer pressure and pressures to have sex or engage in sexual actively enables pupils to consider the range of sources that pressure might come from. Looking at song lyrics, music videos, TV shows and social media content can open up a range of discussions around how sex is portrayed and how this might be different in real life. A meta-analysis by Karsay et al. (2017) found that levels of self-objectification were heightened when playing video games or online social media in relation to that of TV. They explained that this could be because social media and video games require interaction, whereas TV can be watched whilst simultaneously carrying out other activities or unrelated tasks. It is well documented that female characters in video games are often sexualized and the use of avatars and other 'create your own' profile options allows pupils to create a more sexualized or standardized beauty version of themselves (Burgess et al., 2007; Lynch, Tompkins, van Driel, & Fritz, 2016). Therefore, using examples from popular culture can bring pupils' attention to the many influences which may surround them on a daily basis and enable them to be aware of these when making decisions or reflecting on their own self-image.

Key Stage 4

Moving into Key Stage 4, sex education areas to cover may progress to considering pornography, conception, healthy versus coercive relationships, sexting, image sharing, sexual health, pregnancy, fertility, sex and the media and attitudes towards sex as just a few examples. It is vital, however, to be led by what the young people need, as educators may be teaching them things they already know. This can be addressed through a co-design, participatory approach with them (Renold et al., 2023).

When considering sexual health and contraception education it is useful to consider the World Health Organization's definition of sexual health which they present as 'a state of physical, emotional, mental and social well-being in relation to sexuality; it is not merely the absence of disease, dysfunction or infirmity. Sexual health requires a positive and respectful approach to sexuality and sexual relationships, as well as the possibility of having pleasurable and safe sexual experiences, free of coercion, discrimination and violence. For sexual health to be attained and maintained, the sexual rights of all persons must be respected, protected, and fulfilled (2018, p.4). Education around sexual health has moved away from merely being concerned with reducing teenage pregnancy rates and sexually transmitted infections (STIs) to a more holistic approach which considers rights, safety and pleasure.

Sophie Whitehead, whilst speaking to the School of Sexuality, reported that a sex-positive approach to sex education can often be misunderstood as promoting sexual stories or that everyone must engage in sexual activity (Whitehead, 2019). They state that it is about embracing 'the curiosity we have around sex and our own sexual desires is framed as negative or taboo, cloaking the topic in feelings of shame. Interpreting this curiosity through sex positivity reimagines it and dismantles the oppressive framework of taboo and judgement, instead creating space for communication and open exploration.' In Key Stage 4, this curiosity can be supported through the use of anonymous question boxes or online spaces for pupils to share their questions which can be seen by teachers prior to answering so that the teacher has time to consider the question and answer accordingly. Hoyle and McGeeney (2018, p.197) recommend clarifying slang that pupils may hear such as 'giving head' or 'going down' so that pupils understand common sexual terms. One key objective from the statutory RSE guidance (DfE, 2019) is

- that there are choices in relation to pregnancy (with medically and legally accurate, impartial information on all options, including keeping the baby, adoption, abortion and where to get further help).

The current legal status of abortion within the UK is that they are legally available until twenty-three weeks and six days' gestation, through the Abortion Act 1967 in Great Britain, and the Abortion (Northern Ireland) (No.2) Regulations 2020. In Northern Ireland, the abortion law is unconditional until twelve weeks gestation and twenty-four weeks if harm would be caused to the pregnant woman. Whilst individual pupils may have their own values or religious-based views on abortion, it is important that it is taught in a factual and unbiased way. According to the Royal College of Obstetricians and Gynaecologists (RCOG) and the Faculty of Sexual and Reproductive Healthcare (FSRH) (2021), one in five conceptions leads to a woman having an abortion in England and Wales. All women and girls seeking abortion have the right to confidentiality, including those who are under sixteen; however, those who are under sixteen will be encouraged to bring a parent or trusted adult unless this would be harmful to them from a safeguarding perspective. These key facts alongside adoption and keeping a baby need to be explored with pupils to ensure they have an informed and balanced education around pregnancy choices.

Key Stage 5

Despite RSE not being statutory within KS5, it is a vital area for young people, and sex education needs to continue into colleges and sixth-form settings. From the age of sixteen young people can legally consent to sex (this includes sexual intercourse, penetrative sex and any sort of sexual touching) but it is important that they understand that they are the only ones who will know when and if they are ready to engage in sexual activity. At Key Stage 5, some key foci can centre around consent, sexual pleasure, sexual image sharing, healthy relationships, fertility and sexual health. The PSHE Association programme of study also recommends teaching about how to access sexual health advice, diagnosis and treatment in different contexts.

Hoyle and McGeeney (2018, p.22) highlight the importance of young people exploring what 'good sex' is stating that the

RSE curricula have been justifiably criticised for focussing too heavily on the risks of relationships and sex, such as unwanted pregnancy, sexually transmitted infections and sexual violence. Whilst these are important issues for many young people, they are addressed at the expense of exploring the positive and pleasurable aspects of relationships and sexuality such as desire and intimacy. This can leave young people with a good idea of what a 'bad' relationship looks like but with no sense of what it looks or feels like to enjoy relationships and bonds with others, or with no idea about what their own values and priorities are when it comes to relationships.

Therefore, lessons which promote the value of sex and sexual activities as being pleasurable rather than purely as a means of conception are imperative. Allen (2011), however, does warn of the dangers of promoting a 'pleasure imperative' whereby placing pressure upon young people to think that pleasure or orgasm is the end goal or in particular for girls if they do not orgasm from penetrative sex.

Opening up discussion around different types of intimate relationships can support pupils' understanding and reflections of what they look for or are looking for in their own relationships. For instance, the difference between cheating or adultery and an open relationship is open communication and agreed boundaries. For some pupils, intimate relationships will only be discussed within the context of marriage or a committed relationship due to their values, religion or culture. It is important that a range of relationships are discussed as cultural and religious backgrounds can greatly influence a young person's decision-making when it comes to sex or sexual activities; therefore, culturally responsive teaching (Gay, 2020) needs to be considered when planning and delivering lessons.

LGBTQ+ and RSE

Teaching good RSE within an LGBTQ+ context is vital, as many RSE sessions run the risk of becoming heteronormative. The RSE guidance (2020) states that in primary schools 'teaching about families requires sensitive and well-judged teaching based on knowledge of pupils and their circumstances'. This specifically encompasses the LGBTQ+ community, stating that 'care need[s] to be taken to ensure that there is no stigmatisation of children based on their home circumstances'. In terms of secondary education, it states that 'sexual orientation and gender identity should be explored at a timely point and in a clear, sensitive and respectful manner'. It is highlighted that sexual and gender identities have to be accounted for and space should be given for pupils to acknowledge and explore what constitutes healthy same sex relationships in the same way that they are taught about heterosexual relationships. One vital point in relation to RSE and LGBTQ+ education is that this should not be a bolt-on session. These perspectives should be 'integrated appropriately into the relationships and sex education programme, rather than addressed separately or in only one lesson'. This should be embedded across the curriculum and sessions that are taught. Lessons which consider routes to parenthood, fertility and pregnancy choices which are LGBTQ+ inclusive should be included across all key stages. This indicates that LGBTQ+ education is equally as important and valid as all the other aspects of RSE, reinforcing its importance.

LGBTQ+ education has a long history, and many still live with the legacy of Section 28 which stated:

'A local authority shall not –

(a) intentionally promote homosexuality or publish material with the intention of promoting homosexuality;

(b) promote the teaching in any maintained school of the acceptability of homosexuality as a pretended family relationship.'

Section 28 was only abolished in 2003 (2000 in Scotland), making LGBTQ+ education in schools a relatively new phenomenon. However, due to this legacy teaching about LGBTQ+ is vitally important and links to the wellbeing of students from this community. A recent Stonewall report (Stonewall, 2017) found that 45 per cent of LGB students are bullied at school, 61 per cent of LGBT+ young people have self-harmed and 53 per cent of LGBTQ+ pupils stated that they didn't feel that they had a trusted adult they can talk to at school.

These results are contextualized by recent homophobic attacks, as well as the protests that have taken place at various schools in response to the school introducing the 'No Outsiders' (No Outsiders, 2019) programme which supports children to embrace the diversity of the LGBTQ+ community. This highlights the importance of teaching this topic in a sensitive yet robust manner to create a safe space for all children and young people to thrive.

Shock Tactics

Historically, a number of strategies have been used to deliver elements of RSE such as sexually transmitted infections, contraception and online communication with strangers. Often these strategies can include the use of graphic videos, images or negative outcomes to situations in the hope of 'shocking' the learner into refraining from a particular behaviour (such as unprotected sex).

A handbook from the PSHE Association and National Chief Police Council (2021, p.29) found that 'pupils who are upset by a particularly sad (or harrowing) story, film or scenario are unlikely to be able to engage with new learning – it may make an emotional impact but is likely to inhibit the intended learning'. Not only do these shock tactics have the ability to re-traumatize pupils who may have already experienced an adverse childhood experience, but it can also prevent pupils from seeking help with a problem as they deem their situation not to be as serious as the one presented and so do not feel justified in asking for help. In some cases it could also glamorize particular issues.

Sexual Consent

According to Muehlenhard et al. (2016 cited in Willis et al. (2021), 'Sexual consent refers to people's willingness to engage in partnered sexual activity. Typically, one person initiates or requests a sexual behavior, and another person responds based on their willingness to take part in that sexual behavior' (Muehlenhard et al., 2016).

The Sexual Offences Act 2003 developed this further by saying that someone consents to sexual activity if they:

- agree by choice and
- have both the freedom and capacity to make that choice.

In primary schools, consent will have been covered through the RSE curriculum relating to consenting to, for example, what they want to take part in, if they want to hold a friend's hand or allow someone to play with their hair, so pupils should have some baseline understanding of consent before starting secondary school. This work around consent should continue into Year 7 and beyond, reiterating the key point that just because someone does want to hold your hand this time doesn't mean that they will every time and that this isn't a rejection of friendship, just their choice.

Coy et al. (2016) highlight that teaching for and about consent can support both preventing sexual violence and promoting the need for enthusiastic consent, in particular from girls. Jacobson (2018) also notes that girls and boys get different messages from parents about sex and consent. Girls are told that they 'need to keep themselves safe' in contrast to 'boys get the message that sex – having it, or getting it – is tied to being confident, and powerful, and masculine'. It is also important that messages to boys also consider that it is okay for them not to want to have sex.

Many teachers and educators will have come across the Thames Valley Police (2015) 'tea and consent' video which highlights many key issues around sexual consent such as:

- If someone is unconscious, they cannot consent to sex
- Just because someone has consented once doesn't mean it is automatic consent the next time
- Sex cannot be expected at any time and there cannot be coercion
- People have the right to change their mind at ANY point about sexual consent

This video can be useful for Year 9; however, there are more complexities when consenting and communicating about sex than there are about tea. Hancock (2015) puts forward his concerns about the tea and consent video, stating that the video does not consider power dynamics, normative scripting and 'checking in and paying attention'. The video may be a useful introduction to sexual consent and opens up the conversation, providing a vehicle of criticality around consent in KS4 and 5.

The idea of power dynamics within relationships is an important one in sex education from the legalities of age, to positions of authority or balance within friendships. For example, the legal age of sexual consent for sex in the UK is sixteen. Under the Sexual Offences Act 2003, children under the age of thirteen are considered of insufficient age to give consent to sexual activity. Therefore any cases where an under thirteen-year-old is engaged in sexual activity must be reported to the police.

Communication around what enthusiastic consent looks like can be a key discussion point in KS3, 4 and 5. How is consent agreed? Through eye contact, body language, words? Lessons on how consent is negotiated can support pupils' understanding of enthusiastic, positive consent which moves beyond the message of 'no is no'.

In addition, cultural and religious backgrounds can greatly influence a young person's decision-making when it comes to sex or sexual activities; therefore, culturally responsive teaching (Gay, 2020) needs to be considered when planning and delivering lessons. Bearing in mind how the 'tea and consent' video is over-simplified will help you avoid the eye-rolling mentioned in the mental health chapter and will contribute to work in other areas about intersectionality and societal and cultural expectations and their effects on decision-making.

Pupil voice cannot be discounted from sex education. Encouraging pupil voice through surveys, online spaces and discussions within class offers opportunity for pupils to share what they want to know, what they need to know and how best this information can be delivered. It is often useful to ask pupils in KS4 what they wish they'd been taught in KS3 and so on. This can open up key discussions around what is age and stage relevant. Valuing and utilizing pupil voice not only increases pupil engagement but can improve relationships between pupils and teachers and support better communication between pupils and the school (Rudduck et al., 2003).

Conclusion

In conclusion, confidence in teaching sex education is vital for all teachers as it is important that we recognize that quality sex education does not promote sexual activity but instead can offer pupils a safe space to engage with information about their changing bodies, desires, sexuality and sexual identities. The approaches taken are firmly embedded in pedagogy, and the teachers' knowledge of this is an important facet for successful RSE. Whilst the suggestions in this chapter relate to age groups, these are by no means static. The authors would like to highlight that the educator and the sessions should always be planned with the young people, to build on what they already know. In this educational space youth voice is invaluable.

Reflection Questions for You and Your Setting

- What topics or areas do you feel least confident teaching and what support do you need to develop your confidence and the confidence of other staff?
- How is sex education planned within your setting and how does this show a progression of content and skills?
- How is consent taught within your setting and how can we balance LGBT-inclusivity with cultural sensitivity?
- How do you involve the pupils in the design and content of their sessions?

Recommended Resources

- NSPCC: https://learning.nspcc.org.uk/research-resources/schools/relationships-health-and-sex-education-resources
- Sex Education Forum: https://www.sexeducationforum.org.uk
- Hoyle, A. & McGeeney, E. (2018), *Relationships and Sex Education (RSE) Lesson Ideas for the 21st Century*. London: Routledge.
- What's the debate: https://www.whatsthedebate.co.uk/
- Brook: https://www.brook.org.uk/resources/

References

Allen, L. (2011). *Young People and Sexuality Education: Rethinking Key Debates.* Basingstoke: Palgrave Macmillan.

Ashcraft, A. M. & Murray, P. J. (2017), Talking to parents about adolescent sexuality, *Paediatric Clinics of North America*, 64(2), pp. 305–20. https://doi.org/10.1016/j.pcl.2016.11.002

Buni C. (2013), The case for teaching kids 'vagina', 'penis', and 'vulva', *Atlantic*.

Burgess, M. C., Stermer, S. P. & Burgess, S. R. (2007), Sex, lies, and video games: The portrayal of male and female characters on video game covers, *Sex Roles*, 57, pp. 419–33. DOI: 10.1007/s11199-007-9250-0

Buss, D. (2002), Human mating strategies. *Samdunfsokonemen* (4), pp. 48–58.

Childnet (2019), Establishing a safe environment for a high quality PSHE lesson https://www.childnet.com/wp-content/uploads/2019/09/Establishing-a-safe-environment-for-a-high-quality-PSHE-lesson.pdf

Coy, M., Kelly, L., Vera-Gray, F., Garner, M. & Kanyeredzi, A. (2016), From 'No Means No' to 'An Enthusiastic Yes': Changing the Discourse on Sexual Consent through Sex and Relationships Education, in V. Sundaram & H. Sauntson (Eds) *Global Perspectives and Key Debates in Sex and Relationships Education: Addressing Issues of Gender, Sexuality, Plurality and Power* (pp. 84–99). Basingstoke: Palgrave Pivot.

DfE (2019), Relationships education, relationships and sex education (RSE) and health education. Available online: https://assets.publishing.service.gov.uk/government/uploads/system/uploads/attachment_data/file/1019542/Relationships_Education__Relationships_and_Sex_Education__RSE__and_Health_Education.pdf (accessed 22 May 2022).

Establishing a safe environment for a high quality PSHE lesson (2019), Available online: https://www.childnet.com/wp-content/uploads/2019/09/Establishing-a-safe-environment-for-a-high-quality-PSHE-lesson.pdf (accessed 26 June 2022).

Fishman S. (1982), The history of childhood sexuality. *Journal of Contemporary History*, 17(2), pp. 269–83. Doi: 10.1177/002200948201700204

Foucault, M. (1992a), *The History of Sexuality Vol. 1: The Will to Knowledge*, London: Penguin.

Foucault, M. (1992b), *The History of Sexuality Vol. 2: The Use of Pleasure*, London: Penguin.

Foucault, M. (1990), *The History of Sexuality Vol. 3: The Care of Self*, London: Penguin.

Gay, G. (2020), *Culturally Responsive Teaching: Theory, Research, and Practice*.

Hirst, J. (2013), 'It's got to be about enjoying yourself': Young people, sexual pleasure, and sex and relationships education, *Sex Education*, 13(4), pp. 423–36. DOI: 10.1080/14681811.2012.747433

Hoyle, A. & McGeeney, E. (2018), *Relationships and Sex Education (RSE) Lesson Ideas for the 21st Century*, London: Routledge.

Jacobson (2018), Available online: https://www.parentingni.org/wp-content/uploads/2018/05/Consent-article-PDF.pdf

Karsay, K., Knoll, J. & Matthes, J. (2018; 2017), Sexualizing media use and self-objectification: A meta-analysis, *Psychology of Women Quarterly*, 42(1), pp. 9–28.

King-Hill, S. (2021), Assessing sexual behaviours in children and young people: A realistic evaluation of the Brook Traffic Light tool, *Child Abuse Review*. https://doi.org/10.1002/car.2664

King-Hill, S. (2022), Knowledge translation and evidence-informed policy challenges: The implementation of the Brook Traffic Light Tool in Cornwall. *Journal of Sexual Aggression*. https://doi.org/10.1080/13552600.2022.2052770

King-Hill, S. & Woolley, R. (2017), *Sexual Behaviours and Development in Understanding Inclusion: Core Concepts, Policy and Practice*. Routledge-Cavendish. http://eprints.worc.ac.uk/6324/

King-Hill (2023), A student's guide to what you don't know. Available online: https://www.birmingham.ac.uk/schools/social-policy/departments/health-services-management-centre/research/a-students-guide-to-what-you-dont-know.aspx.

Hancock (2015) 'Have You Seen That Tea and Consent Video?' https://bishtraining.com/Have±you±seen±that±tea±and±consent±video

Lynch, T., Tompkins, J. E., van Driel, I. I., & Fritz, N. (2016), Sexy, strong, and secondary: A content analysis of female characters in video games across 31 years. *Journal of Communication*, 66, pp. 564–84. DOI: 10.1111/jcom.12237

Martellozzo, E., Monaghan, A., Davidson, J. & Adler, J. (2020), Researching the effects that online pornography has on U.K. adolescents Aged 11 to 16, *SAGE Open*, 10(1), pp. 215824401989946.

Metcalfe, J. (2017), Learning from errors, *Annual Review of Psychology*, 68(1), pp. 465–89.

Muehlenhard, C. L., Humphreys, T. P., Jozkowski, K. N. & Peterson, Z. D. (2016), The Complexities of Sexual Consent Among College Students: A Conceptual and Empirical Review cited in Willis et al.

No Outsiders (2010), Preparing children for life in modern Britain. Available online: no-outsiders.com (accessed 28 June 2022).

PSHE Association and National Chief Police council (2021), Police in the classroom: a handbook for the police and PSHE teachers. chrome-extension://efaidnbmnnnibpcajpcglclefindmkaj/https://fs.hubspotusercontent00.net/hubfs/20248256/Guidance/Documents/CYP%20police%20in%20the%20classroom%20handbook.pdf

Reynold, E., Milne, B., Bragg, S., Ringrose, J., Timperley, V., Young, H., McGeeney, E., Margolis, R., Hollis, V., & Gill, C. (2023), 'We Have to Educate Ourselves': How Young People are Learning about Relationships, Sex and Sexuality. London: NSPCC. https://learning.nspcc.org.uk/media/3138/sexuality-education-plus.pdf

Rudduck, J. & Demetriou, H., with Pedder, D. & the Network Project Team (2003), Student perspectives and teacher practices: The transformative potential. *McGill Journal of Education*, 38(2), pp. 274–88.

Sex Education Forum (2015), SRE – The evidence. Available online: https://www.sexeducationforum.org.uk/sites/default/files/field/attachment/Evidence%20infographic%20-%20RSE%20day_0.jpg (accessed 27 June 2020).

Stewart, R. (1995), *Philosophical Perspectives on Sex and Love*. New York: Oxford University Press.

Stonewall (2017), chrome-extension://efaidnbmnnnibpcajpcglclefindmkaj/https://www.stonewall.org.uk/system/files/the_school_report_2017.pdf

Whitehead, S. (2019), What Is Sex Positivity? *School of Sexuality Education*. https://schoolofsexed.org/blog-articles/2019/11/4/what-is-sex-positivity (accessed 10 July 2023).

Willis, M., Murray, N. K. & Jozkowski, N. K. (2021), Sexual consent in committed relationships: A dyadic study, *Journal of Sex & Marital Therapy*, 47(7), pp. 669–86. DOI: 10.1080/0092623X.2021.1937417

World Health Organization Sexual and Reproductive Health. (accessed on 30 June 2022); Available online: https://www.who.int/reproductivehealth/topics/sexual_health/sh_definitions/en/

11

Delivering RSE with SEND Pupils

Mel Gadd

Aims of This Chapter

- To explore why RSE is a vital part of your PSHE delivery with SEND pupils.
- To look at what can support effective RSE delivery with SEND pupils.
- To explore what can support you as the RSE practitioner.

Introduction

I have been delivering relationships and sex education (RSE) with young people with additional learning needs, learning disabilities and who are autistic for twenty years. 'A child or young person has special educational needs and disabilities if they have a learning difficulty and/or a disability that means they need special health and education support, we shorten this to SEND' (NHS England, 2015).

My experience is in delivering a targeted, needs-led RSE project that works with small groups of young people in educational and community settings. I co-design bespoke programmes with the students I work with and often work with the same students year on year, building on their skills and knowledge. In this chapter we will explore some of the building blocks to effective RSE delivery with SEND children and young people. These approaches and techniques are also applicable for young people who don't need special health or educational support; you can just add additional layers as appropriate.

Relationships and sex education is learning about the emotional, social and physical aspects of growing up, relationships, sex, gender, human sexuality and sexual health. Good-quality RSE equips children and young people with the information, skills and values to develop safe, fulfilling and enjoyable relationships and to take responsibility for their sexual health and wellbeing both now and in the future, whilst having due regard for friends, partners and other people.

In the UK, education is devolved, so England, Scotland, Wales and Northern Ireland will have a different approach; however, each approach is inclusive of SEND schools and pupils. In England it has been compulsory for relationships education to be delivered in primary settings (Key Stages 1 and 2) and relationships and sex education in secondary settings (Key Stages 3 and 4) since 2020. In September 2022 the Welsh Government brought in a new Relationships and Sexuality Code to support mandatory RSE in Wales. RSE is statutory for primary and secondary education in Northern Ireland, with schools free to design their own curriculum based on guidance and whilst relationships, sexual health and parenthood (RHSP) forms a key part of health and wellbeing delivery in Scotland, it is not currently compulsory.

Let us take a moment to consider what relationships and sex education may mean for the children, young people and families with whom you engage. Many people are concerned that RSE is all about teaching the biological and mechanical aspects of sex, will introduce children and young people to topics that they are not ready for and incite curiosity in inappropriate subjects. For the families and caregivers of individuals who are autistic or who have learning or intellectual disabilities, this concern may well last into adulthood.

Understanding what RSE really is and is not will help us communicate more effectively with parents and caregivers of children and young people. Anxiety about RSE stems from a desire to protect the child or young person and this is especially true if your young person is autistic or has learning disabilities. Imagining a future where your child might display or want to engage in sexual behaviour and/or relationships can be very much beyond your reach if you are dealing with the day-to-day work of parenting. Added to this, many parents and caregivers will not have had good experience of RSE themselves as they may not have been provided with it when they were at school, or their sex education may not have been delivered in a way that we now may consider good practice.

RSE and Safeguarding

'Children who are taught about preventing sexual abuse at school are more likely than others to tell an adult if they had or were actually experiencing sexual abuse' according to a Cochrane review in 2015. Sadly, evidence shows us that children and young people with learning disabilities are at about three times greater risk of sexual abuse and/or sexual assault than their non-disabled peers (Walsh, Zwi, Woolfenden, & Shlonsky, 2015). This is supported by Ward and Rodger (2018): 'There is also a consensus that disabled children are at a greater risk of sexual abuse than their non-disabled peers, and most estimates put this increased risk at around three times that of non-disabled children' (Ward & Rodger, 2018).

The reasons cited for this include:

- They are more dependent on adults and for a longer period of time
- They may be dependent on adults for intimate/personal care
- They may have been taught not to question people in authority
- It is more difficult for them to communicate what's happening to them
- They may be particularly trusting of adults
- They may be isolated from their family due to being institutionalized
- They may have a lack of sexual knowledge and awareness
- They may find it difficult to understand what has happened to them, or indeed realize that they are going through abuse

Although no individual should be responsible for their own protection when it comes to sexual violence, good relationships and sex education do contribute to safeguarding children and young people. Whether it is through teaching young people about consent, how to behave appropriately to others or providing a safe place and person to make a disclosure, we can all work together to make young people's lives safer.

However, it is worth reminding ourselves that a good relationships and sex education programme is always so much more than preventing the 'negative stuff' such as sexual abuse, unplanned and unwanted pregnancy and sexually transmitted infections. It links to other personal development and is an ongoing dialogue, not a one-off piece of work, creating a culture of responsibility and building a circle of resilience counteractive to negative influences. Sex and relationships topics are life skills and are best taught within the context of choice, respect and pleasure.

Prioritizing Inclusivity

Good relationships and sex education, by its very nature, explores the core attributes of inclusivity: rights, kindness, understanding and fairness. However in the past, RSE has not been inclusive enough. For example, until 2003 schools had to contend with Section 28, a law passed in 1988 that prevented schools from teaching about homosexuality. This meant that all sex education was only framed within heterosexual relationships and that young LGBTQ+ people had no education or validation of their sexual orientation and the information they may have needed to know to support healthy relationships and sex. Although repealed in 2003 its effects can still be seen today, with fear and protests about equal representation of same-sex relationships or of transgender identities from a vocal minority.

It is really important to apply the same level of inclusivity to your SEND practice as anyone working with students without learning disabilities. Why is inclusivity so important? Well people are really, really diverse: different ethnicities, gender and gender identities, sexual orientations, impairments and disabilities, religions and cultures. Students who are autistic and/or have learning disabilities are just as likely to have these characteristics as any other human being; however, these characteristics are often not seen as a primary focus for education and/or support. If we don't include representation of people within our education, then we won't engage them fully and even worse can lead them to feeling actively excluded and othered. Also, even if we don't work with very diverse groups of people, our students will need to see representations of a range of people who may live within their communities now or in the future.

Rights-Based Approach

It is absolutely vital to have a rights-based approach to RSE at the heart of your delivery. This is so important when working with SEND students. Many young people with disabilities, whether learning or physical, will not have equitable access to relationships and sex when they grow into adults. This could be due to the challenges of their disability, but more often it is due to societal assumptions about their ability to be sexual and/or in a loving relationship. As many as 70 per cent of adults without disabilities are living as part of a couple compared to 3 per cent of people with learning disabilities. Relationships and consenting sex are a human right and the students we work with need to know that this can be an option in their future.

Needs Assessments

Even though you will have a recommended RSE curriculum for the key stage with which you are working, always undertake a needs assessment before RSE delivery. As the statutory guidance for England tells us in the section on pupils with special educational needs and disabilities, 'high quality teaching that is differentiated and personalized will be the starting point to ensure accessibility'. (DfE, 2019)

Needs assessments are essential when working with SEND young people so we can co-plan our delivery to meet their unique needs and so they can achieve the outcomes we then set. The simplest way to conduct a needs assessment is to communicate with the young person or people and listen and observe what they are both telling you and not telling you and what gaps can you identify. SEND pupils may use a variety of communication methods and you can add RSE symbols and signs to these as needed. Needs assessments with students can take many forms, including:

- One-to-one or group discussions
- Quizzes
- Questionnaires
- Games

When working with SEND pupils I often extend the needs assessments wider to the staff that work with them at school and to their family and caregivers. You can then build up a fuller picture of the needs of the student. This can be particularly useful when the student has different communication abilities and those closest to them can support them to express themselves.

Developmental Stage and Age of Student

Within mainstream education it is fairly normal to have a Year 8 group and assume that they are all twelve to thirteen years old, and therefore have started or will be starting puberty and will have similar needs in regards to RSE topics. In SEND education however, we cannot make this assumption. Students of similar ages will have different developmental abilities and it is usual for there to be a wider range of ability, understanding and experience within a class. It will also be normal for a class to have a broader age range within it too, depending on the abilities of the students. Your needs assessment will take this into account and help you to plan content appropriate to the developmental stage of the student. I advocate a back-to-basics approach when delivering RSE with new students of any age as it can be really easy to assume they have basic knowledge of puberty if they are sixteen years old for example, but if they haven't received comprehensive RSE previously then this knowledge may be absent.

It is not uncommon to work with a group who tell you they already know about topics such as 'what sex is' but when you dig a little deeper you realize they don't know what it is at all. Because we commonly use euphemisms such as 'sleeping together' or 'going to bed with' when talking about sex, SEND students can think they have full understanding but really have a big gap in their knowledge. If you don't get told the information in a way you can understand, then how are you meant to know?

We also have to take into account the biological age of a student. Sometimes staff worry that information may be too advanced for a fourteen-year-old student who has the cognitive ability akin to key stage 1; however, their body will still be growing up and going through puberty and we have to tailor the content to someone who will be managing erections and may be getting the natural urge to masturbate. Ignoring biological changes and urges may mean that problematic behaviour, such as public masturbation, will be more challenging to address at an older age. Going through puberty without understanding that it is normal can also be really frightening for children and young people. No one should have to start their periods or have their voice change without some preparation beforehand.

The Language We Use

When working with SEND students and/or working with students with communication differences, it is really important to think about how you communicate about relationships and sex. How do you talk about sex? Do you commonly use euphemisms and analogies? Or do you speak about it plainly and factually? There is so much hidden meaning in the common language around sex, attraction and love that it can be really confusing for some people. And this really disadvantages them. It is our responsibility to cut through this and share information in the most effective and accessible way possible. I encourage you to practise talking about it as clearly as you can, say what it is, leave as little room for misunderstanding as possible and back this up with visual resources and/or models where appropriate. Whilst you are at it, practise saying things in a neutral or sex-positive way; think about what values or experiences you are bringing into the way you communicate about relationships and sex and how you can manage this within your explanations. This is something you can practise on your own or with colleagues; you can create a script for how to explain sensitive or tricky issues. Then your team can use the same explanations to support the RSE, and as long as these are explanations that are understood, this repetition and reinforcement will support the RSE delivery. It also has the benefit of providing a supported way of talking about these topics for staff who worry about what they can say or not.

Mixed-Sex and Single-Sex Work

Within SEND environments, as well as in wider education, staff often make the common mistake of favouring single-sex work without a thorough assessment of what young people really need to know, delivering contraception or menstruation sessions to young women only or condom or testicle self-examination sessions to young men only. This can lead to a lack of knowledge about the basics of what it means to be a young woman or man and also contributes to a culture of not talking about these issues in front of the opposite sex as if this knowledge is secret, dirty or somehow not their responsibility. As some SEND pupils will usually only learn about the difference in biological sexes if it is explicitly taught to them this needs to be taken into account. Single-sex teaching also assumes that everyone in the group is cisgender and doesn't take into account that trans-men may have periods or should go for cervical screening and that trans-women will need to be mindful of testicular care or prostate health.

In mixed-sex groups young people enjoy sharing their contrasting experiences and often directly challenge each other's assumptions about gender norms, yet in single-sex groups, sessions can be designed to focus on the needs of the sex you are working with and sometimes topics can be explored in more depth, and sometimes with more comfort.

Group Work and One-to-One

Group size can be a decisive factor in delivering successful relationships and sex education group work with SEND students. As I recommend using an active learning approach, this works best with small groups of people with similar abilities and understanding.

Some students will benefit from one-to-one education as their needs may not be met during a group experience or they need tailored support based on their behaviour. One-to-one sessions can feel more intimate, so it is still vital to set a working agreement, boundaries and learning outcomes for the session. I also recommend having an additional member of staff present in these sessions, not only for lone working procedures but to provide additional support to both the teacher and the pupil if needed.

Active Learning

Active learning methods are extremely effective in SEND relationships and sex education, especially for exploring feelings, practicing skills and discussing values. They allow young people to use experiential learning, build on what they already know, learn from each other and learn from the experience of trying something new out. Young people's knowledge, skills and attitudes are developed through using a range of teaching and learning approaches including participatory methods such as brainstorming, case studies, games, simulation and role-play. The nature of these activities enables young people to develop the core skills of communication, working with others and problem-solving, as well as negotiation, empathy, decision-making and investigation skills. Thus the processes involved in learning and its outcomes become as important as the content. However, practitioners must be sensitive to whether the group has the skills necessary to perform the tasks; otherwise, people in the group can feel unconfident or unchallenged. It's essential to communicate and check with the group what they feel happy doing.

Setting a Working Agreement

A working agreement is a key tool in delivering RSE. A working agreement, also known as ground rules or learning contract, is a set of instructions and boundaries created by all the group members that enable them to feel safe and comfortable when taking part in a group, thus allowing all people shared ownership of the learning process. On the face of it, it can feel like a simple and unnecessary exercise but the value of a well-crafted working agreement runs deep. First of all, by asking your group to participate in setting the 'rules' for your RSE you are engaging them in the ownership of the process and they feel listened to from the outset. This alone models good behaviour within interpersonal relationships. By exploring the boundaries and expectations in an RSE session you can introduce concepts such as confidentiality and personal responsibility for disclosure. Reminding the pupils that you are there to help keep them safe contributes to their engagement in the process but also signposts them to trusted adults if they do ever need to seek help or make a disclosure. A working agreement will also support the group process throughout the programme, as participants will support each other to stay within the agreed boundaries of the agreement.

Working agreements are usually created with a group discussion and the content written down, but these activities don't suit everyone. You could use visual images to represent content and create an agreement board or poster, or you could use BSL or Makaton to sign what has been agreed and video the working agreement to play at the start of each RSE session. Taking the time to create an accessible working agreement will pay off in the long run. Although your group does the heavy lifting of setting the working agreement, it is worth considering making sure these issues are raised and included if the group (including you) agree:

- Confidentiality: What does the group agree to in regards to confidentiality? What can staff agree to keep confidential and in what circumstances do they have to break confidentiality? What would happen then?
- Personal disclosure: How open does the group agree to be about personal experiences? Is this setting appropriate to sharing personal information? What personal responsibility do we need to have in choosing what we share? Who could you ask confidential questions to?
- Swearing and rude words: What language boundaries do the group want to place? Is it possible to discuss RSE without using words that some people may find explicit? If explicit language is used within the session, we must agree to not use it in other areas of the school or with younger people.

- Taking time out: Sometimes people need to take time out from participating in order to process information, or if it provokes strong feelings or reactions. Discuss how the group can manage this and enable someone to take some time out if they need to. Sometimes this is just sitting quietly and listening but not actively taking part and at other times this may be designating a separate space for someone to have a breather.

Suggested Session Structure

A RSE session could flow like this:

- Introductions (or a welcoming round if the group knows each other): This helps set the scene so that the participants start seeing themselves as a group
- Ice-breaker to get everyone in the habit of participating
- Information on the session content
- Negotiation of a working agreement or a reminder of what was previously agreed
- Session activities
- Processing the session: A group discussion to encourage the participants to think about what they have done during the activity and what links they can make back to real life outside of the session. There is also the opportunity for assessment here
- Evaluation: To get feedback on the session and to help the practitioner develop their practice
- Ending/closing activity: An activity designed to help close the session and the group to move on and get on with the rest of their day/evening without feeling that they haven't finished the session properly

The Resources We Use

Choosing appropriate resources to use with young people is very important. Care has to be taken when choosing resources, not just because resource budgets are often limited but also to ensure that they are relevant, accurate and meet the needs of your young people. It's likely that no one resource will meet all of your needs so a pick-and-mix approach tends to work best, with your own adaptations to make them relevant for use.

There are a wide range of resources available that support RSE to be delivered in a multitude of ways: visual resources, models, digital resources, written materials – the choice is out there. Your students will have individual communication needs, so a tailored approach works best; however, I often find that if a resource meets the needs of the individual with the most challenging communication needs within the room, then the other students can usually access it too.

In order for your delivery to be inclusive the resources you use should reflect a range of different experiences; all too often resources only show white, non-disabled, heterosexual younger people. Never assume that everyone in your group is heterosexual or cisgender, challenge stereotyping of different groups, never assume that everyone will be able-bodied or will remain so for their whole lives and never assume that everyone won't be or will be sexually active. I have a list of useful resources at the end of the chapter for inclusive delivery.

With practice it becomes easy to adapt relationships and sex education resources for your pupils' needs and use them in your own way. Useful tips for adapting resources include:

- Use image materials for a non-literate group or if you are running a bi-lingual session so that the written words don't exclude anyone
- Always read out any written instructions so that you make sure everyone understands
- Simplify an activity and reduce it down to the essential outcomes
- Always include a wide range of references, use the word partner instead of girl- or boyfriend, use images of people with disabilities and different ethnic groups

The Practitioner

So, you are the lucky member of staff about to deliver RSE to your SEND students? I do not say this lightly; delivering RSE to SEND students is a privilege and a joy. You will go through a journey together where you are both the teacher and the student and you will learn so much. There is no single formal qualification you can undergo that will magically make you into an RSE teacher, although there is a range of excellent training out there to help develop and support your practice. What you're like as a person is probably more important than what you know about sexual health, relationships and sexuality, as knowledge can be gained and built upon. Becoming an effective RSE teacher of SEND students takes a combination of motivation, practice, reflection and support from other people.

Training for Practitioners

Training, it should go without saying, is essential to the development of a relationships and sex education practitioner. Training can not only provide practitioners with the necessary underpinning knowledge but also explore and challenge attitudes and values and develop skills. Regularly updating knowledge, values and skills will help ensure that your practice remains relevant and fresh. There is a wealth of RSE training available, both in person and digital, and I have listed some course providers at the end of the chapter.

Your Support System

A support system for the practitioner is invaluable when delivering relationships and sex education. It is the nature of the work that interesting and challenging new situations constantly arise and it is healthy to seek support and guidance from colleagues and line managers. This is particularly true when working with SEND young people, when the approach has to be flexible and you may have more scrutiny from colleagues and parents about content, delivery and appropriateness. I always advise a team approach with RSE planning and delivery; you can then share the load and bounce ideas off each other. If a piece of work is likely to be too complex or explicit for the students, then the team can work together to achieve balance.

Having supportive work colleagues with whom you can share practice can be helpful on a day-to-day basis; however, scheduled support and supervision should always be prioritized. To ensure creativity and development, practitioners have said that they find it useful to have contact with other RSE practitioners – at meetings, in the workplace, attending seminars, both face to face and online and conferences. Sharing practice (without breaking confidentiality) will help the practitioner reflect on their delivery and what changes, if any, to make to future work.

There are many formal and informal support networks available to relationships and sex education practitioners. Some practitioners set up their own informal support network – meeting for coffee to discuss practice and share ideas can be an excellent form of support for developing good practice and many new ideas start off in this way. I have recommended some support networks at the end of the chapter.

Monitoring and Evaluation

In order to ensure that your RSE is relevant and on track it is important that your RSE is regularly evaluated, and that progress is monitored and experiences are shared. This process should involve young people, the practitioners, parents and caregivers and you can include wider circles of influence too such as support workers, school nurses, care staff, etc. Progress through a RSE programme can be measured by connecting your evaluation to the learning outcomes you set.

The most obvious way to find out what young people get out of the RSE programme is to ask them. Often SEND students are not asked to give feedback on their learning processes so listening to their opinions and feedback is an action that can support longer-term engagement. The participatory methods involved in active learning can allow opportunities for less- and pre-verbal young people to demonstrate what they have learnt and understood. Additional markers such as parental feedback and observed behaviours and/or attitudes can also be recorded. Evaluating the work and consulting with young people are important and, again, model good interpersonal relationship skills of checking in and giving weight to the young people's feelings and opinions. We gain valuable information that will help us improve our delivery and keep it fresh and engaging. There are a range of evaluation methods in the recommended resources, and using a range of methods will be more interesting and inclusive for your young people.

A good test of a successful session is to ask yourself if you are enjoying engaging with the RSE you are delivering. The chances are if the answer is no, then neither is the group!

Questions for Reflection for You and Your Setting

- Why do you want to deliver relationships and sex education?
- Is there a will to do this work? Does your school support you?
- Do you have the knowledge and skills to deliver this work? Do you need training? Can you shadow someone else for a while?
- Do you have someone to help you? Who is your team and what is your support structure?
- Do you have access to the resources you need?

Recommended Resources

Daisy & Desmond
A range of anatomical models and cloth puppets for use in RSE
Bodysense.org
Books beyond words
Books with no words addressing issues such as relationships, sexual abuse and sexual health
www.booksbeyondwords.co.uk
CHANGE accessible booklets

A series of booklets: Sex and Masturbation, My Pregnancy My Choice, Parenting, You and Your Baby, You and Your Child, Friendships and Relationships, LGBTQ+, Safe Sex and Contraception, Understanding Sexual Abuse

changepeople.org

Condom demonstrator

A blue plastic penis model for condom education. Also useful for masturbation education

FPA.org

Great Relationships and Sex Education. 200+ Activities for Educators Working with Young People

Hoyle, A. & McGeeney, E. 2020

Routledge, London

Jiwsi: A Pick 'n' Mix of Sex and Relationships Activities. Mel Gadd & Jo Hinchliffe, 2007, FPA – available as a free download from:

www.sexeducationcompany.org/adnoddai-a-linciauresources-and-links

Makaton Resource Vocabulary

Sex Education Signs & Sex Education Symbols

The Makaton Charity 2008

Masturbation, Autism and Learning Disabilities: A Guide for Parents and Professionals

Mel Gadd 2021 Jessica Kingsley Publishers

Picture Yourself 1 & 2

Hilary Dixon and Ann Craft, illustrations by David Gifford Me-and-us

Sets of line drawings and photographs for use in sex and relationships work

www.bodysense.org.uk

Online Pornography and Illegal Content – An Easy Read Guide

Developed by Care Management Group, CHANGE and Choice Support

choicesupport.org

Sexuality and Severe Autism. A practical guide for parents, caregivers and health educators.

Kate E Reynolds 2014

Jessica Kingsley Publishers

www.jkp.com

Talking Together … About Growing Up

Lorna Scott and Lesley Kerr-Edwards 2010

FPA

www.fpa.org.uk

Talking Together … About Sex and Relationships

Lorna Scott and Lesley Kerr-Edwards 2010

FPA

www.fpa.org.uk

What's Happening to Tom?
What's happening to Ellie?
Kate E Reynolds 2015 Jessica Kingsley Publishers
Brook www.brook.org.uk
Sex and relationships information, services and training for young people under twenty-five and for professionals
Cwmni Addysg Rhyw – Sex Education Company www.sexeducationcompany.org
RSE social enterprise working with young people with vulnerabilities and/or learning disabilities and with adults with learning disabilities. Provides project work, consultation and training. If you work in North Wales we also provide an RSE practitioners' network.
Claire Lightley Lightley Consulting clairewithwings@gmail.com
RSE Trainer and consultant, specializes in working with people with learning disabilities
Mencap www.mencap.org.uk
National charity supporting people with learning disabilities and their families
National Autistic Society www.autism.org.uk
National charity supporting autistic people and their families
The Proud Trust: https://www.theproudtrust.org/
Training and information for staff supporting LGBTQ+ young people
The Sex Factor: https://www.chf.org.uk/Sex_Factor_Brochure.pdf
Relationship and Sex Education for staff working with children and young people with complex neurodisabilities
Supported Loving:
https://www.choicesupport.org.uk/about-us/what-we-do/supported-loving
Supported Loving promotes positive relationships for people with learning disabilities and provides resources, training and a practitioner support group

References

Department for Education (2019), *Relationships Education, Relationships and Sex Education (RSE) and Health Education*. Available online: https://assets.publishing.service.gov.uk/government/uploads/system/uploads/attachment_data/file/1019542/Relationships_Education__Relationships_and_Sex_Education__RSE__and_Health_Education.pdf

Mencap (2019), *Sexuality and Relationships – What We Think*. Available online: https://www.mencap.org.uk/about-us/what-we-think/relationships-and-sex-what-we-think

NHS England (2015), *NHS England Special Educational Needs and Disability (SEND)*. England.nhs.uk. Available online: https://www.england.nhs.uk/learning-disabilities/care/children-young-people/send/

The National Archives (2011), *Local Government Act 1988*. Legislation.gov.uk. Available online: https://www.legislation.gov.uk/ukpga/1988/9/section/28/enacted

Walsh, K., Zwi, K., Woolfenden, S. & Shlonsky, A. (2015), School-Based Education Programmes for the Prevention of Child Sexual Abuse, *Cochrane Database of Systematic Reviews* (4). DOI: 10.1002/14651858.cd004380.pub3

Ward, M. & Rodger, H. (2018), *Child Sexual Abuse in Residential Schools: A Literature Review Independent Inquiry into Child Sexual Abuse*. IICSA Research Team. Available online: https://www.iicsa.org.uk/key-documents/7747/view/child-sexual-abuse-residential-schools%3A-a-literature-review-november-2018.pdf

12

Image Sharing and Digital Resilience

Emily Setty and Victoria-Marie Pugh

Aims of This Chapter

- To consider how digital criticality and resilience can be developed through PSHE.
- To consider the nature of contemporary youth digital sexual culture, as pertains the practice of sexual image sharing among young people and understand the contexts in which image sharing takes place.
- To explore the distinctions between abusive/non-consensual sharing and developmentally normative practices of 'digital intimacies'.

Introduction

Now more than ever, young people communicate, express themselves and learn about the world around them from online or social media sources. Given the complexities of these sources, it is important that we support our young people to develop criticality and resilience so they can navigate, cope with and benefit from their experiences online. According to the UK Council for Child Internet Safety (2020), 'Digital resilience is the ability to understand when you are at risk online, knowing what to do if anything goes wrong, and being able to recover from difficulties or upsets.' Manning (2021) develops this idea further by stating that 'digital resilience is developed through four connected elements: understanding when you are at risk, knowing what to do to seek help, learning from experiences, and having appropriate support to recover'. This process may not be as simple as teaching each one in sequence but needs to be continually revisited throughout the curriculum.

The guidance document 'Education for a Connected World' (UK *Council for Internet Safety*, 2020) provides a framework for ways to equip young people for a digital life and explores eight key areas. Its goal is not only to support the teaching of online safety but to go beyond these basics to promote safe and empowering behaviours which link to the wider aspects of PSHE such as community, but also to healthy relationships and online reputation.

1   Self-image and identity
2   Online relationships
3   Online reputation
4   Online bullying
5   Managing online information
6   Health, wellbeing and lifestyle
7   Privacy and security
8   Copyright and ownership

For the purposes of this chapter, we will be focusing on digital sexual image sharing, and ways to support digital criticality and promote digital resilience. It goes without saying that there are many more areas to cover to create a relevant and meaningful media literacy curriculum and there will be signposts to useful resources at the end of the chapter to support this.

Digital Sexual Image Sharing

Teaching about digital sexual image sharing among young people is stipulated as part of the Department for Education (DfE) statutory guidance for schools on Relationships, Sex, and Health Education (RSHE) (DfE, 2019). The guidance directs schools to teach about 'online and media'. The learning outcomes in this category that have implications for teaching about digital sexual image sharing include for pupils to know about 'their rights, responsibilities, and opportunities online, including that the same expectations of behaviour apply in all contexts, including online'. At the same time, it also requires pupils to know that 'any material someone provides to another has the potential to be shared online … [and] not to provide material to others that they would not want shared further … ' This lack of privacy rights online does not reflect what is typically expected in offline interactions and, therefore, indicates that online interactions come with a distinct set of rights and responsibilities (Setty and Dobson, in press). The guidance also states that pupils are to know 'what to do and where to get support to report material or manage issues online' and 'that creating and viewing indecent images of children (including those created by children) is a criminal offence which carries severe penalties including jail'.

A vast body of evidence has accumulated regarding the nature of digital sexual image sharing among youth, as well as how best to intervene to prevent and respond to the issue. This includes numerous surveys conducted in the UK and other countries to estimate the prevalence of image sharing. Findings vary, but a meta-analysis found that 14.8 per cent of young people report sending images and 27.4 per cent report receiving them, with rates increasing with age (Madigan et al., 2018). This meta-analysis also found that 12 per cent of young people say they have forwarded an image without consent and 8.4 per cent say that they have had their own image forwarded without consent. There is, therefore, a substantial proportion of young people directly involved in image sharing, including non-consensual sharing. It seems not to be normative, in the sense that not all young people are taking and sharing images. As will be seen below, however, studies indicate that the phenomenon is *normalized* in young people's 'post-digital' youth sexual cultures and that abusive behaviours take place within gender inequitable peer social contexts. These contexts create conditions of risk and harm for young people that need to be addressed in RSHE.

Young people's socio-sexual development and lives have been transformed by contemporary digital media. Their experiences are both individually heterogenous and shaped by social and cultural dynamics. While the practices may seem new, however, there is a need to connect the risks and challenges that young people face in digital contexts to non-digital contexts and conceive of 'post-digital' intimacies whereby the distinctions between online and offline are blurred and (re)mediated by one another. There is a need for schools to create open lines of dialogue about young people's perspectives and experiences, free from blame, shame or punishment, and deep critical engagement with the norms and expectations that shape young people's choices, actions, and experiences in sexualized digital environments.

While technology provides a tool for self-expression, experimentation and discovery, it also, through its affordances, creates new conditions for potentially harmful experiences and practices. The technology should not be unduly maligned in these regards; instead, young people should be educated in 'digital sexual citizenship' (Albury, 2017) in which the focus is on youth sexual culture itself and how young people operate and make decisions for themselves and one another from an ethical perspective.

Abusive image sharing has, however, been conceived of as part of a continuum of 'digital intimacies' for youth, which also comprises normative behaviours and experiences of using digital platforms to forge connection, build intimacy and manage interpersonal relationships (McGeeney and Hanson, 2017). It involves a wide range of online behaviours and practices including sexually explicit image sharing; taking and sharing selfies; flirting and meeting partners; and creating, accessing and circulating sexual content online (Scott et al., 2020). Digital intimacies may not be inherently harmful for youth (see Wolak and Finkelhor, 2011). Research indicates that young people participate in image sharing for various reasons, not always sexual, and can experience it positively (Anastassiou, 2017; Cooper et al., 2016). Digital technology seems, therefore, to be part of how young people form positive relationships and healthy sexual development including how they express themselves and build intimacy, sometimes as an alternative to physical sex (British Pregnancy Advisory Service, 2018; Katz and Asam, 2020; Phippen, 2017; McGeeney and Hanson, 2017; Vanwesenbeek et al., 2018).

Some evidence suggests that consensual image sharing is more common among young people than aggravated or abusive sharing (Bianchi et al., 2016, 2017). Youth digital sexual culture is, however, complex and characterized by 'grey areas' of subtle, indirect pressures and expectations in the absence of direct pressure, force or coercion (Cooper et al., 2016; Garcia-Gomez, 2017; Ringrose et al., 2012; Setty, 2019, 2020b; Thomas, 2018). Extensive evidence shows that girls are disproportionately likely to be victims of and boys are disproportionately likely to be perpetrators of non-consensual and abusive image sharing behaviours (e.g. see Ringrose et al., 2021a, 2021b; Setty et al., in press). This evidence shows that girls are also more likely to experience negative impacts of abuse and to blame themselves for abuse and are less likely to report their experiences.

For boys, meanwhile, image sharing can affirm their masculinity, increase their social status and support peer bonding (Coffey and Roberts, 2021; Ringrose et al., 2021a, 2021b; Setty, 2019, 2020a; Symons et al., 2018). They have been found to share images of girls to obtain social reward and capital, thus facilitating non-consensual further sharing of the images (Berndtsson and Odenbring, 2020, p.6; also see De Keseredy and Schwartz, 2016; Setty et al., in press). Boys do, however, also face some risks. While there is less perceived stigma around male bodily expression, studies have found that some boys have faced marginalization and shaming, for example, as 'unattractive', 'desperate' or 'creepy', but that this is often trivialized as 'banter' (Ravn et al., 2021; Ringrose and Harvey, 2015; Setty, 2020a, 2020b). This context means that some boys say they would not share images themselves.

It is important, nevertheless, to avoid the heteronormativity that typically pervades narratives surrounding youth sexual image sharing, whereby the issue is conceived of just in terms of abusive power dynamics between boys and girls. A UK study indicates that significantly more non-binary and bisexual youth begin romantic relationships online and significantly more gay and bisexual young people had asked someone out online compared to those who were heterosexual (McGeeney and Hanson, 2017). Other studies show that image sharing is more common among LGBT+ compared to heterosexual and cis-gender young people (Gámez-Guadix et al., 2015; Gámez-Guadix and de Santisteban, 2018; Van Ouystel et al., 2020). These differences may be because LGBT+ youth use social media more and may be more likely to consider it a safe space. Bauermeister et al. (2014) found that young gay and bisexual men engage in more consensual sharing than heterosexual. It has been argued that LGBT+ individuals may be more accepting of consensual sharing in sexual and romantic life.

A stronger articulation of the distinction between consensual and non-consensual image sharing can be made with age and should be developed across the key stages. It also foregrounds youth agency and autonomy and can challenge notions that abusive behaviours are determined by technology rather than by individual choice and decision-making. It can support empathy, perspective taking, and prosocial bystander intervention and the development of positive digital footprints. Developing this idea of autonomy and empowerment can support the continued development of digital resilience by providing the pupil with the tools to be able to make decisions about their own actions online or through sharing of images or often just promote the need to stop and think before acting.

What Does This Look Like in the Classroom?

The PSHE curriculum creates an ideal opportunity for pupils to explore the challenges and opportunities which digital spaces can offer. Although work around what information to share, keeping passwords and personal information safe and respectful communication online is often covered in primary schools, it is essential that these concepts are built upon and relevant topics explored within secondary and college settings.

In terms of creating a spiral curriculum throughout your setting, the initial building blocks pertain to general rights and responsibilities online and the normative contexts that may impact young people's abilities to exercise their rights and may cause young people to behave harmfully and irresponsibly and to blame victims of abuse. The nuances and complexities of these cultural processes and social norms as well as gender norms can be further explored and unpacked in terms of the specifics of the continuum of digital intimacies as young people progress into subsequent key stages.

Education around digital sexual image sharing should take place early in KS3 to equip young people with the skills, competences and outlooks they require for navigating contemporary digital sexual cultures safely and ethically. This needs to begin with a clear articulation of rights and responsibilities regarding privacy and consent online and the obligations that young people have to behave respectfully towards one another. Lessons which clearly explore a range of scenarios and situations of consent and what it looks like should be integrated into lesson discussions and opportunities or exploration of a range of outcomes planned. For example, using activities that encourage pupils to reflect on the things they do online, the ways they interact and how this makes them feel can be a useful way for pupils to identify situations which are positive for them and those which pose challenges or encourage negative feelings.

Lessons should also address online sexual harassment and sexualized and gender-based bullying among young people, with clear messaging about what is and is not acceptable. This can be linked with protected characteristics and work around the Equality Act (2010). It should also address the gender and sexual norms that shape digital sexual culture and specifically challenge the attitudes that underpin abuse. Often these lessons can be introduced through the use of scenarios, pictures or fake text conversations in order for pupils to safely discuss key issues through a distanced approach rather than using personal anecdotes.

Going into Key Stages 4 and 5, young people can continue to be educated about the continuum of digital sexual behaviours and can start to explore the distinction between consensual and non-consensual behaviours. Education can focus on strengthening their digital sexual citizenship in terms of their ability to identify their own boundaries and respect those of others. Throughout, it is imperative to avoid overly legalistic or abstract and decontextualized educational approaches and messages. Instead, RSHE needs to engage with the realities of youth digital sexual culture and support young people to navigate the complexities and 'grey areas' of what they may encounter and experience. A key aspect of this approach is to challenge and avoid perpetuating all forms of shame, stigma and victim blaming and focus on creating dialogue and the conditions for young people to report any experiences of abuse.

Wider PSHE sessions can also explore the ways in which advertising, fake news and photo editing can be experienced by young people and the tools they can use to make choices about how they want their data to be used or which adverts they want to see. Organizations such as Media Smart provide useful information for teachers and pupils as well as resources and videos to support aspects of life online.

By the end of Key Stage 5, pupils should understand the distinctions between consensual and non-consensual image sharing and should have an appreciation of the nuanced nature of consent whereby pressures and expectations may be subtle and indirect. They should be ready and able to challenge victim blaming and the stigma and shame directed to vulnerable groups. They should be knowledgeable about the options for reporting and seeking support and should feel confident to pursue these options. Encouraging the development of critical awareness of social norms that shape contemporary digital intimacies and the role they can play in tackling the normative contexts that create conditions of risk for young people is a vital area and links strongly to safeguarding. SEND pupils may be at heightened risk of harm in online sexual culture and RSHE needs to sensitively tackle the issue without reifying SEND pupils as inherently vulnerable in an overly protectionist approach. Instead, and as is the case for all young people, these pupils need to be equipped to navigate contemporary digital life safely and to understand how to identify and report abuse.

The Project deShame (2017) survey found that the top barriers to reporting online sexual harassment were being too embarrassed, worrying about what would happen next, and worrying about being targeted by those involved. When asked specifically why they would not seek help from a teacher, the most common response was that they were worried that their school would overreact. Jorgensen et al. (2019, p.32) likewise found that young people want trustworthy and secure avenues for reporting abusive image sharing and some said they were 'too embarrassed' to report their experiences and described teachers as 'awkward'. They expressed a preference for more personal and communicative approaches rather than teachers or parenting 'shouting' or 'having a go' at them (2019, p.35). Other research similarly identifies the value of youth-led and participatory solutions and making available a range of options for support while respecting privacy and avoiding judgement and victim blaming (Quayle and Cariola, 2019). It may be that this personal approach can be achieved through specific PSHE lessons which cover signposting external agencies in addition to quality pastoral care.

These issues with educating about image sharing were highlighted in the Ofsted review into sexual abuse in schools (Ofsted, 2021). It is important, therefore, for RSHE to identify abusive behaviours and seek to engender ethical digital sexual cultures among youth (Albury, 2017; Dobson, 2019). Young people report wanting practical advice to help them deal with real life situations that focus on helpful competences in terms of managing their relationships online (Katz and Asam, 2020; McGeeney and Hanson, 2017; Phippen, 2017; Setty, 2020). Döring (2014) describes a 'safer sexting approach' as aiming to foster young people's individual skills in resisting peer pressure and making conscious decisions about if, when, how and with whom to have sex and/or to sext consensually and responsibly. Albury (2017) similarly argues that educators should focus on developing students' skills in recognizing and negotiating affirmative consent. This involves promoting the model that 'no' is the default and that both parties need to engage in a process of establishing voluntary, meaningful and explicit consent. It requires a participatory approach on the part of learners, who must be part of identifying problems and solutions (Jorgensen et al., 2019; Lee et al., 2018).

Conclusion

It is important that online resources and social media are not villianized as for many pupils this is a key source of mental health support, communication with friends and support with academic work. It is also important, however, that teachers ensure that they have the necessary skills to be able to navigate the risks and challenges which they may face and that a strong and spiral digital literacy curriculum is in place.

Reflection Questions for You and Your Setting

- How does your setting develop digital resilience within PSHE and/or the wider curriculum?
- What different forms does digital sexual image sharing take and what might be the motivations for participating in different image sharing behaviours (consensual and non-consensual)?
- What roles do young people play in image sharing culture, including but beyond those directly involved in taking and sharing an image?
- What other messages do young people need to hear about image sharing, beyond 'just say no' and 'sexting is wrong/illegal or stupid'?

Recommended Resources

Teaching toolkit by Project deShame based on research with young people about online sexual abuse and harassment. The research covered perspectives on topics concerning non-consensual sharing of intimate images and videos, exploitation, coercion and threats, sexualized bullying and unwanted sexualization. The toolkit focuses on reporting while encouraging young people to discuss ways to challenge harmful online behaviour with the use of films, audio stories and workshops. https://www.childnet.com/what-we-do/our-projects/project-deshame/i-am-an-educator/

Suite of resources including workshop slides and school policy suggestions to tackle sexual harassment and image-based sexual abuse, co-created by UCL and the School of Sexuality Education with the Association of School and College Leaders. The resources aim to challenge online and offline sexual violence and create conditions for young people to engage in change. https://www.ascl.org.uk/Microsites/IBSHA/Resources

The School of Sexuality Education offers a range of policies available for tackling online sexual harassment via a whole school approach. The charity offers an extensive range of training and in-school workshops on all topics on the RSHE curriculum (including digital sexual image sharing) and offers policy and guidance documents for school leaders. https://schoolofsexed.org/guidance-for-schools

References

Albury, K. (2014), Porn and sex education, porn as sex education, *Porn Studies*, 1(1–2), pp. 172–81.

Albury, K. (2017), Just because it's public doesn't mean it's any of your business: Adults' and children's sexual rights in digitally mediated spaces, *New Media and Society*, 19(5), pp. 713–25.

Anastassiou, A. (2017), Sexting and young people: A review of the qualitative literature, *The Qualitative Report*, 22(8), pp. 2231–9.

Barter, C., Stanley, N., Wood, M., Lanau, A., Aghtaie, N., Larkins, C. & Øverlien, C. (2017), Young people's online and face-to-face experiences of interpersonal violence and abuse and their subjective impact across five European countries, *Psychology of Violence*, 7(3), pp. 375.

Bauermeister, J. A., Yeagley, E., Meanley, S. & Pingel, E. S. (2014), Sexting among young men who have sex with men: Results from a national survey, *Journal of Adolescent Health*, 54(5), pp. 606–11.

Berndtsson, K. H. & Odenbring, Y. (2020), 'They don't even think about what the girl might think about it': Students' views on sexting, gender inequalities and power relations in school, *Journal of Gender Studies*, 30(1), pp. 91–101.

Bianchi, D., Morelli, M., Baiocco, R. & Chirumbolo, A. (2016), Psychometric properties of the Sexting Motivations Questionnaire for adolescents and young adults, *Rassegna di Psicologia*, 33(3), pp. 5–18.

Bianchi, D., Morelli, M., Baiocco, R. & Chirumbolo, A. (2017), Sexting as the mirror on the wall: Body-esteem attribution, media models, and objectified-body consciousness, *Journal of Adolescence*, 61, pp. 164–72.

Brenick, A., Flannery, K. M., & Rankin, E. (2017), Victimization or entertainment? How attachment and rejection sensitivity relate to sexting experiences, evaluations, and victimization, in Wight, M.F. (Ed.), *Identity, Sexuality, and Relationships Among Emerging Adults in the Digital Age* (pp. 203–25). Hershey: Information Science Reference/IGI Global.

British Pregnancy Advisory Service. (2018), *Social Media, SRE, and Sensible Drinking: Understanding the Dramatic Decline in Teenage Pregnancy*, Straford-Upon-Avon: BPAS. Available online: https://www.bpas.org/media/3037/bpas-teenage-pregnancy-report.pdf

Casas, J. A., Ojeda, M., Elipe, P. & Del Rey, R. (2019), Exploring which factors contribute to teens' participation in sexting, *Computers in Human Behavior*, 100, pp. 60–9.

Choi, K. S., Cho, S. & Lee, J. R. (2019), Impacts of online risky behaviors and cybersecurity management on cyberbullying and traditional bullying victimization among Korean youth: Application of cyber-routine activities theory with latent class analysis, *Computers in Human Behavior*, 100, pp. 1–10.

Clancy, E. M., Klettke, B. & Hallford, D. J. (2019), The dark side of sexting – Factors predicting the dissemination of sexts, *Computers in Human Behavior*, 92, pp. 266–72.

Cooper, K., Quayle, E., Jonsson, L. & Svedin, C. G. (2016), Adolescents and self-taken sexual images: A review of the literature, *Computers in Human Behavior*, 55, pp. 706–16.

Crofts, T., Lee, M., McGovern, A. & Milivojevici, S. (2015), *Sexting and Young People*, Basingstoke: Palgrave Macmillan.

DeKeseredy, W. S. & Schwartz, M. D. (2016), Thinking sociologically about image-based sexual abuse, *Sexualization, Media, and Society*, 2(4), pp. 1–8.

de Ridder, S. (2017), Social media and young people's sexualities: Values, norms, and battlegrounds, *Social Media and Society*, 3(4), pp. 1–11.

Department for Education (DfE) (2019), *Statutory Guidance on RSE for Schools in England*, London: DfE. Available online: https://www.gov.uk/government/publications/relationships-education-relationships-and-sex-education-rse-and-health-education

Department for Education (DfE) (2021), *Sexual Violence and Sexual Harassment between Children in Schools and Colleges*, London: DfE. Available online: https://assets.publishing.service.gov.uk/government/uploads/system/uploads/attachment_data/file/1014224/Sexual_violence_and_sexual_harassment_between_children_in_schools_and_colleges.pdf

Dobson, A. S. & Ringrose, J. (2016), Sext education: Pedagogies of sex, gender and shame in the schoolyards of tagged and exposed, *Sex Education*, 16(1), pp. 8–21.

Dobson, A. S. (2018), Sexting, intimate and sexual media practices, and social justice in schools, in A. S. Dobson, N. Carah, & B. Robards (Eds.), *Digital Intimate Publics and Social Media* (pp. 93–110), Cham: Palgrave Macmillan.

Dobson, A. S. (2019), 'The things you didn't do': Gender, slut-shaming, and the need to address sexual harassment in narrative resources responding to sexting and cyberbullying, in H. Vandebosch, & L. Green (Eds.), *Narratives in Research and Interventions on Cyberbullying among Young People* (pp. 147–60), Cham: Springer.

Döring, N. (2014), Consensual sexting among adolescents: Risk prevention through abstinence education or safer sexting, *Cyberpsychology: Journal of Psychosocial Research on Cyberspace*, 8(1), p. 9.

Firmin, C. E. (2020), School rules of (sexual) engagement: government, staff and student contributions to the norms of peer sexual-abuse in seven UK schools, *Journal of Sexual Aggression*, 26(3), pp. 289–301.

Gámez-Guadix, M. & De Santisteban, P. (2018), 'Sex pics?': Longitudinal predictors of sexting among adolescents, *Journal of Adolescent Health*, 63(5), pp. 608–14.

Gámez-Guadix, M., Almendros, C., Borrajo, E. & Calvete, E. (2015), Prevalence and association of sexting and online sexual victimization among Spanish adults. *Sexuality Research and Social Policy*, 12(2), pp. 145–54.

García-Gómez, A. (2017), Teen girls and sexual agency: Exploring the intrapersonal and intergroup dimensions of sexting. *Media, Culture and Society*, 39(3), pp. 391–407.

Grobbelaar, M. & Guggisberg, M. (2018). Sexually explicit images: Examining the lawful and unlawful new forms of sexual engagement. In M. Guggisberg & J. Henricksen (Eds.), *Violence against Women in the 21st Century: Challenges and Future Directions* (pp. 133–60), Hauppage, NY: Nova Science Publishers.

Harder, S. K. (2021), The emotional bystander – sexting and image-based sexual abuse among young adults, *Journal of Youth Studies*, 24(5), pp. 655–69.

Harvey, J. & Ringrose, J. (2016), Competition, accountability and performativity: Exploring schizoid neo-liberal 'equality objectives' in a UK primary school. In: E. Reimers & L. Martinsson (Eds.), *Education and Political Subjectivities in Neoliberal Times and Places* (pp. 63–81). London: Routledge.

Henry, N. & Powell, A. (2018), Technology-facilitated sexual violence: A literature review of empirical research. *Trauma, Violence, and Abuse*, 19(2), pp. 195–208.

Henry, N., Flynn, A. & Powell, A. (2018), Policing image-based sexual abuse: Stakeholder perspectives. *Police Practice and Research*, 19(6), pp. 565–81.

Jørgensen, C. R., Weckesser, A., Turner, J. & Wade, A. (2019), Young people's views on sexting education and support needs: Findings and recommendations from a UK-based study. *Sex Education*, 19(1), pp. 25–40.

Katz, A. & El Asam, A. (2020), Look at me: Teens, sexting and risks, *Internet Matters*. Available online: https://www.internetmatters.org/wp-content/uploads/2020/06/Internet-Matters-Look-At-Me-Report-1.pdf

Krieger, M. A. (2017), Unpacking 'sexting': A systematic review of nonconsensual sexting in legal, educational, and psychological literatures, *Trauma, Violence, and Abuse*, 18(5), pp. 593–601.

Lee, N., Hewett, A., Rübner Jørgensen, C., Turner, J., Wade, A. & Weckesser, A. (2018). Children and sexting: The case for intergenerational co-learning, *Childhood*, 25(3), pp. 385–99.

Lippman, J. R. & Campbell, S. W. (2014), Damned if you do, damned if you don't … if you're a girl: Relational and normative contexts of adolescent sexting in the United States, *Journal of Children and Media*, 8(4), pp. 371–86.

Lloyd, J. (2019), Response and interventions into harmful sexual behaviour in schools. *Child Abuse and Neglect*, 94, p. 104037.

Madigan, S., Ly, A., Rash, C. L., Van Ouytsel, J. & Temple, J. R. (2018), Prevalence of multiple forms of sexting behavior among youth: A systematic review and meta-analysis. *JAMA Pediatrics*, 172(4), pp. 327–35.

Marcotte, A. S., Gesselman, A. N., Fisher, H. E. & Garcia, J. R. (2020), Women's and men's reactions to receiving unsolicited genital images from men. *Journal of Sex Research*, 58(4), pp. 1–10.

McGeeney, E. & Hanson, E. (2017), *Digital Romance: A Research Project Exploring Young People's Use of Technology in Their Romantic Relationships and Love Lives*, London: National Crime Agency and Brook. Available online: https://www.basw.co.uk/system/files/resources/basw_85054-7.pdf

McGlynn, C. & Rackley, E. (2017), Image-based sexual abuse. *Oxford Journal of Legal Studies*, 37(3), pp. 534–61.

McGlynn, C., Rackley, E. & Houghton, R. (2017), Beyond 'revenge porn': The continuum of image-based sexual abuse. *Feminist Legal Studies*, 25(1), pp. 25–46.

Naezer, M. & van Oosterhout, L. (2021), Only sluts love sexting: youth, sexual norms and non-consensual sharing of digital sexual images. *Journal of Gender Studies*, 30(1), pp. 79–90.

Phippen, A. (2017), Young people and digital lives, In A. Phippen (Ed.), *Children's Online Behaviour and Safety* (pp. 43–62), London: Palgrave Macmillan.

Project deShame (2017), *Young People's Experiences of Online Sexual Harassment: A Cross-Country Report from Project deShame*, London: Childnet. Available online: https://www.scie-socialcareonline.org.uk/young-peoples-experiences-of-online-sexual-harassment-a-cross-country-report-from-project-deshame/r/a110f00000RCyeaAAD

Quayle, E. & Cariola, L. (2019), Management of non-consensually shared youth-produced sexual images: A Delphi study with adolescents as experts. *Child Abuse and Neglect*, 95, p. 104064.

Ravn, S., Coffey, J. & Roberts, S. (2021), The currency of images: Risk, value and gendered power dynamics in young men's accounts of sexting. *Feminist Media Studies*, 21(2), pp. 315–31.

Ricciardelli, R., & Adorjan, M. (2019), 'If a girl's photo gets sent around, that's a way bigger deal than if a guy's photo gets sent around': Gender, sexting, and the teenage years, *Journal of Gender Studies*, 28(5), pp. 563–77.

Ringrose, J., Gill, R., Livingstone, S. & Harvey, L. (2012). A qualitative study of children, young people and 'sexting': A report prepared for the NSPCC. Available online: https://eprints.lse.ac.uk/44216/1/__Libfile_repository_Content_Livingstone%2C%20 S_A%20qualitative%20study%20of%20children%2C%20young%20people%20 and%20%27sexting%27%20%28LSE%20RO%29.pdf

Ringrose, J. & Harvey, L. (2015), Boobs, back-off, six packs and bits: Mediated body parts, gendered reward, and sexual shame in teens' sexting images *Continuum Journal of Media and Cultural Studies*, 29(2), pp. 205–17.

Ringrose, J., Regehr, K. & Whitehead, S. (2021a). Teen girls' experiences negotiating the ubiquitous dick pic: Sexual double standards and the normalization of image based sexual harassment. *Sex Roles*, 85, pp. 558–76.

Ringrose, J., Whitehead, S. & Regehr, K. (2021b), 'Wanna trade?': Cisheteronormative homosocial masculinity and the normalization of abuse in youth digital sexual image exchange. *Journal of Gender Studies*, 31(2), pp. 243–61.

Scott, R.H., Smith, C., Formby, E., Hadley, A., Hallgarten, L., Hoyle, A., Marston, C., McKee, A. & Tourountsis, D. (2020), What and how: Doing good research with young people, digital intimacies, and relationships and sex education. *Sex Education*, 20(6), pp. 675–91.

Setty, E. (2018), Young people's attributions of privacy rights and obligations in digital sexting culture. *International Journal of Communication*, 12, pp. 4533–52.

Setty, E. (2019), Meanings of bodily and sexual expression in youth sexting culture: Young women's negotiation of gendered risks and harms, *Sex Roles*, 80(9), pp. 586–606.

Setty, E. (2020a), 'Confident' and 'hot' or 'desperate' and 'cowardly'? Meanings of young men's sexting practices in youth sexting culture. *Journal of Youth Studies*, 23(5), pp. 561–77.

Setty, E. (2020b), *Risk and Harm in Youth Sexting Culture: Young People's Perspectives*. London: Routledge.

Setty, E. & Dobson, E. (2023), Department for education statutory guidance for relationships and sex education in England: A rights-based approach? *Arch Sex Behav*, 52, pp. 79–93. https://doi.org/10.1007/s10508-022-02340-5

Setty, E., Ringrose, J. & Regehr, K. (in press), Digital sexual violence and the gendered constraints of consent in youth image sharing, in M. Horvarth, & J. Brown (Eds.), *Rape: A Challenge to Contemporary Thinking – 10 Years on*. London.

Strassberg, D. S., Cann, D. & Velarde, V. (2017), Sexting by high school students. *Archives of Sexual Behavior*, 46(6), pp. 1667–72.

Symons, K., Ponnet, K., Walrave, M. & Heirman, W. (2018), Sexting scripts in adolescent relationships: Is sexting becoming the norm? *New Media and Society*, 20(10), pp. 3836–57.

Thomas, S. E. (2018), 'What should I do?': Young women's reported dilemmas with nude photographs, *Sexuality Research and Social Policy*, 15(2), pp. 192–207.

Tolman, D. L., Anderson, S. M. & Belmonte, K. (2015), Mobilizing metaphor: Considering complexities, contradictions and contexts in adolescent girls' and young women's sexual agency. *Sex Roles*, 73(7), pp. 298–310.

UK Council for Internet Safety (2020), *Sharing Nudes and Semi-Nudes: Advice for Education Settings Working with Children and Young People. DCMS and UK Council for Internet Safety*. Available online: https://www.gov.uk/government/publications/sharing-nudes-and-semi-nudes-advice-for-education-settings-working-with-children-and-young-people

van Ouytsel, J., Walrave, M., De Marez, L., Vanhaelewyn, B. & Ponnet, K. (2020), A first investigation into gender minority adolescents' sexting experiences. *Journal of Adolescence*, 84, pp. 213–18.

Vanwesenbeeck, I., Ponnet, K., Walrave, M. & Ouytsel, J. V. (2018). Parents' role in adolescents' sexting behaviour. In: M. Walrave, J. van Ouystel, K. Ponnet, & J. Temple (Eds.), *Sexting* (pp. 63–80), Cham: Palgrave Macmillan.

Wolak, J., & Finkelhor, D. (2011), *Sexting: A Typology*, Durham, NH: Crimes against Children Research Center. Available online: https://scholars.unh.edu/cgi/viewcontent.cgi?article=1047&context=ccrc

Wolak, J., Finkelhor, D., Walsh, W. & Treitman, L. (2018), Sextortion of minors: Characteristics and dynamics. *Journal of Adolescent Health*, 62(1), pp. 72–9.

13

Financial Literacy

Nicola Butler

Aims of This Chapter

- Highlight the need for a basic understanding of fundamental financial and economic vocabulary.
- Explore key concepts and sociological influences which impact upon personal finances.
- Emphasize the need for financial education considering economic trends, 'good debt versus bad debt' and the rise in 'Buy Now Pay Later' (BNPL) loans.

Introduction

Following the campaign for compulsory Relationships and Sex Education in secondary schools and colleges, the PSHE Association continues to press for the 'E' in PSHE Education – representing economic wellbeing and careers – to be statutory as well (Campaigning, 2022). This chapter explores how and where we can introduce this to our learners, especially considering the current economic and financial concerns around the rising cost of living. Recent statistics from The Money Charity state, 'People in the UK owed £1,773.2 billion at the end of February 2022. This is up by £66.4 billion from £1,706.8 billion at the end of February 2021, an extra £1,255.32 per UK adult over the year' (Statistics Archive – The Money Charity, 2022). In 2017, this figure was £107 billion (Household debt in Great Britain – Office for National Statistics, 2022).

How important is it, therefore, to support the current generation to make the right decisions for their future financial security? The annual Young Person's Money Index published by the London Institute of Banking & Finance (LIBF) lays bare the opinions of our young people. The statistics below are taken from their 2021–2 findings (Young Persons & Money Index | The London Institute of Banking & Finance, 2022):

- Anxiety in young people about finance has increased to 81 per cent from 67 per cent last year
- 67 per cent say that Covid-19 has made them feel more anxious about money that rises to 73 per cent among fifteen- to sixteen-year-olds
- Overall, 72 per cent want to learn more about money and finance in school that rises to 85 per cent among seventeen- to eighteen-year-olds

Asked at what age they would like to start learning about money:

- 56 per cent said between the ages of eleven and fourteen
- 25 per cent said between the ages of fifteen and eighteen
- 8 per cent said from the age of ten
- 15 per cent said ten and under

As you can see the majority are asking us to teach them from Key Stage 3, but are we facilitating this? Learners need to be aware of the necessity to ensure a balance between income and expenditure is maintained to achieve financial sustainability throughout their lives. Some pupils may have already experienced the highs and lows of financial and economic instability within their home environment. They should be encouraged to discuss their experiences as they would the rest of their PSHE/RSHE.

The classroom is an environment that offers this opportunity for all pupils, but it is rarely taken for financial matters. There are a multitude of topics which are more openly talked about now compared to only a few years ago; however, money remains a taboo subject for many people. Alongside the PHS, the E, incorporating financial sustainability, is therefore fundamental to our learners' long-term wellbeing. Mind (2022) explains the link between money and mental health, highlighting the importance of this curriculum content in line with Chapter 4 of this book.

At the time of writing (April 2022) inflation is at 9 per cent (against a government target of 2 per cent), Russia is at war with Ukraine and fuel costs are spiralling; consequently, the nation is struggling with the rising cost of living (Office for National Statistics 2022b). Rishi Sunak, then Chancellor of the Exchequer, cut fuel duty to absorb some of the cost and the Bank of England increased interest rates to the highest rates for thirteen years, to curtail consumer spending. The tax burden is at 36 per cent of GDP (up from 33 per cent before Covid), the highest it has been since the 1940s; National Insurance is about to rise and the continuing implementation of the government triple-lock guarantee for pensions may force the state pension age to rise sooner than planned. If all this has your head in a spin and makes you wish you were more informed, then this chapter will give you an insight into why we need to financially educate our young people in their quest to become healthy, confident, enterprising and ethically informed citizens of the UK and the world (Donaldson, 2015).

Social acceptability of debt has changed immensely over the last forty years and financial education has not kept pace. Young people are under increasing pressure and influence through social media to always look and be at their best. The early temptation and ease of obtaining credit to support this lead to higher levels of debt at a younger age. Add to this the lack of understanding of living costs, taxes, benefits and where to get free advice once they become financially independent, it is hardly surprising that we live in an era of increasing personal debt. It is imperative that we include it in the curriculum, from an understanding of basic current and savings accounts to where to obtain help. They should be more informed, and we can start this process in our classrooms and should do so.

I find the growth of 'buy now, pay later' services, such as those from Klarna and Clearpay, particularly worrying. This is a topic we must explore in depth – making sure children can look past the glossy marketing and social media presence of these companies and see them for what they are – credit providers, which carry the same risks as any other. It is easy to see how the rise in this 'BNPL' culture could drive impulse purchases and put people in debt and severe financial difficulties. Indeed, my concern is not just how young people, once they turn eighteen, might start using these services, but also how they can impact parents and families. When you look at the world from this perspective, you see why we must teach personal finance, its wider relevance and impact on living.

Consideration of welfare state benefits, the array and complexity of them, is a critical area for pupils of all academic levels and backgrounds. Again, this has not been a key area of learning, but it is a crucial part of the safety net of life. By the end of Key Stage 5, learners should be able to access and apply the fundamental financial tools to take them confidently and comfortably into their adulthood. Whether that is understanding the need to start a pension as soon as they start working, knowing the process of paying back their student loans, accessing benefits and further education funding if they need it, or just the basics of setting up home on their own, we can facilitate the basics through financial capability education. It does not, and should not, need to be left to chance any more.

Teaching Financial and Economic Skills in PSHE

Before embarking on financial matters, we should ensure an inclusive setting for learners from different socio-economic backgrounds. For example, Sharia Law prohibits the payment of interest. Establish good ground rules from the start by encouraging learners not to make judgements about one another or, as the teacher, not making assumptions about pupils based on their economic background.

The most appropriate term for teaching the 'E' is Autumn. The months running up to Christmas must be budgeted for and planned – consider the extra expenses this incurs alongside the increasing energy costs of the winter. Struggling with debt links into other areas discussed in this book. If we educate our learners to manage their money, this will help with their future relationships, mental health, planning and their digital financial experiences.

During almost ten years of teaching this subject I have accessed a variety of resources to adapt my resources and methods to the needs of my learners. Young Money, Barclays Life Skills and LIBF are the best place to start, see recommended resources at the end of this chapter. There are, of course, others, and once you start teaching this topic you may find that your preferences will differ. However, they will save you time initially with planning and supporting your knowledge gaps.

Topic Structure

Whilst the following structure and ideas suggestions are for each age group, it will depend on the current level of financial education your learners have received and their ability. You will also find some learners are keen to discuss situations that have happened to them or that they know of, but be mindful to ensure that private or confidential information is not shared in a public setting and offer pupils the opportunity to talk to a trusted adult privately about any money worries. Learner discussion will inform your content and may lead you into other areas not necessarily covered in the order below.

Allocated time is also a huge factor and will depend on your setting. If you are short on time the focus needs to be on budgeting, good debt versus bad debt and referring to the easy availability of credit. In addition, it is important to signpost learners as to where they can get help and support with managing their finances and debt via charitable organizations, such as the Citizens Advice Bureau, Money Helper and Step Change.

Year 7: Introduction to Their Finances and Savings Accounts

By the age of eleven you will find a considerable proportion of learners will have at least one savings account, and any pupils born between 1 September 2002 and 2 January 2011 will have a tax-free savings account called a Child Trust Fund (Child Trust Fund, 2022). This was a government initiative of £250 per child. From discussions with my learners many of them do not know they have this so it will come as a welcome surprise. Although the scheme closed in 2011, parents are still able to top up these accounts with up to £9,000 per year. Savings accounts are therefore an excellent place to start with pupils in Year 7.

Activities and Discussion Suggestions

Financial services is a fast-paced, ever-evolving environment. In my practice I have found that customer inertia means learners have their accounts at the same financial institutions as their parents, grandparents, or carers, but is this really the best place for their money? Investigating different accounts, both online and in branch, is an interesting and interactive task for all. What are the crucial factors for them? Interest rates, customer service, accessibility and ease of use are just a few suggestions for discussion.

Pupils can be encouraged to research children's current accounts with a variety of banks and building societies, simultaneously considering the following questions: Why do we need to save? What are the benefits? What are interest rates? Who offers the best home for their money? Why? What is required to open a new account?

A number of pupils may also be using prepaid cards, topped up by their parents for them to use for bus fares, lunches and general expenses when they are out with their friends. Here they can consider what the benefits are for pupils of cash versus cards. This will be an introduction to budgeting, which can then be explored further in Year 8.

Year 8: Current Accounts and Budgeting

At this point, learners will be more aware of the need for money as part of their everyday life, and a few may even be young carers themselves and already be expected to manage some of the day-to-day spending in their household – it is important that we give them the tools to support this. From the age of thirteen, the savings' accounts discussed in Year 7 may be transferred into current accounts, often referred to as Youth Accounts, a type of current account for teenagers. Now that our young people will have access to a debit card, what does this mean for them? What are debit cards, and how are they used? Research and discuss the variety of youth accounts available – which one is the best for their situation?

Current accounts also come with mobile phone banking apps. Most pupils will have phones and may be tempted to access these apps. Learners could research different banking apps. What are the advantages/disadvantages of using these? What are the main concerns of having their financial activity on their phone? Financial fraud is an interesting concept here; learners enjoy investigating examples of this online if you have access to the internet in your setting.

Budgeting and saving for specific purchases at various times of the year are the next stage of financial education. What are the benefits of budgeting? There are initial links to the Mathematics Numeracy Curriculum here. You may also want to start to link it to mental health (see Chapter 4) and tentatively introduce the concept of debt to be developed in Year 9 and beyond. Planning for the future (Chapter 14) may also be a consideration for some more advanced learners. Ask learners to think of something they would like to buy, then consider their income and expenditure. Encourage a discussion around income from chores at home, pocket money and gifts from family. Then ask them what they regularly spend and how much they can afford to save towards their purchase. Finally calculate how long it will take them to save up for their purchase.

Year 9: Part-Time Jobs, Gambling and an Introduction to Economics

Aged thirteen, learners are allowed to work part-time and some may now want to start earning their own money. Although they are not entitled to minimum wage and will not pay National Insurance until they are sixteen (gov.uk 2022e), this is a suitable time to introduce income from part-time jobs. A number of learners may start working for family members or be encouraged into work to gain extra family income. Earning your own money means you also need to know how to manage it.

Activities and Discussion Suggestions

They may be paid in cash at this stage and may need to visit bank branches to pay the money in. Where is the safest place to store cash? What is the advantage of paying their cash in at the bank? Why should they be encouraged to do this? Inflation could be introduced here – how does this affect our cash if we store it in our money box? Use the Bank of England website for the current rate of inflation and access the inflation calculator (Bank of England, 2022). To protect the purchasing power of our money we must endeavour to earn more in interest than the current rate of inflation. At the time of writing (May 2022), it is almost impossible to do this from a standard savings account. Learners can use price comparison websites to compare the rate of inflation to the interest rate on their savings account. If there is a negative difference between the inflation rate and the interest rate, there is a decline in the 'real' value of their savings; this means the current monetary value (nominal value) is adjusted for the effects of inflation. This may be their first foray into economics at a time when they are considering their options for GCSE and so may also be used to support their choices for the future.

Learners will also need to consider what added costs they may incur in getting to and from work. Will they need to bring or buy lunch? How often and when will they get paid? Does the timing of pay affect their spending habits? Will they have to work in advance of getting paid and what are the consequences to their budget if they do?

As learners start earning their own money now is a suitable time to introduce the notion of gambling. Most learners have played online games where they are encouraged to use virtual money to buy and sell football players or to buy loot boxes where contents are unknown. However, they may not hold what they want when opened and quite often they are required to pay additional funds to get what they want or to expand their portfolios further. There are news stories associated with parents unwittingly receiving huge bills for gaming purchases (Johns, 2020). These games introduce the concept of risk versus reward and identification of early links to addiction. They are not, however, officially considered as gambling so are not regulated by the Gambling Commission (Kleinman, 2022). You may wish to introduce a lesson on the facts around gambling: age requirements, effects on our finances and whether the risk is purely a financial one. Care must be taken with this topic to remain mindful of individuals that may already be affected by gambling. Signpost learners to the NHS website for further help and support (NHS 2021). Visit the Gambling Commission website for up-to-date information on gambling trends.

Years 10 and 11: How Do External Factors Affect Our Personal Finances?

By now, learners are maturing and if they have had a grounding in financial and economic topics as presented here then they should be encouraged to consider the wider economic environment. How much of what goes on in their own home life is based on important financial decisions? Here, I would like to encourage pupils to discuss the effects of rising prices and the cost of living alongside what they can do to help in their own homes.

Suggested Tasks, Activities and Discussions

Learners should now be ready to identify the costs of running a home. Sharing your own life experiences and asking them to think about their own home environment, to determine what they need to consider, will highlight the cost of living that goes unrecognized before they leave home. Create a virtual home with them and identify the costs of running it. Consider the obvious bills but also the less obvious such as TV licence, council tax, insurance and any costs involved with pets they may have.

A basic economic and finance lesson involving an investigation into Consumer Price Inflation (CPI) and how it is measured using the consumer basket of goods is encouraged. A brief guide can be found on the ONS (Office for National Statistics) if you are not familiar with this concept (Tucker and Gooding, 2017). Research and consider what is in the current basket and why. Reflect on how a rise or fall in inflation affects the purchasing power of the money going into their household; what can they do to help. What are the wider impacts of a rise or fall in inflation?

Borrowing is much more socially acceptable than it was in the 1970s and 1980s. Families rely on credit cards to supplement their income and balance their budgets. What are credit cards? What place do they have in our finances, if any? An investigation lesson is useful here on the issues around the increasing levels of UK credit card debt and 'buy now pay later' (BNPL) schemes. Identify the variety of products available and how suppliers make them easily affordable through credit options.

Mindful of rising debt levels, how do interest rates affect the cost of these debts? Pupils can consider the interest rate earned (AER – Annual Earnings Rate) on savings and the interest rate paid (APR – Annual Percentage Rate) on borrowing, comparing the two and ascertaining why one is higher. How does this impact on where they save their money and how much attention they pay to this?

Learners can now consolidate and individually reflect on their own personal circumstances. How are they impacted by rising interest rates and inflation? Have their parents made cutbacks in certain areas? Do they consider they are living on a tight budget? How can they contribute to keeping costs down? The BBC Investigation of so-called 'vampire devices' (Cieslak and Gerken, 2022) will help them identify the savings they could make whilst also encouraging sustainability (Chapter 15). Follow this up with a calculation of how many hours their family are working just to pay for these devices.

Lastly, research where can people go for money and debt advice? Signpost learners to The Citizens Advice Bureau, Step Change Debt Charity or Money Helper, all of which offer free debt advice. There are also organizations that charge for debt advice, and learners may want to compare fees.

Learners should now recognize that there are numerous factors at play when budgeting to balance income against expenditure. Understanding the impact of external factors such as inflation and interest rates is imperative to financial sustainability. You can find information on consumer price inflation in the UK from the Office for National Statistics.

Key Stage 5: Preparation for Life beyond School

Here we must consider a variety of options including student loans, apprenticeships and leaving and setting up home, but it is worth noting that not all learners will go to university following Key Stage 5 education. This is a crucial time for learners as they will be making big life decisions. Financial aspects will form a large part of this so we should facilitate teaching and learning as we would, for example, with the writing of personal statements. Turning eighteen also gives them access to additional financial products, and most parents and carers I have spoken to over the years have stated that they wished they had had some financial education before being let loose into the world. Any decision to borrow should always first consider the ABC of borrowing; is it affordable, what is the benefit and what are the consequences of not repaying the loan?

Suggested Tasks, Activities and Discussions

Student loans are often seen as a negative aspect of university given the levels of debt incurred at the end of study. However, with previous knowledge of budgeting and an understanding of the repayment structure of student loans, learners will be able to make an informed decision beyond the final figure.

Before considering this though, we must introduce the idea of 'good debt versus bad debt'. Martin Lewis, money saving expert, explains this in his video of the same name (Lewis, 2012). This topic forms a large part of the course I deliver, both through the LIBF resources and at every opportunity with all pupils. It is the precursor to any form of borrowing, therefore a key concept to financial education. Once learners grasp this they are immediately at an advantage when they go it alone. Borrowing money should be seen as an investment: If it helps the borrower to increase their wealth in the long term then it is good debt. Are student loans therefore good debt? Ask learners to think about a selection of borrowing products and consider whether they are good debt or bad debt; mortgage, overdraft, credit cards, hire purchase are some examples.

Student loans are in two parts: the tuition loan pays the fees for learning and the maintenance loan supports the living expenses while at university. Both are not repaid until the borrower reaches the required earnings threshold. The long-term management of these loans and the fact they are investing in their future mean it is considered as good debt, even though they are currently repaid for up to thirty years before they are written off. From 2023, however, to reduce the bill to taxpayers, the repayment period is being extended to forty years and concern has been raised about the impact of this (Shearing, 2022). A further report likens it to a 'working-life-long graduate tax' (Goodwin, 2022).

In addition, consideration must be given to the student current account selected at this point. A key learning outcome here is what learners are enticed into borrowing in addition to student loans. Student current accounts offered by banks entice teenagers with promises of free gifts, interest-free overdrafts and other offers. Learners need to be careful that they get the right one for their needs and not be attracted to the 'freebies'. The idea of an interest-free overdraft is great; however, the reality of paying it back after they have had the benefit of it is not. If learners can budget their loans and grants efficiently over the three terms per year, they should not need to use the overdraft, or at the most, dip in and out of it. Research and discuss with learners the various offers and the ways banks use incentives to entice them to open an account with them (Cavaglieri, 2022).

They may also be tempted to get a credit card as they are now of an age to borrow. Although credit cards have the advantage of offering added consumer protection when buying online, they must be repaid in full every month for them to be considered good debt. Making the minimum repayment each month leads to long-term hardcore debt and high rates of interest. I would recommend investigating with learners the advantages and disadvantages of credit cards, how the interest and fees are allocated, any interest-free periods and how quickly the overall debt can increase with interest (Money Supermarket, 2022). At eighteen, learners will also currently qualify for a Lifetime ISA (Individual Savings Account). This account offers a savings account with a potential for a government bonus of up to £1,000 per year. There are limited providers offering this account but if learners intend to buy their own home at a point in the future, it is an excellent choice for their savings and one well worth researching. Consider the advantages and disadvantages of this type of savings account, along with the providers offering the accounts – should they open one? What is an ISA? How does contributing to this affect other tax-free savings accounts? What identification will they need to open one? Why do they need to prove their identity?

Discussing the Lifetime ISA will also lead your group into the possibility of owning their own home. As a student it is more likely they will be renting initially. Investigate the advantages and disadvantages of renting or buying; do learners know if their home is rented or mortgaged? How will the interest rates and the economy affect any decision-making? Why would this have influence?

Buying or renting a home is a big topic and I recall a recent lesson when I was teaching the Baccalaureate, rather than in a pastoral or mathematics setting. The learner was our head girl at the time and was completing her destination passport, a baccalaureate task which encourages them to take ownership of their future by contacting employers, constructing budgets and considering what they will realistically need to know to successfully reach their career and life goals. We were discussing how they will afford to pay rent and bills at university then progressed onto renting or buying in the future. As a previous bank manager and current finance teacher I was able to take it a step further and we looked at different types of mortgages. At the end of the lesson, she came to me and thanked me for what she felt was 'the most useful lesson she had ever had'. Whilst I am sure this was not the case, it certainly re-enforced what learners want and need from their PSHE education, especially in the current environment. Owning your own home, the purchasing process and the financial implications are beyond the realms of a PSHE setting; however, the costs involved of being self-sufficient post education can certainly be covered here. A guest speaker could be called upon if appropriate. A number of the big banks will offer support with this. We have encouraged guest speakers from a variety of roles to speak to our sixth form over the years. The recommended resources contain a selection of charities and financial institutions to contact.

Another key topic for learners to understand is when to start a pension. It is likely to be the furthest financial consideration from their minds, but should it be? The message here is that it is never too soon to start contributing to a pension. By starting as soon as you commence working, you build up the largest pension pot possible for your retirement at a time when it will have the least impact on your take-home pay. By saving a small amount from your salary each month, employees are less likely to notice the deduction than if they leave it until they are on a higher salary. Ask learners to consider the lifestyle they would like when they retire. If they leave it until later to start their contributions, what will the impact be on their net pay (what goes into their bank after deductions) to achieve this lifestyle, specifically at a stage of their life cycle when they may have other financial commitments. Research how financially advantageous it is to start investing in a pension sooner rather than later. It is important to note that although apprentices may not earn a full wage while they are learning, they are still entitled to contribute to a workplace pension. Since 2012, auto-enrolment means if employees meet a certain criterion, they will be enrolled onto the pension scheme of the company where they work. Apprentices may not necessarily earn the minimum amount, but this does not mean they are exempt. Although not obliged to, apprentices earning over a certain amount can opt in to pay and consequently their employer will contribute too (Department for Work and Pensions, 2022).

The concept of insurance as a transfer of financial risk for unforeseen events introduces life assurance, car insurance, critical illness cover and payment protection insurance (PPI). Whilst PPI has had a lot of bad press, learners need to understand that it was the mis-selling that caused this, not the product, and that it plays an important part in financial planning. More information can be found on the Money Helper Website (MoneyHelper, 2022).

Assessment and Reflection

Successful teaching and learning of financial literacy will be evident in the savings and current accounts learners choose and how confident they feel about their own finances. Through the variety of tasks discussed a core understanding of the costs involved when running a household and the perils of bad debt should be evidenced. At any point throughout the progression of topics learners must be given the opportunity to ask questions, debate with each other and do their own research to meet their required depth of knowledge. In addition, as part of their Corporate Social Responsibility (CSR) programmes many financial service providers offer quizzes, games and targeted information to develop young people's understanding of the financial environment.

How far have you developed a basic understanding of financial literacy with your groups? How can you develop that understanding and use of vocabulary? Do you have sufficient opportunities and resources to explore key concepts and sociological influences which impact upon personal finances? Are you able to emphasize the need for financial education considering economic trends, good debt versus bad debt and the rise in 'Buy Now Pay Later' (BNPL) loans? What changes can you implement straight away into your system and what needs more long-term planning? How can you share the tasks presented in this chapter with your teams to make best use of them?

In my experience, PSHE is taught in mixed ability groups and consequently learners from diverse backgrounds and abilities must be able to access a wide variety of resources. I hope that you find the recommendations and suggestions in this chapter supportive of this. In addition, there is a list below of further organizations and charities that can be accessed for extra support.

Questions for Reflection for You and Your Setting

- To what extent have you developed a basic understanding of financial literacy with your groups? How can you develop that understanding and use of vocabulary?
- Do you have sufficient opportunities and resources to explore key concepts and sociological influences which impact upon personal finances?

- How can you emphasize the need for financial education considering economic trends, good debt versus bad debt and the rise in 'Buy Now Pay Later' (BNPL) loans?
- What changes can you implement straight away into your system and what needs more long-term planning?
- How can you share the tasks presented in this chapter with your teams to make best use of them?

Recommended Resources

https://www.moneyhelper.org.uk/en/family-and-care/talk-money/how-to-talk-to-your-children-about-money

https://www.capitalone.com/bank/money-management/financial-tips/teaching-kids-about-money/

https://www.natwest.com/life-moments/teaching-kids-about-money.html

https://www.young-enterprise.org.uk/youngmoneychallenge

https://barclayslifeskills.com/

https://www.libf.ac.uk/

https://www.young-enterprise.org.uk/teachers-hub/financial-education/financial-education-programmes/my-money-week/

https://www.nationaldebtline.org/

https://www.stepchange.org/

Home | Bank of England

https://www.citizensadvice.org.uk/debt-and-money/get-help-with-gambling-problems/

https://www.citizensadvice.org.uk/

https://www.moneyhelper.org.uk/en

https://www.klarna.com/uk/

https://www.moneysavingexpert.com/

https://www.gamblingcommission.gov.uk

References

Bank of England (2022), *Inflation Calculator*. Available online: https://www.bankofengland.co.uk/monetary-policy/inflation/inflation-calculator (accessed 26 May 2022).

Barclays Life Skills (2022), *LifeSkills | Developing Work and Life Skills*. Available online: https://barclayslifeskills.com/ (accessed 24 May 2022).

Cavaglieri, C. (2022), *Student Bank Accounts*. Available online: https://www.which.co.uk/money/banking/student-and-graduate-bank-accounts/student-bank-accounts-ablvm7t6pdjr (accessed 27 May 2022).

Cieslak, M. and Gerken, T. (2022), *Energy Supplier Counts Cost of Devices on Standby*. Available online: https://www.bbc.co.uk/news/technology-61235367 (accessed 27 May 2022).

Deparment for Work and Pensions (2022), *What Is Auto Enrolment?*. Available online: https://www.gov.uk/government/news/what-is-auto-enrolment (accessed 23 April 2022).

Donaldson, G. (2015), *Successful Futures*. [ebook] OGL. Available online: https://gov.wales/successful-futures-review-curriculum-and-assessment-arrangements (accessed 23 April 2022).

Goodwin, H. (2022), '*Graduate Tax*': Students to Pay off Loans into Their 60s under New Plans. Available online: https://www.thelondoneconomic.com/politics/graduate-tax-students-to-pay-off-loans-into-their-60s-under-new-plans-313307/ (accessed 15 June 2022).

gov.uk. (2022b), *Student Loans Company*. Available online: https://www.gov.uk/government/organisations/student-loans-company (accessed 27 May 2022).

gov.uk. (2022c), *Gambling-Related Harms Evidence Review: Summary*. Available online: https://www.gov.uk/government/publications/gambling-related-harms-evidence-review/gambling-related-harms-evidence-review-summary (accessed 27 April 2022).

gov.uk. (2022d), *Child Trust Fund*. Available online: https://www.gov.uk/child-trust-funds (accessed 23 April 2022).

gov.uk. (2022e), *Child Employment*. Available online: https://www.gov.uk/child-employment (accessed 7 May 2022).

Johns, T. (2020), *Dad Horrified at £4,642 Gaming App Bill*. Available online: https://www.bbc.co.uk/news/business-53272411 (accessed 25 May 2022).

Kleinman, Z. (2022), *Fifa Packs and Loot Boxes 'Not Gambling' in UK*. Available online: https://www.bbc.co.uk/news/technology-49074003 (accessed 14 June 2022).

Lewis, M. (2012), *Martin Lewis – Good Debt Bad Debt Quiz*. Available online: https://www.youtube.com/watch?v=aOQhZQrNrZk (accessed 27 May 2022).

The London Institute of Banking and Finance (2022a), *Student Investor Challenge*. Available online: https://www.libf.ac.uk/study/financial-education/student-investor-challenge (accessed 23 April 2022).

The London Institute of Banking and Finance (2022b), *Young Persons' Money Index*. Available online: https://www.libf.ac.uk/study/financial-education/young-persons-money-index (accessed 23 April 2022).

Mind (2022), Available online: https://www.mind.org.uk/information-support/tips-for-everyday-living/money-and-mental-health/ (accessed 24 May 2022).

Money Helper (2022), *Insurance*. Available online: https://www.moneyhelper.org.uk/en/everyday-money/insurance (accessed 27 May 2022).

Money Supermarket (2022), *Advantages and Disadvantages of Credit Cards: What Are the Pros and Cons of Getting a Credit Card?* Available online: https://www.

moneysupermarket.com/credit-cards/advantages-and-disadvantages/ (accessed 27 May 2022).

NHS (2021), *Help for Problem Gambling*. Available online: https://www.nhs.uk/live-well/ addiction-support/gambling-addiction/ (accessed 26 May 2022).

Office for National Statistics (2022a), *Consumer Price Inflation, UK*. Available online: https://www.ons.gov.uk/economy/inflationandpriceindices/bulletins/ consumerpriceinflation/latest (accessed 26 May 2022).

Office for National Statistics (2022b), *The Rising Cost of Living and Its Impact on Individuals in Great Britain*. Available online: https://www.ons.gov.uk/ peoplepopulationandcommunity/personalandhouseholdfinances/expenditure/ articles/therisingcostoflivinganditsimpactonindividualsingreatbritain/ november2021tomarch2022 (accessed 23 May 2022).

Office for National Statistics (2022c), *Household Debt in Great Britain*. Available online: https://www.ons.gov.uk/peoplepopulationandcommunity/ personalandhouseholdfinances/incomeandwealth/bulletins/ householddebtingreatbritain/april2016tomarch2018 (accessed 24 May 2022).

PSHE Association (2022), *Campaigning*. Available online: https://pshe-association.org. uk/our-vision/campaigning (accessed 23 May 2022).

Shearing, H. (2022), *Students to Pay off Loans into Their 60s, Plans Say*. Available online: https://www.bbc.co.uk/news/education-60498245 (accessed 15 June 2022).

The Money Charity (2022), *Statistics Archive*. Available online: https://themoneycharity. org.uk/money-statistics/ (accessed 26 May 2022).

Tucker, J., & Gooding, P. (2017), *Consumer Price Indices, a Brief Guide*. Available online: https://www.ons.gov.uk/economy/inflationandpriceindices/articles/ consumerpriceindicesabriefguide/2017 (accessed 25 May 2022).

Wearn, R. (2021), *More than 17 Million Have Used Buy Now, Pay Later Services*. Available online: https://www.bbc.co.uk/news/business-59433904 (accessed 23 April 2022).

Young Enterprise (2022), *Young Money – MMW Resource Hub*. Available online: https://www.young-enterprise.org.uk/MMW/ (accessed 24 May 2022).

14

Planning for the Future

Victoria-Marie Pugh and

Sophie-Lauren McPhee

Aims of This Chapter

- To differentiate between the role of CEAIG coordinator and PSHE lead in careers education.
- To explore the place of careers education within the PSHE curriculum.
- To establish the right approach to careers education within PSHE.

Introduction

Careers education is an important and often undervalued aspect of the curriculum. De Botton (2021) states: 'At its best, careers education takes care of the future part. It is about helping young people to find their best next step in a world of uncertainty. It opens up pathways based on aspiration and skill rather than circumstance and stereotype. And it is fundamentally inclusive, removing barriers and rebalancing towards high-quality technical and vocational education.' However, according to Paul Joyce, Deputy Director, Further Education and Skills (2020), careers education in many schools is quite patchy and not of good quality according to inspection findings. He also pointed out that not all schools are not 'fulfilling their duties under the Baker clause'.

The Baker Clause (2017) was introduced as part of the Further Education Act 2017. It states that schools must allow colleges and training providers access to every student in Years 8–13 to inform them about approved technical education qualifications and apprenticeships. Guidance in relation to this is clear with DfE stipulations, setting out the following:

We expect the school to provide opportunities for visits from a range of providers of Key Stage 4, post-16 options and post-18 options, including T Levels, apprenticeships, traineeships, technical and vocational qualifications, applied qualifications and higher technical skills courses. Visiting providers should include further education colleges, studio schools, university technical colleges, institutes of technology and a range of providers of apprenticeships and technical options, including Independent Training Providers (ITPs).

Schools and colleges are also expected, by the Department for Education, to use the Gatsby Benchmarks (2013). The Gatsby Benchmarks are an internationally recognized framework that defines the best careers provision. Although the benchmarks are non-statutory, they are designed to offer careers guidance to all twelve- to eighteen-year-olds and students aged up to twenty-five with an education, health and care plan (EHCP).

The benchmarks are:

- A stable careers programme
- Learning from career and labour market information
- Addressing the needs of each pupil
- Linking curriculum learning to careers
- Encounters with employers and employees
- Experience of workplaces
- Encounters with further and higher education
- Personal guidance

A study by the University of Derby (2021), funded by Gatsby, followed sixteen schools and colleges in the North East of England which had implemented the Gatsby Benchmarks within their curriculum. The results found an increase in career readiness scores and a positive correlation between the number of benchmarks held and GCSE's grades 9–4. Notable differences in engagement in class were also reported by teachers.

Although careers education is not part of the statutory RSHE curriculum, it is part of the programme of study from the PSHE Association. This programme of study covers careers education as part of the living in the wider world section which covers KS1–5. Careers education should be covered in primary schools along with work around tackling stereotypes in jobs and careers; however, this needs to continue into Year 7. Many schools, due to time constraints or staffing, begin any significant careers lessons after GCSEs, but this is too late as pupils need time and guidance to support them in their choices and to survey the wide variety of options available to them. A study by the Education Endowment Foundation (2018) found that employer engagement in education enhanced young people's understanding of personal routes into careers and enabled young people to gain the skills needed in employment, supporting the jump from education to job and increasing attainment.

The Role of the CEAIG Coordinator

Many secondary education providers now employ Careers Education, Information, Advice and Guidance (CEAIG) coordinators, either as a stand-alone position or as an additional responsibility. This person would typically audit the quality of both curricular and extra-curricular careers education, coordinate and monitor work experience, organize careers events within school/college (such as alumni events, where ex-pupils and students return to give presentations on their jobs, or mock interviews with employers), and external visits to workplaces or careers fairs. They may also organize a series of events to mark National Careers Week, which takes place every year in March. There are other tools that they can draw upon that, as long as pupils have access to a computer, can be explored during form time, such as the National Careers Service and the 'Find an apprenticeship' search tool on the government website. Furthermore, there are also platforms that schools and colleges can subscribe to which pupils can use to find out information about higher education and apprenticeship providers. Overall, the CEAIG coordinator must ensure that the Gatsby Benchmarks are being met for every pupil within the curriculum and beyond it, so that they 'understand enough about career options to enable them to make informed decisions' (Gatsby Charitable Foundation, 2014).

The Role of the PSHE Teacher

A PSHE teacher's role is to supplement the work of the CEAIG coordinator with lessons that seek to explore the topic of careers in more depth. There are external organizations that provide off-the-peg lesson plans that can help with this at all secondary key stages, such as Barclays Life Skills, whose lesson plans and activities can be adapted to fit the mode of delivery, whether through tutor time, drop-down days or timetabled lessons – it would be worth consulting the CEAIG coordinator as to who will assume responsibility for communicating plans with staff if not being delivered through timetabled PSHE. Barclays Life Skills also provides resources for the linked themes of wellbeing and financial capability, both of which will impact on, or be impacted by, career choices, plus helps students to develop useful character attributes for the workplace, such as self-confidence and assertiveness.

It is clear to see, then, that like all others, careers is a PSHE topic that cannot be taught in isolation without reference to the rest. Another example of this is encouraging more pupils from ethnic minorities into politics when teaching about parliament and government, as 'in 2021 about 14% of the UK population was from an ethnic minority background', but 'in October 2021 … 6.6% of Members of the House of Lords were from ethnic minority groups' (House of Commons Library, 2021).

The PSHE Association has linked sustainability to careers by publishing a set of lesson plans for Key Stage 3 produced by the Environment Agency called 'Careers for change', pupils can be signposted to diversity, equity and inclusion groups within specific fields, such as the 'Decolonise Architecture' movement, and lessons about First Aid can be concluded by signposting pupils to the various youth programmes offered by St John Ambulance.

However, the power of teacher ideas and experience when planning PSHE careers lessons cannot be undervalued – an off-the-peg lesson is good for those colleagues who are new to teaching PSHE, or if a lesson plan is required quickly, but like all PSHE topics, the best lessons will be those which amalgamate ready-made high-quality lesson plans, consultation with experts, up-to-date research, the needs of pupils in individual contexts and using individual teacher ideas and experience. For example, creating a lesson around the difference between knowledge and skills, to show pupils the benefit of all academic subjects in terms of the skills they help cultivate, so that they do not approach lessons with the narrow view that only those subjects with knowledge content directly linked to their chosen career are important. In it, pupils can discuss how every subject on the mainstream curriculum helps someone who wants to become a doctor, such as learning how to maintain a steady beat in music lessons – vital when administering CPR! Another example is a lesson about workplace behaviour and culture, which supports the work of the wider pastoral team on whole-school behaviour management and school culture. At Key Stage 4 it could be study skills, using sixth formers to give guidance following their experience with GCSEs.

At Key Stage 5, we really need to focus on getting pupils workplace-ready, an issue highlighted by Andrew Bernard in his book *The Ladder*, a handbook and toolkit for CEAIG coordinators and those who support them in their role, such as PSHE leads. Whilst work experience helps serve this purpose, some schemes only take place in school holidays, and in term-time, pupils – and their parents or carers – may be reluctant to take time away from studies on a weekly basis. Back at the start of 2020, it was being reported that 'the proportion of teenagers working in Saturday jobs has almost halved in the past 20 years as staffing tills, stacking shelves and delivering newspapers have gone out of fashion and people have turned online to earn cash' (Booth, 2020), and since then, the national lockdowns during Covid-19 will have meant that there have been even fewer opportunities for pupils to practise skills in clear, calm and respectful communication, smart personal presentation, managing under pressure, prioritizing and so on in a workplace context. The Change Your Mind programme mentioned in Chapter 5 can really help here, as it provides pupils with work experience during the school day, leaving pupils with their evenings and weekends free for academic study, rest and leisure.

Inclusive Careers Education

As well as providing consistent and high-quality careers education, which begins before pupils enter secondary school or college, the provision also needs to be inclusive.

According to the Apprenticeships in England by industry characteristics 21/22 (gov.uk, 2022) data, the number of female students entering health care or social work apprenticeships far exceeds those of male students. Likewise, the number of male students entering construction, public administration and manufacturing apprentices exceeds those of females.

When we look at A-level subject intake data from Joint Council for Qualifications (2019) it is a similar story.

In 2019:

- Over 70 per cent of physics and computing A-level entrants were male.
- Over 70 per cent of psychology and English A-level entrants were female.

So why is there such a gender divide in subject and career uptake? One historically suggested reason as to why girls and women may not study or entered into STEM jobs is that girls typically do not do as well in mathematics. However, Gjersoe (2018) highlights that this is simply not true and girls typically match or exceed boys in mathematics classwork; the difference, however, is that girls do not seem to perform as well in tests. She notes that this was reported to be due to lower levels of confidence and test anxiety.

This is where a fully rounded and inclusive careers curriculum could support the tackling of stereotypes, confidence and aspirations. Friedman and Laurison (2015) found that children of those in higher-paid professional jobs were more likely to follow into these careers. The social and cultural capital that these pupils have due to parent/carer understanding of the education systems, filling in university or job applications puts these pupils at an advantage overall. They found that barriers of class outweigh those of race, religion and sexual orientation and therefore careers education can help to provide the tools needed for those pupils who do not have the advantage of this capital. Lemahieu (2019) stated: 'Young disabled people aged 16–24 are more likely than other groups to end up Not in Employment, Education or Training (NEET).' This highlights the importance of quality careers education and information about a range of industries, qualifications and skills.

Change Your Mind – A Case Study (Sophie McPhee)

At the start of each academic year, I tell each new Change Your Mind (CYM) cohort of Year 12 pupils that CYM operates as a business, and they should consider the programme not as a school extra-curricular or enrichment activity, but think of it as an organization for whom they work. The structure is that I am the Programme Director, overseeing operations within our school and helping other schools and colleges in the UK and beyond set up the programme through in-house pupil and staff training and staff-only webinars, my colleague in the PSHE department is my deputy, assisting with running the programme at our school, and the pupils are the regular employees split up into teams, with several of them appointed to be line managers, acting as the go-between and monitoring and managing around five pupils each.

Each team plans and delivers in local primary schools one workshop related to an aspect of health and wellbeing. Because the content is only as prescriptive as the titles of the segments within each workshop, pupils of all ability levels and backgrounds can access the programme. In my work setting up CYM in over 130 school and college hubs so far, I have run training days in schools where pupils tell me their aspirations for the future do not stretch beyond the confines of their own town, in private schools set in the Devon countryside, and in city-based Sikh and Catholic faith schools, to name a few examples.

Alongside all of the usual employability skills, such as teamwork, communication, leadership, initiative and so on, and alongside reinforcing the standards we expect from pupils every day anyway, such as smart presentation, polite manner and punctuality, Change Your Mind gives young people access to situations and opportunities that are unique, authentic and not necessarily offered elsewhere. Through the programme, my students have been able to appear on the internationally broadcast Teacher Toolkit podcast; they have appeared at the School and Public Health Nurses' Association annual conference in the form of a pre-recorded video, written an article which appeared in the Wellbeing in International Schools magazine, and received verbal feedback on one of their workshops from digital detoxing expert Tanya Goodin, author of several books on the subject.

However, some of the most valuable experience comes from more mundane occurrences: during a recent workshop, one of my Year 12s asked a Year 6 class to write an A-Z of words related to hygiene. 'Off you go', he said – without giving them any paper. Other pupils have really had to summon their confidence – and volume – to get a class to quieten back down after a discussion activity. The advantage of making mistakes and lacking in confidence within the context of Change Your Mind is that it is offering an authentic workplace experience with the security blanket of being supported by a teacher they know and trust who provides them with extensive feedback after each session. You will be able to see, therefore, that this programme alone helps schools and colleges meet several of the Gatsby Benchmarks and it is flexible enough to be adapted according to context.

Change Your Mind offers pupils the opportunity to test out the minutiae of unspoken workplace etiquette (such as taking your coat off before delivering a presentation), to finding new avenues of enjoyment (one pupil told me he was now considering working with children thanks to CYM) and push out of their comfort zone in a supportive environment. It is the opportunity to practise standards and skills encouraged back at school and college in a real-life context which contributes to true personal development, as these pupils attest:

> I am proud to say that taking part in Change Your Mind throughout Year 12 has significantly improved my organisation and timekeeping skills as I hoped when applying. As well as improving my ability to present and speak publicly, the course has changed for the better my approach to my learning and professionalism. I am confident this improvement behind the scenes will be invaluable to me in the future and I am grateful for the fact that Change Your Mind has enabled me to become the best version of myself.
>
> Pupil, Queen Mary's Grammar School

> I highly recommend the Change Your Mind programme. It opened my eyes to something I thought I'd never be able to do – standing in front of people doing a presentation.
>
> Pupil, Dover Christ Church Academy

Conclusion

Whilst careers education provision across the curriculum is improving, The Careers and Enterprise Company found when compiling their 2021 report *Trends in Careers Education* that 'PSHE continued to be the subject most closely related to careers learning', so it is important that the PSHE lead recognizes their role in supporting the work of their school or college's CEAIG coordinator. Thankfully, gone are the days when, as was once reported by a pupil, young people are told that their ambitions – in this particular case, to be a professional cricketer – are unrealistic, or careers education was limited to a brief visit to the local careers advice centre and a week's work experience at the end of Year 11. Now, all pupils from all backgrounds are exposed to all of the post-16 and post-18 pathways available to them, there are specialist lesson plans and resources for SEND pupils and care leavers and employers themselves are making active strides in diversifying workplaces, such as the Birmingham Architectural Association's 'Women in Architecture' focus group, breaking down barriers for marginalized young people ahead of them entering the job market. Of course, the world of careers, much like everything else that we teach about in PSHE, is constantly evolving, with the most recent large-scale change being the move towards hybrid working after the pandemic-induced national and international lockdowns. PSHE practitioners have a very important role to play in bringing together the different threads of the PSHE curriculum through careers education.

Questions for Reflection for You and Your Setting

- Which of the Gatsby Benchmarks are strengths and areas for development in your school or college?
- How can you support the work of your school/college's CEAIG coordinator through the PSHE curriculum?
- How can you make sure that your careers education is inclusive – free from glass ceilings and stereotypes?

Recommended Resources

Barclays Life Skills: https://barclayslifeskills.com/educators/lessons/

Bernard, A., *The Ladder* (2021), Crown House Publishing. Andrew Bernard ('Bernie') also delivers workshops in schools about aspirations through https://innovativeenterprise.co.uk/

Change Your Mind: qmgschangeyourmind.wordpress.com

'Find an apprenticeship' search tool: https://www.gov.uk/apply-apprenticeship

Future First: https://futurefirst.org.uk/

Inner Drive: https://www.innerdrive.co.uk/

National Careers Service: https://nationalcareers.service.gov.uk/

National Careers Week: https://nationalcareersweek.com/

PSHE Association: https://pshe-association.org.uk/

St. John Ambulance: https://www.sja.org.uk/get-involved/young-people/

The Careers and Enterprise Company: careersandenterprise.co.uk

Unifrog: https://www.unifrog.org/

References

Birmingham Architectural Association. Available online: https://brumarchitecture.com/

Booth, R. (2020), Proportion of young people in Saturday jobs halves in 20 years', *The Guardian*. 4th January. Available online: https://www.theguardian.com/society/2020/jan/04/proportion-of-young-people-in-saturday-jobs-halves-in-20-years (accessed 18 June 2022).

de Botton (2021) cited in The Careers and Enterprise Company (2021), *Trends in Careers Education 2021*. Available online: https://www.careersandenterprise.co.uk/media/xadnk1hb/cec-trends-in-careers-education-2021.pdf (accessed 18 June 2022).

Friedman, S., Laurison, D. & Miles, A. (2015), Breaking the 'class' ceiling? Social mobility into Britain's elite occupations, *The Sociological Review (Keele)*, 63(2), pp. 259–89.

Gatsby (2013), 'Good Career Guidance.' Available https://www.gatsby.org.uk/education/focus-areas/good-career-guidance

Gatsby Charitable Foundation (2014), *Good Career Guidance*. Available online: https://www.gatsby.org.uk/uploads/education/reports/pdf/gatsby-sir-john-holman-good-career-guidance-2014.pdf (accessed 18 June 2022).

Gjersoe, N. (2018), Bridging the gender gap: why do so few girls study STEM subjects? *The Guardian*, 8th March. Available online: https://www.theguardian.com/science/head-quarters/2018/mar/08/bridging-the-gender-gap-why-do-so-few-girls-study-stem-subjects (accessed 6 June 2022).

House of Commons Library (2021), *Ethnic Diversity in Politics and Public Life*. Available online: https://commonslibrary.parliament.uk/research-briefings/sn01156/ (accessed 18 June 2022). https://d2tic4wvo1iusb.cloudfront.net/documents/guidance/Employer_Engagement_in_Education.pdf?v=1629121309

Lemahio, R. (2019), *Good Career Guidance Perspectives from the Special Educational Needs and Disabilities*. Available online: sectorhttps://www.goodcareerguidance.org.uk/assets/file?filePath=send/good-career-guidance-perspectives-from-the-send-sector.pdf (accessed 18 June 2022).

Technical and Further Education Act (2017). Available at https://www.legislation.gov.uk/ukpga/2017/19/section/2 (accessed 18 June 2022).

15

Sustainability and PSHE

Elena Lengthorn, Sarah Dukes and Georgina Beard

Aims of This Chapter

- To identify potential opportunities to embed sustainability in your PSHE practice.
- To build confidence in climate crisis discussions.
- To recognize the value of and opportunities for nature connection in PSHE.

The foreword of the DfE's statutory guidance on Relationships Education, Relationships and Sex Education (RSE) and Health Education guidance recognizes the importance of teaching children how to be physically and mentally healthy and the role of the curriculum content in fostering wellbeing and happiness, and yet the guidance does not include, in our time of nationally declared climate emergency, any content explicitly related to education for sustainable development (ESD).

In spite of that there is a huge appetite for ESD from young people, evidenced by the ongoing School Strikes for Climate, Teach the Future and SOS UK and a responsibility, ethically and legislatively, for educators to be embedding ESD into our teaching practice. There have been a series of parliamentary readings, led by Lord Knight of Weymouth, calling for an amendment of the Education Bill to include 'instils an ethos and ability to care for oneself, others and the natural environment, for present and future generations'. As well as making provision for a 'sustainable citizenship education' for the secondary curriculum (DfE, 2019), Rackley (2020) encourages us to think beyond the curriculum to question our safeguarding responsibility in light of climate change and its potential impacts.

The United Nations Sustainable Development Goals (UN SDGs), the descendants of the Millennium Development Goals, were adopted by 193 countries in 2015 and proceed until 2030, and they provide a scaffolding of seventeen interconnected targets to end poverty, reduce inequality and tackle climate change. Of particular relevance to teachers of PSHE is Goal 4: Quality Education, target 4.7: '4.7 By 2030, ensure that all learners acquire the knowledge and skills needed to promote sustainable development, including, among others, through education for sustainable development and sustainable lifestyles, human rights, gender equality, promotion of a culture of peace and non-violence, global citizenship and appreciation of cultural diversity and of culture's contribution to sustainable development' (UN, 2015).

This broad target, one that the UK and 192 other UN member countries have committed to, highlights that ESD is a responsibility for all educators, and moving sustainability beyond the curriculum confines of Geography and Science is essential.

April 2022 saw the UK Government publish a policy paper entitled 'Sustainability and Climate Change: a strategy for the education and children's service systems'. It recognizes the important role the DfE plays in 'all aspects of sustainability' (DfEb, 2022), giving specific emphasis to the reduction of the education environmental footprint. It contains, in its opening context setting, a reminder that the strategy has been developed in the context of the UK's legislative requirements and work in relation to the UN SDG's, among other frameworks.

The launch of this new policy paper coincided with an announcement that the government has approved plans for a new GCSE in Natural History. This new qualification will enable pupils to develop a rich understanding of the natural world: from their own local wildlife, environment and ecosystem to critical global challenges like climate change, biodiversity and sustainability. Research from Natural England (2020) confirms that increased nature connectedness improves wellbeing and pro-environmental behaviours (in both domestic and conservation actions) and recognized that these outcomes rely on a combination of both contact and connection with nature, something that the new GCSE may enable but that PSHE can already drive forward.

The policy paper and the new GCSE in Natural History approval are statements of commitment to ESD and have been warmly welcomed by some, yet criticized by others, for not going far or fast enough in our time of declared climate and ecological emergency. The re-stated government advice on impartiality has been recognized as sending a message of fear about what educators can and cannot explore in lessons with Ashley Hodges, CEO of Young Citizens, suggesting this may lead to difficult conversations being avoided or simplified (Young Citizens, 2022).

PSHE and the new statutory guidance provide opportunities that can be harnessed for ESD and we have attempted to exemplify some ways that you might do that with confidence in this chapter, through a variety of activities that are deliberately transferable across the key stages, highly inclusive and adaptable for the different educational needs of your young learners. From considerations of core theme 2: Relationships in terms of our connections with the more-than-human and with nature, to core theme 3: Living in the Wider World in terms of the development of green skills for employability, as well as the crucial consideration of mental health with regards eco-anxiety and climate grief linked to core theme 1: Health and wellbeing (PSHE Association, 2019).

Discussing the Climate Crisis

Dr Tina Fawcett, Senior Researcher, Environmental Change Institute, University of Oxford, reassures us: 'To have a climate conversation you don't need to be an expert in everything or to live an irreproachably low carbon life. You just need to be yourself and to engage others in genuine discussion. Climate conversations can be many things – surprising, moving, creative, uplifting, challenging – but they are always worthwhile' (Talk Climate Change, 2022: para 13).

It is essential that our learners talk about climate change. We *must* give pupils dedicated time within the classroom to discuss the climate crisis in a meaningful way – its causes, the effects and how we tackle it – plus opportunities to acknowledge pupils' very real concerns. PSHE is a perfect opportunity to do just that. Talking can help students comprehend and voice the complex, challenging, and potentially overwhelming topic of climate breakdown, plus provide the tools to act. As Dr John Cook puts it, 'One of the most powerful things that individuals can do to confront climate change is to talk with others about it' (Talk Climate Change, 2022, para 9).

The existential thought of climate breakdown alone is enough to cause panic; our pupils are increasingly *directly* affected, too, through extreme weather events such as flooding. Dedicated PSHE time for pupils to discuss how their emotional wellbeing may be affected will *in itself* help pupils to understand and process; it will also begin to enable pupils to develop strategies to cope, allow them to identify and articulate a range of emotions accurately and sensitively, and build resilience.

This section will look at various discussion formats you could use within your classroom, ranging from small group discussions to whole-class debates, plus explore what could be discussed, when and why.

What to Discuss – Our Initial Objectives

It is important to establish what the climate crisis is. All pupils will be aware of the term 'climate change' but their understanding may be at different stages. The discussion format to use here is a mini-group debate (see debate formats). Starting in small groups will enable pupils to build their confidence gradually, and allow the teacher to visit the groups, check and correct understanding, and get to know their class.

Our first objective is to find out what students already know and establish a shared understanding of concepts and terminology, as there is a lot of potentially tricky jargon – BBC Newsround's handy 'What Do All the Words Mean?' video and article is a good starting place.

Objectives: What is climate change? What do I already know? What do we need to find out? Do I understand the key concepts and terminology around climate change?

- KS3: climate change, global warming, renewable energy, consumerism
- KS4: IPCC, run-away climate change, emissions, green jobs, mitigation, adaptation
- KS5: feedback loop, geoengineering, global mitigation, tipping point

After clarifying what climate change is, pupils can consider why it is important, who is affected and what we can do about it. A good debate format here is 'agree, build, challenge'. This further enables confidence to grow in a smaller group setting, and gives pupils a scaffold to help verbalize and structure their debate.

There are valuable opportunities to keep this predominantly pupil-led, with the plenary of each lesson focusing on what groups would like to explore next, perhaps encouraging pupils to bring in their own articles, news reports and documentary ideas as the basis for next lesson's discussion. When considering the content for discussion, why not focus on pupils' own experiences within their own local environment? Look for articles from the local newspaper, radio or local TV news. Giving inspiring or controversial quotations can also be a good starting point.

Climate change can be a divisive and emotive topic – it is important to remain sensitive to other people's opinions whilst establishing the very real and most up-to-date science: make sure you fact-check your statistics. Employ student knowledge and build on prior learning across key stages, utilizing any KS5 eco-activists and science experts to facilitate the discussion. The climate and our environment are taught specifically within the Geography & Science curriculum: there might be an appropriate summative article or reading material that these departments would prefer you use.

Empowering Pupils to Act

Discussions can lead to action, and action can be followed with discussions. The following sections give you ideas for activities to galvanize your students.

Mini-group debates: Get pupils in groups of four or five, and allocate each a role (have these displayed on your board, along with a count-down timer):

- Chief: keeps everyone on task; knows the overall objective; and encourages groups to reach a conclusion.

- Note taker: takes notes; can summarize where the group are at certain points; and help get group back on target.
- Dictionary & fact checker: in charge of finding out what new words mean – really important when dealing with the jargon surrounding climate breakdown. Using a laptop or phone to find definitions and check facts is invaluable when busting the many myths.
- Envoys: Once groups have carried out a task, one person from each group is selected as an 'envoy' to explain and summarize to a new group, find out what the new group thought, decided or achieved, then return to the original group to feed back.

The agree, build and challenge (ABC) questioning method can be used to encourage discussion and thinking around the climate crisis and pupils' responses to it, encouraging students to agree with other student views, build upon each other's ideas and challenge each other's opinions. Allocate pupils into small groups of about four, ideally mixing up your pupils to allow them to build resilience outside of their comfort zone and become open to a range of opinions from people other than their usual friendship group. Sentence stems can be used, such as 'I agree with …. because ….'; 'I would argue the same thing, because ….'; 'This is an interesting point, because … '; 'I would like to build on …..'s point, because ….'; 'I agree with …. and would like to add also that ….'; 'This is a good argument, and to make it even stronger, I would say …..'; 'I don't think …. Is right, because ….'; 'I would like to challenge this because ….'; 'My view is different, because … '; and 'I think that is incorrect, because ….'

Socratic debate: Hosting a whole-class Socratic debate is a fantastic way to create a serious, lively discussion around our declared climate crisis, elevating its status to that of an emergency. Pupils love to participate – once you have established the format and rules, given students time to prepare and reassured pupils (and yourself) that awkward silences are okay, there will be no looking back! A Socratic debate is a form of cooperative group discussion where students help one another understand a key idea or concept through asking and answering questions. Students are responsible for facilitating the discussion, whilst also practising how to listen to one another. Move your tables to form an inner group (six to eight pupils works well), with an outer group facing in. The inner group leads the discussion; the outer group participates through listening and note taking (supplying a specific focus linked to your objective works well here; e.g. make a note when the group discusses emotions; facts and figures; differences of opinions; misinformation; etc).

Firstly, give students time to prepare by reading and annotating a text, writing down key questions, or researching a topic (either at the start of the lesson, or utilize a whole lesson prior to the debate). Next, give all students an overall objective or learning question to focus their discussion (this could be pupil-generated at Key Stages 4 and 5), and have questions prepared to drop into the discussion every now and then, to keep the talk flowing. The inner group can start by reading aloud prepared material or discussing the first question; encourage everyone else (including you!) to add a comment or ask a question by first raising their hand and waiting to be invited to speak.

Avoid giving students direct answers – lead them to reach the answer themselves, by offering questions instead of answers. At the end, encourage the group to reach an agreement, and incorporate time to reflect on and evaluate the content of the debate. This works well as a pupil-led activity, such as nominating a student to write the feedback on the board. There are some good examples of what a Socratic debate looks like in practice on YouTube.

Sample questions include:

How does climate change affect us? How does it affect others?

Are we aware of the risks of climate change?

Are there students who have directly been impacted by an event attributable to climate change?

Are there children who are at greater risk of eco-anxiety?

What Next? Post-Discussion Reflection and Feedback

Eco-anxiety is a very rational fear based on events and stories from around the world, underpinned by the weight of evidence that our climate is changing (Hickman et al., 2021). After each discussion, it is important to give time and space within the lesson for pupils to process the content, ideas and emotions that have been raised.

One way to do this is through personal, reflective writing; display the following on the board, and ask students to choose one or two to write about.

- The most memorable moment of the discussion for me was …
- The saddest part for me was ….
- The most beautiful, or interesting or unusual part of our discussion was …
- This reminded me of … (in my life, or that of other people I know)
- This reminded me of … (in books, or films, or stories, or TV programmes)
- What I find most unusual or interesting about climate change is …
- A question I have about climate change of ask the group/the teacher/the whole class …

Another way is for the 'envoy' from each group to feed back to groups or the whole class, or pupils can write ideas onto the whiteboard or a large sheet of paper, which can be added to after each lesson, to see your overall journey. The summative class discussion can lead to ideas for the next lesson.

Pre-Teach Listening Skills

It might feel like a scary challenge to host a series of debates, especially when the PSHE class in front of you might include students you've never taught before – what if it turns into noisy chaos? To overcome this, the most important thing to do when building a culture of talk is to teach listening skills:

- What does a good listener look like? (Nods; look of concentration; possibly eye contact).
- What does a good listener sound like? (Asks questions; uses names; builds on opinions). This can be turned into a set of reminders that are stuck onto the wall, and can be referred back to throughout subsequent discussion lessons. Creating scaffolds for talking is incredibly useful, too: sentence stems, question prompts and suggested connectives to help the discussion develop (see 'agree, build, challenge').

Host your debate outside: 'It's well-known that getting outdoors in nature can be good for people's health and well-being' (Robbins, 2020). Not only is 'nature connectedness ... positively related to an individual's conservation pro-environmental behaviours' but also 'contact with nature is good for people's general health and nature connectedness is good for their wellbeing' (Matin et al., 2020). Connecting with nature is crucial, and it would be fantastic if you could hold some or all of your discussion in any green outside space your school may have, such as a playing field or science garden. Alternatively, there are ways to bring nature into your classroom – play birdsong through tree.fm, or bring in some pot-plants or flowers.

Eco-Anxiety to Empowerment – Facilitating the Journey

Acknowledgement of Anxiety

Eco-anxiety is a term defined in the *Oxford Dictionary* as 'extreme worry about current and future harm to the environment caused by human activity and climate change'. This area covers a hugely broad spectrum, not just considering current harm to the environment but future (potentially unknown harm) too. Eco-anxiety is rising, as the general acknowledgement of the unravelling climate crisis becomes all the more apparent. Media coverage of the climate emergency, its planet-wide impacts and a growing sense of urgency to act are being sensed by our pupils, alongside a slow, limited response to this crisis.

'Previous studies have found that 45% of children suffer lasting depression after surviving extreme weather and natural disasters. Eco-anxiety predicated on climate change, she suggests, is a very rational fear based on events and stories from around the world, underpinned by the weight of evidence that our climate is changing' (Hickman, 2019, para 3).

Eco-anxiety is necessary when considering any teaching around climate change. While this subject is emotional and difficult to tackle, it should not be avoided. Why is this difficult? As teachers, we like to plan having most of the answers to questions raised. However, here we must accept that we have neither of these things. You are not leading conversations or activities; you are hosting them. You will not have all the answers to pupil questions or be able to fix their concerns; instead, you are providing the space and time for young people to gain a realization they are not alone. You are aiding their participation in a hugely valuable essential journey.

Be brave and acknowledge the conversations, the emotions and variety of direction in which the lessons lead you. Finally remember you are not just a teacher in the room, but an individual who is also part of this journey and you are also not alone!

Informing and Exploring – Fact Finding

Well-informed young people will make good choices, be able to adapt, cope with change and ultimately become creative and empowered to act! As teachers, usually the first place to start is informing (teaching), as we already know the content pupils need to acquire. However, in terms of climate change, it is the reverse. We have some content, but this is changing with new information from a wide variety of sources to consider on a regular basis. So how do we plan and deliver some engaging lessons that support the pupils' learning?

Here the practice of 'hosting' a lesson rather than teaching becomes extremely powerful. Planning a lesson to include a mixture of discussions and debates already detailed alongside practical activities to explore will not only inform pupils but begin to increase their own connection with the natural environment itself!

Broadly, there are two areas when it comes to exploring to understand more: researching information around climate change, its impacts and the wider Sustainable Development Goals, or hands-on activities. For both, consider things young people already have a natural interest in exploring and be mindful that you may need to plan for different options, as the weather can be variable for outdoor activities.

Suggested General Lesson Format

- Introduction may start with some discussion and debate as detailed earlier. This may have been a previous lesson.

- Generation of some questions that students are looking to answer – try to keep these broad, allowing students to see where their research takes them. The question generator can assist with this too.
- Choose a suitable research activity for your group ability, SEND needs, circumstances, weather.
- Allow plenty of time for the research or activity; you may find it diverts off into new directions of exploration.
- Set out key rules for activity – especially when working outside or with equipment.
- Remember the learning aim of the lesson is for students to be exploring more about climate change, biodiversity, wider impacts to our planet and an opportunity to connect to nature. This is deliberately broad.

Below are some suggestions which can be individual PSHE lessons, a sequence of PSHE lessons, or build towards a larger project over time.

Researching Information

While all of the research activities below can be conducted indoors, it is worth considering that many of these could be undertaken outside too. Utilizing iPads or other such technology would allow pupils to work in an outdoor environment and get a bit closer to nature in the process (see 'Recommended resources' later for links to support).

- Analysis of data and reports: There are lots of great websites and places where you can find reports about changing species and ecosystems. Pupils can review reports, pick out key findings, summarize facts and figures.
- Environmental review: As part of the Eco-Schools programme pupils complete a review of the school, which is a great tool to use. This is in a pupil-friendly format and split into sections which could work with groups. Pupils could even complete the same survey at home or other environments to compare and contrast.
- Waste investigation: Try counting by type, weight and location to establish the main offenders and problems. This could be an indoor or outdoor activity. Pupils can then map the waste around school, and research ways to dispose of it in an environmentally friendly way.
- Researching climate change and the wider global impacts – websites and teaching resources: Many organizations like WWF, Transform Our World and Thoughtbox have prepared lessons around exploring this broad subject. With pre-planned resources that can be used as individual or a series of lessons exploring climate change, empowerment, a wide variety of different global impacts, habitats, a carbon footprint calculator, citizenship, which are mostly

free for teachers to access. Any of these great materials will enable pupils to increase their understanding while supporting time-poor teachers.

- Article investigation: Pupils could research media stories and articles on the environment, which can be compared and contrasted for discussions and debates.
- Environmental pictures: Pupils can research to find a given number of pictures that demonstrate good/bad environmental practices. Findings from the research can be used for displays, discussions or to provoke further debates.
- Energy investigation: Pupils can review the quantity, type and locations of lighting around school. They can monitor timings around what is on and when. This could be mapped, quantified or even costed. Comparisons between school areas, households and even the country can extend the review further.
- Nature documentaries: Pupils can watch to collect facts and contrast environments. Again, these can provoke more discussions or create informative displays around school.

Hands-on Exploration

A more hands-on approach to investigation and researching is a great way of getting your young people to connect with the natural environment at the same time as really immersing themselves in the learning.

- Nature mapping: Pupils create a map of the school including details of all natural areas, green spaces and wildlife discovered around the site. This could be during one lesson or over several weeks. Another version of this would be a site tree map. For detailed maps, you could try asking students to identify species found.
- Live observations of wildlife and birds: Take pupils outside to observe the natural environment, nature walks, bug investigations, hedge reviews or generally just what is under their feet. What do they see, hear, smell and feel? They will need to record their findings and find ways of identifying species. Perhaps try different sites for comparisons such as comparing school grounds and with a local area. Do different areas have different impacts upon the senses – if so, why might that be? If you struggle for greener areas to visit, try some online sites of live bird tables, bird boxes and owl boxes available. This activity is suitable for a wide variety and age range of pupils, at KS3 mapping and recording findings, KS4 comparing and contrasting findings, KS5 evaluating and considering the conservation of these delicately balanced ecosystems.
- Photographing or drawing nature around us: A nice task to connect young people to the outdoors is to get them to photograph, sketch or draw the things they see. This could link to the nature map above. Different pupils could look at

different plants, wildlife or areas. Maps can then be compared and contrasted for discussions. Use the pictures with pupils to consider what feelings or mind-sets they evoke, do different pictures, species or surroundings change this?

- Tree journals: Pupils select a tree (individually, groups, classes). They can create a journal about their chosen tree over a given time period. What it looks like, feels like, the weather, area, time of year. This activity can also link to creating a site tree map.

- Sounds of nature: There are many ways to access the sounds in nature. One would be to sit and listen and create a sound map of what they hear around them over a given time period. Pupils can use their findings to understand more about the environment around them. Other ways could include listening to recorded sounds of nature such as birds, marine animals or trees.

- String journey: Take pupils on a walk with a piece of string each. While walking pupils collect things and tie them to the string as they go. Different types of journeys can be undertaken and contrasted.

- Build a habitat to observe: Building bird tables, bird or bat boxes, wildlife ponds all provide great ways for young people to research and learn more about the requirements for local wildlife. Pupils can observe and monitor these habitats over time. This is a longer project and needs more planning.

- Grow plants to observe: Planting flowers or vegetables to look after and observe over time. Pupils learn about the requirements to nurture the plants and the efforts that go into growing something. They can consider the environments required, different varieties, species and methods to grow things. There is an opportunity to link further to finding out about food production in different climates or regions; pupils could then investigate how much food they need to produce for their family, school, town or country.

- Track and monitor waste and electricity on site: Pupils can monitor their chosen topic over a given time period at school across site. Pupils can monitor different areas and research average school or household use to compare and contrast. This could enable pupils to look for ways to calculate the school's carbon footprint.

- Bring the outside in: Having objects such as pine cones, flowers, leaves or something similar while hosting debates and discussions. This can simply help pupils connect to nature in a deeper way during these activities too as well as becoming a mindfulness activity – pupils can have a chance to reset.

- Undertake a whole school survey: Pupils could create questions around travel, lunches, electricity, waste, water, outdoor areas and use the data collected to present back to the school community, create a display, posters or make an action plan, all of which could be shared with another school locally or even abroad to contrast, or perhaps with local stakeholders too.

Combining research and hands-on activities would give students a real immersive experience to find out more about climate change and the environment. Students could look at their local natural habitats and then contrast with the UK and other countries through wider research, or the other way round. The key is that they are learning through their own exploration.

Turning Research into Action

Once the research or exploration has taken place, pupils will naturally progress to ideas of how to act. It is key these are captured either throughout the process or at the end:

- Create an action plan – a large piece of paper with sticky notes of all the pupils' ideas is quick and simple.
- A drawing wall – use a long piece of paper, pupils can draw (sometimes easier than writing) ideas. This could be used to capture conversations from earlier discussions and debates too.
- Pinterest board – pupils add articles, pictures, anything they have found on a wall or a long piece of paper. This could be done in one go or left for them to collect over a long period of time.
- Box to collect ideas/anonymous thoughts/feelings, etc.
- Orally present findings back to group, or in small groups.
- Use a range of graphs, charts and tables of data to display findings for others to view.

Empowerment – Action Stations

Now seize the energy! Nothing is more powerful than engaged young people who are ready to act. This is the ideal situation to arrive in following debates, discussions, researching and exploring, channelling this into practical actions will lead to empowered and motivated pupils who can make a difference!

Using everything the pupils have discovered so far on their journey, you now need to facilitate by helping them to decide areas to focus upon. Pick one or several actions to take forward. It is really important at this stage to understand that all actions are good no matter how big or small, results can be slow and every achievement should be celebrated.

The key outcome here is that pupils have travelled through a learning journey, gathering information and making outdoor connections to help them kick-start the care process. This in turn is generating motivated young people who are actively looking for ways to tackle the climate emergency.

Alongside this learning, it is important to recognize that pupils are also developing life skills in tackling anxiety and concerns by seeking information allowing them to move to a more motivated mind-set. These pupils will be informed, empowered and able to make good choices to support a more sustainable way of living. Just as climate psychology shows us, the antidote to climate grief is the doing!

Moving Forward – Suggested Action Ideas

- Inform the wider school community: posters, assemblies, use of data collated, displays (photographs taken, drawings), school newspapers and webpages
- Competitions involving a wider group of pupils, such as collecting crisp packets, growing sunflowers
- Introduce green rewards at school: certificates, merits, awards, prizes all for green actions
- Pledges: get all pupils and staff to pledge a change then display them
- Waste reduction: new recycling areas, bin monitors, canteen reviews, food awareness
- Writing to an MP: letters, postcards, pictures, all a great use of persuasive writing skills, with lots of information you have discovered to back it up
- Create an allotment area: groups of young people can tend and work on this, you can have tutor group growing competitions, engage the school canteen, compost and pick your own sessions. There are many opportunities to involve the wider community too
- Write a speech to engage others on the climate emergency or for parliament
- Join a wider eco-scheme: there are many schemes with awards such as Eco-Schools, Forest Schools
- Declare a climate emergency at school
- Increase biodiversity on your school site: create ponds, plant trees and hedging, make a nature trail, a science garden or perhaps a green corridor
- Create a school travel plan to include clean ways to walk and travel to school
- Introduce bird ID or other wildlife signage around your site; you could include scannable QR codes for pupils to learn more
- Create or run a quiz to encourage the wider school community to learn more about the things you have discovered too

Finally, now celebrate the successes! As a teacher, enabling the pupils to review their progress is not only the last part of the journey, but perhaps the most enjoyable. Look for ways to display, show and shout about what the pupils have achieved and how this will enable young people to change their actions to live in a more sustainable way going forward.

Conclusion

We find ourselves in an urgent situation that we didn't plan for or choose, but nonetheless have an opportunity, as educators, to respond to and support our young people through. We don't need to be experts to open up these crucial conversations and actions on behalf of our planetary community.

We recognize that facing our climate reality can be just as difficult for us as teachers, and we wanted to remind you that you are not alone in finding this hard. There are some helpful strategies on how to manage and support eco-anxiety in the recommended resources section.

It is never too late to start helping nature and there is never a wrong time to include ESD in your PSHE curriculum. It is relevant to all of us, all the time. You might, however, like to use a UN International observance date or series of dates to hook your ESD lessons to e.g. 22nd April – Earth Day, 5th June – World Environment Day, 4th October – World Habitat Day, or perhaps tie your focus in with the next Conference of the Parties (COP) event, held annually in November.

David Attenborough, in his address to the UN Security Council in 2021, reminded delegates that our response to the climate crisis requires 'unparalleled levels of global cooperation' (Attenborough, 2021). As educators we have the chance to teach, model, nurture and disseminate. Let's get to it!

Recommended Resources

The 'Talk Climate Change' website is an excellent starting point for teachers and pupils – full of inspiring and helpful advice and encouragement from climate leaders, activists and communication experts across the globe: https://talkclimatechange.org/advice

BBC Newsround – lots of useful articles and videos focusing on climate change and its impact: https://www.bbc.co.uk/newsround

BBC Newsround's handy 'What Do All the Words Mean?' video and article: https://www.bbc.co.uk/newsround/58985263

IPCC https://www.ipcc.ch

National Geographic: https://www.natgeokids.com/uk/

The Climate Signals website allows users to explore what climate change looks like on the ground, in your region, state, or neighbourhood and specifies the long-term climate trends and physical processes at work: https://www.climatesignals.org

The Survival Game – Nicky Singer

Friends of the Earth on Eco-Anxiety: https://friendsoftheearth.uk/climate/how-cope-eco-anxiety

New Scientist on Eco-Anxiety: https://www.newscientist.com/article/2220561-stressed-about-climate-change-eight-tips-for-managing-eco-anxiety/

The 'Transform our world' website is great for teachers with lessons, activities, action plans and an opportunity for participate in youth voices: https://www.transform-our-world.org/

WWF has a great collection of resources, pre-planned lessons and many activities students can join in, including live lessons too: https://www.wwf.org.uk/get-involved/schools, https://www.wwf.org.uk/get-involved/schools/walrus-from-space

The RSPB website contains up to date annual birdwatch results which can support data and fact finding: https://www.rspb.org.uk/about-the-rspb/about-us/media-centre/press-releases/the-rspb-big-garden-birdwatch-2022/

The Eco-Schools programme: https://www.eco-schools.org.uk/

Thoughtbox is a great organization with a whole range of pre-planned resources and lessons: https://www.thoughtboxeducation.com/

Live Bird cam in Devon: https://www.youtube.com/watch?v=SLNKVjKgXJc

Website links to listen to the environment: https://www.tree.fm/ https://sounds.bl.uk/Environment

Climate Signals website for real time climate change impacts: https://www.climatesignals.org

BBC documentaries including Blue Planet, Green Planet, Life of Earth, Natural World.

References

Attenborough, D. (2021), *Sir David Attenbrough speech to the UN Security Council* [web streamed], United Nations, 23 February 2021.

DfE (2019), Relationships and sex education (RSE) and health education. Department for Education. UK Government. Available online: https://www.gov.uk/government/publications/relationships-education-relationships-and-sex-education-rse-and-health-education (accessed 25 May 2022).

DfE (2022a), Political impartiality in schools. Department for Education. UK Government. Available online: https://www.gov.uk/government/publications/political-impartiality-in-schools/political-impartiality-in-schools (accessed 25 May 2022).

DfE (2022b), Sustainability and climate change strategy. Department for Education. UK Government. Available online: https://www.gov.uk/government/publications/sustainability-and-climate-change-strategy (accessed 25 May 2022).

Gayle, D. (2022), Fridays for future school climate strikes resume across the world. *The Guardian Newspaper*, 25 March 2022. Available online https://www.theguardian.com/environment/2022/mar/25/fridays-for-future-school-climate-strikes-resume (accessed 25 May 2022).

Hickman, C. (2019), *Press Release. Rise of 'Eco-Anxiety' Affecting More and More Children Says Bath Climate Psychologist.* Available online: https://www.bath.ac.uk/announcements/rise-of-eco-anxiety-affecting-more-and-more-children-says-bath-climate-psychologist/ (accessed 18 May 2022).

Hickman, C., Marks, E., Pihkala, P., Clayton, S., Lewandowski, E., Mayall, E., Wray, B., Mellor, C. & van Susteren, L. (2021), Climate anxiety in children and young people and their beliefs about government responses to climate change: A global survey, *Lancet Planetary Health*, 5(12), pp. e863–e873. https://doi.org/10.1016/S2542-5196(21)00278-3

Martin, L., White, M., Hunt, A., Richardson, M., Pahl, S. & Burt, J. (2020), Nature contact, nature connectedness and associations with health, wellbeing and pro-environmental behaviours, *Journal of Environmental Psychology*, 68, pp. 101389. ISSN 0272-4944. https://doi.org/10.1016/j.jenvp.2020.101389

Natural England (2020), A summary report on nature connectedness among adults and children in England (March 2020). Available online: http://publications.naturalengland.org.uk/publication/6005041314136064 (accessed 25 May 2022).

Natural England (2022), A summary report on nature connectedness among adults and children in England: Analyses of relationships with wellbeing and pro-environmental behaviours. Available online: http://publications.naturalengland.org.uk/publication/6005041314136064 (accessed 25 May 2022).

OCR (2022), OCR Natural History. *OCR*. Available online: https://teach.ocr.org.uk/naturalhistory (accessed 25 May 2022).

Oxford Dictionary. Available online: https://www.oed.com/view/Entry/59377#eid1336326950 (accessed 24 May 2022).

PSHE Association (2019), Programme of study for PSHE Education Key Stages 1–5. *PSHE Association*. Available online: https://fs.hubspotusercontent00.net/hubfs/20248256/Programme%20of%20Study/PSHE%20Association%20Programme%20of%20Study%20for%20PSHE%20Education%20(Key%20stages%201%E2%80%935)%2c%20Jan%202020.pdf?hsCtaTracking=d718fa8f-77a8-445b-a64e-bb10ca9a52d8%7C90ef65f6-90ab-4e84-af7b-92884c142b27 (accessed 13 June 2022).

Rackley, K. (2020). Climate change – a safeguarding issue? *GA Magazine*. Geographical Association. Sheffield. Available online: https://www.researchgate.net/publication/348920518_Climate_change_-_a_safeguarding_issue_GA_Magazine (accessed 25 May 2022).

Robbins, J. (2020), Ecopsychology: How immersion in nature benefits your health, *European Centre for Environment & Human Health at the University*. Available online: https://e360.yale.edu/features/ecopsychology-how-immersion-in-nature-benefits-your-health Report can be accessed at: https://www.nature.com/articles/s41598-019-44097-3 (accessed 25 May 2022).

SOS UK (2021), Schools Sustainability Survey 2019-20 & 2020-21: Research into Pupils' views on Environmental Sustainability. SOS UK. Available online: https://uploads-ssl. webflow.com/6008334066c47be740656954/60ed9cbf1015d467b321cea7_20210707_ Schools%20Sustainability%20Survey%202019-20%262020-21_FINAL.pdf (accessed 25 May 2022).

Talk Climate Change (2022). Available online: https://talkclimatechange.org/advice (accessed 25 May 2022).

Teach the Future (no date), Current climate education is inadequate. Teach the future. Available online: https://www.teachthefuture.uk/ (accessed 25 May 2022).

Turney, C. (2019), UK becomes first country to declare a 'climate emergency,' *The Conversation*, 1st May. Available online: https://theconversation.com/uk-becomes-first-country-to-declare-a-climate-emergency-116428 (accessed 25 May 2022).

UN (2015), Sustainable development goals: Quality education. *United Nations*. Available online: https://www.un.org/sustainabledevelopment/education/ (accessed 25 May 2022).

Weymouth, J. (2021), Education (Environment and Sustainable Citizenship) Bill [HL] Volume 813: debated on Friday, 16 July 2021. *Second Reading*. Available online: https://hansard.parliament.uk/lords/2021-07-16/debates/C5939A80-DD61-4EE4-BB46-F0A23C713E2B/Education(EnvironmentandSustainableCitizenship) Bill(HL) (accessed 25 May 2022).

Young Citizens (2022), Responding to the Government's guidance on political impartiality in schools. *Young Citizens*. Available online: https://www.youngcitizens. org/news/responding-to-the-governments-guidance-on-political-impartiality-in-schools/

Index